W9-CIG-582

HÉLÈNE CIXOUS

Key Contemporary Thinkers

Published

Jeremy Ahearne, *Michel de Certeau: Interpretation and its Other*
Peter Burke, *The French Historical Revolution: The Annales School 1929–1989*
Simon Evnine, *Donald Davidson*
Graeme Gilloch, *Walter Benjamin*
Andrew Gamble, *Hayek: The Iron Camp of Liberty*
Phillip Hansen, *Hannah Arendt: Politics, History and Citizenship*
Christopher Hookway, *Quine: Language, Experience and Reality*
Douglas Kellner, *Jean Baudrillard: From Marxism to Post-Modernism and Beyond*
Chandran Kukathas & Philip Pettit, *Rawls: A Theory of Justice and its Critics*
Lois McNay, *Foucault: A Critical Introduction*
Philip Manning, *Erving Goffman and Modern Sociology*
Michael Moriarty, *Roland Barthes*
William Outhwaite, *Habermas: A Critical Introduction*
Susan Sellers, *Hélène Cixous: Authorship, Autobiography and Love*
Georgia Warnke, *Gadamer: Hermeneutics, Tradition and Reason*
Jonathan Wolff, *Robert Nozick: Property, Justice and the Minimal State*

Forthcoming

Alison Ainley, *Irigaray*
Sara Beardsworth, *Kristeva*
Michael Best, *Galbraith*
Michael Caesar, *Umberto Eco*
James Carey, *Innis and McLuhan*
Colin Davis, *Levinas*
Eric Dunning, *Norbert Elias*
Jocelyn Dunphy, *Paul Ricoeur*
Judith Feher-Gurewich, *Lacan*
Kate and Edward Fullbrook, *Simone de Beauvoir*
Adrian Hayes, *Talcott Parsons and the Theory of Action*
Sean Homer, *Fredric Jameson*
Christina Howells, *Derrida*
Simon Jarvis, *Adorno*
Paul Kelly, *Ronald Dworkin*
Carl Levy, *Antonio Gramsci*
John Preston, *Feyerabend*
Harold Noonan, *Frege*
Nick Smith, *Charles Taylor*
Geoff Stokes, *Popper: Politics, Epistemology and Method*
Ian Whitehouse, *Rorty*
James Williams, *Lyotard*

HÉLÈNE CIXOUS

Authorship, Autobiography and Love

Susan Sellers

Polity Press

First published in 1996 by Polity Press in association with Blackwell Publishers Ltd.

2 4 6 8 10 7 5 3 1

Editorial office:
Polity Press
65 Bridge Street
Cambridge CB2 1UR, UK

Marketing and production:
Blackwell Publishers Ltd
108 Cowley Road
Oxford OX4 1JF, UK

Blackwell Publishers Inc.
238 Main Street
Cambridge, MA 02142, USA

ISBN 0-7456-12547
ISBN 0-7456-12555 (pbk)

A CIP catalogue record for this book is available from the British Library and the Library of Congress.

Typeset in $10\frac{1}{2}$ on 12 pt Palatino
by Best-set Typesetter Ltd., Hong Kong
Printed in Great Britain by TJ Press Ltd, Padstow, Cornwall

This book is printed on acid-free paper.

For Sue Roe

Contents

Acknowledgements

I should like to thank Margaret Whitford for her help, support and encouragement throughout the writing of this book.

Elizabeth Fallaize, Judith Still and Nicole Ward Jouve all offered invaluable advice at different stages of the project. I am indebted to them for their careful and apposite criticisms.

Thanks are also due to Marguerite Sandré for help with materials, and to Deborah Jenson, Catherine MacGillivray and Donald Watson for generously allowing me to work from their translations.

The author and publishers gratefully acknowledge: Antoinette Fouque and the Editions Des femmes for translation of extracts from *L'Ange au secret*, Paris, 1991, *Jours de l'an*, Paris, 1990, *La*, Paris, 1979, *Manne aux Mandelstams aux Mandelas*, Paris, 1988 and *(With) Ou l'art de l'innocence*, Paris, 1981, and for permission to quote from *Vivre l'orange/To Live the Orange*, Paris, 1979; Carol Barko (translator) and Schocken Books for quotations from *Inside* copyright © 1986 by Schocken Books Inc. reprinted by permission of Schocken Books Inc. a division of Random House Inc., New York; Hélène Cixous and the Théâtre du Soleil for translation from *L'Histoire terrible mais inachevée de Norodom Sihanouk Roi du Cambodge*, Théâtre du Soleil, Paris, 1985 and *L'Indiade ou l'Inde de leurs rêves*, Théâtre du Soleil, Paris, 1987; Harvard University Press for quotations from *'Coming to Writing' and Other Essays*, Cambridge, Mass., 1991; Jo Levy (translator) and Calder Publications for English translation copyright © Jo Levy 1985 and the Editions Des femmes copyright © 1977 for extracts from *Angst* reproduced by permission of the copyright holders and the Calder Educational Trust, London; Catherine MacGillivray (translator) and *Qui Parle: A Journal of Literary Studies* for quotations from 'Hélène Cixous: Writings on the Theatre'; The Open University Press for quotations from *Writing Differences: Readings from the Seminar of Hélène Cixous*, Milton Keynes, 1988; Presses Universitaires de Vincennes for translation from *Hélène Cixous: Chemins d'une écriture*, Saint-Denis, 1990; Betsy Wing (translator) and University of Minnesota Press for English translation copyright © 1986 of quotations from 'Sorties', in *The Newly Born Woman*, Minneapolis; Betsy Wing (translator) and University of Nebraska Press for quotations from *The Book of Promethea*, Betsy Wing's translation and introduction © 1991 by the University of Nebraska Press (originally published as *Le Livre de Promethea* © Editions Gallimard, Paris, 1983).

Preface

My aim in this introductory study of Héléne Cixous' work is to explore the development of her fictional and dramatic writing in the context of her theory of *écriture féminine*. Although Cixous is primarily known in the English-speaking world for her work as a feminist and literary critic,[1] this in fact constitutes only a small proportion of her œuvre. Of her books published to date,[2] thirty-six are works of fiction or drama. In choosing to focus here on her literary texts, I am hoping, therefore, to redress this imbalance. None the less, since I intend to read her fictional and dramatic writing in the light of her work on *écriture féminine*, my discussion will, necessarily, also encompass the main points of her theoretical and critical contribution.

For the purposes of this study I define Cixous' 'theory' of *écriture féminine* as an/other writing. This phrase is drawn from Cixous' own delineations. I argue that while Cixous' early fiction does not, on a first reading, appear to fulfil her criteria for an *écriture féminine* since it is concerned with the writing self, this self-exploration is the necessary precursor to the later writing which thus mirrors more completely her descriptions of *écriture féminine*.

My argument concerning the development of Cixous' literary œuvre is substantiated by her article 'From the Scene of the Unconscious to the Scene of History: Pathway of Writing'.[3] In this article, Cixous outlines her autobiography as a writer. She describes how the foreign, multilingual environment into which she was born,[4] the war in Algeria and her father's premature death from tuberculosis when she was eleven years old 'became the causes and opportunities for my writing' (p. 16). She suggests: 'my writing was born in

Algeria from a lost country of the dead father and foreign mother' (p. 16) and stresses 'foreignness, exile, war, the phantom memory of peace, mourning and pain' (p. 16) as crucial factors in her writing. Of these various influences, Cixous locates her father's death as the most important in her decision to write:[5]

> I believe that one can only begin to advance along the path of discovery . . . from mourning and in the reparation of mourning. In the beginning the gesture of writing is linked to the experience of disappearance, to the feeling of having lost the key to the world, of having been thrown outside. Of having suddenly acquired the precious sense of the rare, of the mortal. Of having urgently to regain the entrance, the breath, to keep the trace. (p. 19)

The correlation between loss and self-definition as the prerequisite for writing will form the subject of this study.

Although there is clearly a link between Cixous' autobiography and the genesis of her writing which both informs and sheds light on her work, my account will take as its focus the progression of the *written* subject as this figures in her fictional and dramatic texts. As will be discussed in detail in the Introduction below, Cixous identifies in language the oppressive structures of meaning and narration that organize our lives as well as the potential to deconstruct these procedures and rewrite them in other, non-coercive and thus liberatory ways. For Cixous, the literary text is the key domain of this venture, and she sees in the fictions of such writers as the Brazilian novelist Clarice Lispector the model for alternative relations to differences. Thus, while Cixous' autobiography is clearly a major motivating element in her work, this account will focus on the textual development of Cixous' œuvre, tracing the progression from the preoccupation with self-identity in the early fiction to the increasing affirmation, in Cixous' later work, of other possibilities for meaning and relating.

In 'From the Scene of the Unconscious' Cixous draws a link between the missing and thus symbolic father and language. She explores this link through a reading of Clarice Lispector's short story 'Sunday, Before Falling Asleep'.[6] In Lispector's story, Cixous writes, the father, through his gift of the word 'ovomaltine', functions as 'a magic door' to the child protagonist that 'opens on to the other world' (p. 17). 'Ovomaltine' is:

> the mysterious thing with the foreign name that opens the path to pleasure. Before the father, in order to please him, one goes to a place

> to discover America, to say *extraordinary words*. The key to the secret words 'ovomaltine' or 'the top of the world' is in His possession. (p. 18)

This world of language, Cixous continues, is also domain of the mother, but as music, rhythm; 'm'other, my other' (p. 19) – familiar and *already* other.[7] Language is both a compensation for and a means of living – through inscribing – loss:[8] 'everything is lost except words. This is a child's experience: words are our doors to all the other worlds' (p. 19).

In 'From the Scene of the Unconscious', Cixous explores how these various antecedents – the situation and timing of her birth, language, her father's death – which inform the early fiction gave way to a mode of writing seeking to protect and safeguard life:

> perhaps knowing that we are mortal and saving each minute, consecrating it to life, is the task that animates certain writings. As for me joining the party of life is itself my political party. . . . I am on the side of those who have a drive towards redemption, protection, reanimation, reincarnation. I dream of protecting the living and the dead. For one can also kill the dead, one can bury them, erase them to infinity. (p. 20)

Writing preserves life – 'writing follows life like its shadow, extends it, hears it, engraves it' (p. 20) – while inscribing knowledge of loss and death. Cixous details her own experience of this progression. She suggests that she began writing in order to overcome her personal experience of loss: 'one writes from death towards death in life' (p. 21). She was, she explains, in 'hell', a hell formed from her own confrontation with death and the 'primitive primordial chaos' (p. 21) that accompanies the struggle for self-definition: 'hell is incomprehension, it is dreadful mystery, and also the demonic or demoniac feeling of being nothing, controlling nothing, of being in the unformed, tiny before the immense' (p. 21). Writing offered itself as the way through this hell, towards a present in which it became possible to *record* non-comprehension:

> this is what paradise is, managing to live in the present. Acceptance of the present that occurs, in its mystery, in its fragility. It means accepting our lack of mastery. . . . It is not rest, but relentlessness, the unceasing effort to be there. (p. 22)

Cixous argues that only by writing *through* her personal hell was she able to write: 'not in order to mourn the past, but to become prophet of the present' (p. 22). Such a task, she stresses, requires constant work, since it entails celebrating the present while remembering that for many it is still a hell:

> one must not forget. . . . It is in one's interest to write in order both to feel the passing of, and not to forget that there is, hell. Writing is (should be) the act of remembering what is, in this very instant, of remembering what has never existed, remembering what could disappear, what could be forbidden, killed, scorned, remembering far off, minimal things, turtles, ants, grandmothers, the good, first and burning passion, nomadic peoples, people who are exiled little by little, flights of wild ducks. (p. 22).

It is at this point in 'From the Scene of the Unconscious' that Cixous broaches the question of the other for the writer. For, in order to remember, and inscribe the present which *includes* the sufferings of others, the writer must find ways of writing those whose experiences s/he does not or cannot share. Citing Clarice Lispector's disclosure of her difficulty comprehending, from her superior economic and social position, the plight of her character Macabea (p. 24),[9] Cixous argues that this problem has been central to her own writing: 'how to arrange oneself in order to write about the Khmers? This is a question that has come back to me under its thousand different faces for the last twenty years' (p. 24).[10]

Cixous believes her personal answer to this question has come through her more recent experience of writing for the theatre:[11]

> it's only very recently that I've begun to try out an answer. It's a matter of letting them speak, the Macabeas, the Khmers. . . . I've found something which has moreover been granted me: it is the theatre that helps me let them speak. (p. 24)

Cixous suggests the theatre offers a medium in which it is possible for writers to let go of their own language and allow space for the languages of those they are writing (p. 24). She argues that this relinquishing of the language of the self is something she achieved only gradually:

> there is a certain path of development to follow: there is the path of the self, one must develop in oneself out of oneself. In the theatre one can only work with a self that has almost evaporated, that has transformed itself into space. (p. 24)

Cixous' account of the evolution of her writing here, from the necessary exploration of her own unconscious/other to an increasing engagement with the others of culture and history,[12] as well as the crucial role played by the theatre in this process, will form the background to my study.

The writer's 'I', Cixous continues:

> is an I that has come to bring itself into accord with the world's difficulties. But it is not given, it must be formed. It seems to me that there is an entire span of time, the time of the ego, through which one must pass. One must become acquainted with this self, make a descent into the agitated secret of this self, into its tempests, one must cover this complex route with its meanderings into the chambers of the unconscious, in order to then emerge from me towards the other. The ideal: less and less of me and more and more of you. This cannot be a conscious aim. The meaning of this journey comes once it's over but the itinerary is inevitable. (p. 24)

I propose to follow the self-preoccupation of Cixous' early work, in order to show how its engagement with the various forces that create the self gives rise, in the later fiction, to a writing 'I' that is no longer dependent on the other for definition, and which is thus able to undertake the writing of 'you':

> one must reach this state of 'de-egoization', this state of without-me, of dispossession of me, that will make the *possession* of the author by the characters possible. (p. 28)

I shall argue that this 'I', which refuses the glorifications available to the self in writing and which seeks, instead, to encounter and inscribe the other, is the hallmark of an *écriture féminine*. As Cixous puts it:

> thus can one someday hope to arrive at this point of accomplishment where the self will hold fast, will consent to erase itself and to make space, to become, not the hero of the scene, but the scene itself: the site, the occasion of the other. (p. 25)

I have organized my argument as follows. In the Introduction I outline in detail Cixous' 'theory' of *écriture féminine*. This delineation then provides a framework for tracing the progression of Cixous' œuvre in terms of a feminine or other writing. Chapters 1–5 follow the development of Cixous' fiction and drama in chronological order, beginning with the early work, continuing with the main period of theatrical writing, and concluding with the most recent fictional texts. As Cixous has written over thirty works of fiction and drama, I have chosen to focus the various stages of my argument around the discussion of selected texts in order to avoid a merely superficial reading of each work.

Since my argument in this book concerns the relationship between Cixous' creative writing and her delineation of an *écriture féminine*, I have preferred to base my discussion of her texts on her own 'theoretical' and 'critical' writings, analysing her fiction and plays in the context of her descriptions of *écriture féminine* and referring the reader, where necessary, to the works of those philosophers and critics – such as Sigmund Freud, Jacques Lacan and Jacques Derrida – whose ideas she both draws upon and challenges.

In addition to her delineation of an *écriture féminine*, which will be discussed in detail in the Introduction below, Cixous has pioneered a corresponding mode of feminine reading. The clearest exposition of Cixous' reading practice is given in the 'Conversations' in *Writing Differences: Readings from the Seminar of Hélène Cixous.* [13] Here Cixous explains how Freudian theory and poststructural accounts of language (p. 144) combine with close attention to the text's composition:

> we work very close to the text, as close to the body of the text as possible; we work phonically, listening to the text, as well as graphically and typographically. (p. 148)

These theoretical and formal 'tools', she stresses, are not employed to fit the text to a predetermined 'grid' (p. 147), but are used to hear the text's specific meanings:

> we aren't looking for the author as much as what made the authors take the particular path they took, write what they wrote. We're looking for the secret of creation, the same process of creation each one of us is constantly involved with in the process of our lives. (p. 148)

The theoretical and critical aids adopted are suggested by the text itself, and Cixous underlines the need for a variety of approaches if we are to apprehend all its complex meanings and operations. This plurality of approaches entails a number of perspectives, including a theoretical overview and the careful reading of the words on the page (p. 148).

As will be discussed in the Introduction, for Cixous the literary text presents a space in which diversity can disturb and challenge the desire for unicity and control. Cixous' own texts are sensitive to the multifarious possibilities of their meanings, and seek to reinscribe this multiplicity in ways which inevitably frustrate the reader's longing for coherence and self-substantiation. My reading of Cixous endeavours to follow this feminine mode, employing contemporary literary theory, Cixous' own insights into the genesis of her work, and a detailed and variform examination of the texts' composition. Since my aim is to explore Cixous' fiction and theatrical writing in the light of her work on *écriture féminine*, it appears vital to adopt a reading position that will remain open to the processes and opportunities for meanings within the texts, rather than seek to impose any pre-established conclusion. At the same time, to avoid a purely descriptive summary of my reading, it seems important to have an at least provisional schema as a guide: hence my decision to follow the line of development suggested by Cixous' article. The pitfalls of adopting Cixous' own reading practice and account of her writing – namely, that such an approach prevents the critic from furnishing other, negative interpretations – are hopefully circumvented by the inherently plural and open nature of Cixous' descriptions.

Introduction

In *The Newly Born Woman,*[1] Cixous warns of the dangers in attempting to 'theorize' *écriture féminine*, a process, she argues, that will inevitably reduce, distort or obliterate its essential features:

> at the present time, *defining* a feminine practice of writing is impossible with an impossibility that will continue; for this practice will never be able to be *theorized*, enclosed, coded, which does not mean it does not exist. (p. 92)

The importance of feminine writing for Cixous is precisely its capacity to circumvent the binary structures embedded in our current, 'masculine' system of thinking, whereby whatever is designated as different or other is appropriated, devalued, excluded.[2] Cixous believes a feminine writing will challenge the present modes of perception and representation, and thus herald into being a new schema to replace the existing hegemony.

Before turning to Cixous' descriptions of *écriture féminine*, it is important to understand her concept of masculine and feminine and to examine in more detail her view of writing's revolutionary potential.

The economies of masculine and feminine

Cixous' notion of masculine and feminine is most easily explained with reference to Freud's theory of castration.[3] In *The Newly Born*

Woman, Cixous argues that Freud's reliance on his own view of sexual identity is reductive, since it derives from the very concept of biological 'destiny' that has hamstrung men as well as women throughout history.[4] Cixous suggests that Freudian psychoanalysis is based on :

> the formidable thesis of a 'natural', anatomical determination of sexual difference–opposition. On that basis . . . [it] implicitly back[s] phallocentrism's position of strength. (p. 81)

Both sexes, Cixous stresses, 'are caught up in a web of age-old cultural determinations that are almost unanalyzable in their complexity' (p. 83). She refutes the 'voyeur's theory' (p. 82) adopted by Freud as 'a story made to order for male privilege' (p. 81), insisting that sexual difference cannot be delineated 'simply by the fantasized relation to anatomy' (p. 82). Cixous does not, however, believe that this means the Freudian model should be abandoned. She argues that it provides a helpful account of the way sexual difference is organized in response to patriarchal 'law', and hence an opportunity to understand and challenge its tenets.[5] Thus, while she criticizes Freudian psychoanalysis for its 'mirror economy' (p. 94) and complicitous privileging of man's narcissistic need to love *him*self, she believes its theories can be usefully adopted. Cixous suggests that Freud's descriptions offer an instructive insight into the way our innate bisexuality is structured according to a single, masculine libido.[6] She condemns his insistence on and allegiance to castration, which she sees as illustrative of his reverence for a 'glorious phallic monosexuality' (p. 85), and concludes there is 'no *woman's* reason' (p. 85) to comply with its system of repressions.

It must be noted that Cixous' reading of Freud in *The Newly Born Woman* depends to some extent on a simplification of his position since it ignores both the contradictions in his work and his investigations into 'natural' and constructed sexual identity.[7] Cixous' messianic reading should be viewed in the context of the radical and militant debates for women's liberation taking place in France in the early 1970s (*The Newly Born Woman* was written in 1973).

Cixous describes what she sees as the two possible responses to patriarchal law in terms of gender 'economies'.[8] In her essay 'Extreme Fidelity',[9] she illustrates her description with reference to the legend of the quest for the Holy Grail and the story of the Fall in Genesis. She argues that when Perceval, the key protagonist in the Arthurian legend, arrives at the court of the Fisher King he does not, as the law has decreed, dare to question what is happening until the crime he could have prevented has already been committed.[10] Cixous contrasts Perceval's masculine position of adherence to the law with Eve's response in the Garden of Eden. Unlike Perceval, who represses his desire to ask questions since this would contravene what he has been taught, Eve follows her desire and defies God's incomprehensible prohibition not to eat from the Tree of Knowledge. Eve's refusal, Cixous writes, creates for herself and the world the opportunity for knowledge, innovation and uncensored choice. For Cixous, these two responses of masculine allegiance to the law and feminine willingness to risk its prohibitions exemplify the poles of behaviour open to every one of us. For convenience, and as an approximation of the way these positions are adopted by men and women within a system in which men ostensibly have more to gain from allegiance, Cixous employs the labels masculine and feminine to suggest the way these positions tend under patriarchy to divide. However – and this is important in connection with Cixous' work on *écriture féminine* – she stresses that the terms are merely markers and can – perhaps should – be exchanged for others. In 'Extreme Fidelity' she writes:

> what I call 'feminine' and 'masculine' is the relationship to pleasure, the relationship to spending, because we are born into language, and I cannot do otherwise than to find myself before words; we cannot get rid of them, they are there. We could change them, we could put signs in their place, but they would become just as closed, just as immobile and petrifying as the words 'masculine' and 'feminine' and would lay down the law to us. So there is nothing to be done, except to shake them . . . all the time. (p. 15)

This comment on the difficulties of the terms masculine and feminine is noteworthy, since they do at times appear confusing and imprecise. The insistence that masculine and feminine relate to ways of living, for example, is complicated by Cixous' call to women to explore and write the sex-specific experiences of our bodies (see *The Newly Born Woman*, p. 51). The confusion may explain the disappointment of those readers who seek in Cixous a feminist campaigner only to discover that many of her examples of *écriture féminine* are by men. It should again be emphasized that *The Newly Born Woman* was written at the height of feminist debates in France, and that although Cixous remains loyal to women's causes her more general interest is in the constructions and motivations of the *human* subject.[11]

Although Cixous suggests that women, as a result of our relegation by the patriarchal order, are more likely to adopt a feminine position than men, she stresses that we all perpetually fluctuate between gender roles, sometimes assuming defensive, masculine postures that seek to close down, appropriate and control, at other times adopting a more open, feminine response willing to take risks, and at other times combining elements of each.[12]

For Cixous, the key difference between a feminine and masculine comportment involves our relationship to others. A feminine approach to the other, in contradistinction to the appropriation or destruction of the other's difference necessitated by masculine attempts to construct a subject position of mastery, entails locating and maintaining a relation in which both self and other can exist.

Cixous believes that biological sex differences nevertheless play a role in determining our choice of gender. She argues in *The Newly Born Woman* that patriarchy has defined and thus appropriated sexual 'difference', privileging and imposing male constructions and an attendant masculine response. She stresses that women's sexuality has been repressed, excluded or neutered in this process. For Cixous, the differences between male and female entail the possibility of different insights, understanding and ways of relating. She finds in women's sex-specific experiences of pregnancy and childbirth, for example, the potential for a radically different connection to the other, to subjectivity and love:[13]

> really experiencing metamorphosis. Several, other, and unforeseeable. That cannot but inscribe in the body the good possibility of an alteration. It is not only a question of the feminine body's extra resource, this specific power to produce some thing living of which her flesh is the locus, not only a question of a transformation of rhythms, exchanges, of relationship to space, of the whole perceptive system. . . . It is also the experience of a 'bond' with the other, all that comes through in the metaphor of bringing into the world . . .
>
> There is a bond between woman's libidinal economy – her *jouissance*, the feminine Imaginary – and her way of self-constituting a subjectivity that splits apart without regret. (p. 90)

Cixous suggests that women's sex-specific relation to the origin engenders a freer and more expansive economy than is currently possible for men. Thus, while she stresses that feminine writing, like femininity, is potentially the province of both sexes, she nevertheless locates in women's writing the repressed 'history' of our experiences (*The Newly Born Woman*, p. 97) an important source for change.

Feminine writing

Cixous' vision of an *écriture féminine* can therefore be described as feminine in two senses. First, although Cixous insists that *écriture féminine* is the domain of both sexes, the fact that she believes women are currently closer to a feminine gender than men means she views women's inscription of our sexuality and history as containing the potential to explode masculine thinking and initiate changes in its process of government (*The Newly Born Woman*, p. 95). Secondly, since a feminine subject position, with its refusal of masculine fear and self-defensive appropriation of the other's difference, necessarily entails new forms, Cixous argues that the hallmark of *écriture féminine* is its willingness to defy the masculine and seek new relations between subject and other *through writing*. Not only can writing exceed the binary oppositions that currently structure our thinking and thus create new modes of relations between subject and object, self and other, but, Cixous stresses, through such transformations, feminine writing will enable corresponding changes in our social and political systems (*The Newly Born Woman*, p. 83). Feminine writing is:

> a place . . . which is not economically or politically indebted to all the vileness and compromise. That is not obliged to reproduce the system. . . . If there is a somewhere else that can escape the infernal repetition, it lies in that direction, where *it* writes itself, where *it* dreams, where *it* invents new worlds. (*The Newly Born Woman*, p. 72)

One of the difficulties I have been confronted with in this study is the discrepancy between Cixous' insistence on the impossibility of theorizing *écriture féminine* and the very powerful and detailed descriptions of this she is able to give. The passages from *The Newly Born Woman* in particular set up an expectation that Cixous' own writing will present a space in which these delineations can take root and a new 'order' finally emerge. Reading Cixous' fiction, especially the early fiction, after such inspirational descriptions of *écriture féminine* can be a disappointing experience. Although, as Chapters 1 and 2 (below) will show, there are senses in which Cixous' early work fulfils her criteria of feminine writing, the relentless, claustrophobic exploration of the fragmented 'I' – far from encouraging and enabling the reader – can produce a bewildered retreat to more conventional textual pleasures with a feeling little short of relief. While the writing of the 1980s is arguably very different, even this only tentatively envisions an alternative: the final scene of *L'Histoire terrible mais inachevée de Norodom Sihanouk roi du Cambodge* ('The Terrible but Unfinished Story of Norodom Sihanouk King of Cambodia'), for example, ends with no more than a *hope* that the surviving elements can combine to create a new form (see Chapter 4 below).

Cixous' vision of an *écriture féminine* involves a number of components. These include the writer's position, the process and purpose of writing, the relationship between writing and its subject, the nature of meaning, and genre. I propose to examine each of these in turn.

The writer's (feminine) position

An important aspect of Cixous' conception of *écriture féminine* is her insistence on writing the body. This can be fruitfully contextualized in terms of Lacan's theory of human development. Cixous refutes what she sees as Lacan's either/or logic of complete separation from the m/other, and argues for the continuing impact of the body in adult life.[14] This insistence on the body translates into Cixous' view of *écriture féminine* in three ways.

First, Cixous stresses that women's bodies – including our perceptions of ourselves and our sex-specific experiences as women – have been appropriated and imaged by men. In *The Newly Born Woman*, she urges women to break with these restrictive definitions and to express our discoveries in writing: 'we have turned away from our bodies. Shamefully, we have been taught to be unaware of them. . . . Woman must write her body' (p. 94). She suggests that women's inscription of our 'awakenings' (p. 94) will explode the 'partitions, classes, and rhetorics, orders and codes' (p. 94) of the patriarchal symbolic, opening this to 'other' possibilities (p. 97).

Secondly, Cixous argues that language is itself a body function. In 'Conversations' in *Writing Differences* she stresses: 'language is a translation. It speaks through the body. Each time we translate what we are in the process of thinking, it necessarily passes through our bodies' (pp. 151–2). Speech and writing involve the transformation of thoughts through a complex network of nerve impulses, chemical messages and muscle movements, and Cixous suggests that this physiological activity, together with the continual body functions of breathing, pulse, the impact of body drives, stress and hormonal changes, influence our use of language. A writer's attempt to repress these bodily activities is a falsification of the nature of the signifying operation, and, Cixous insists, an endeavour to control meaning in accordance with masculine requirements (p. 179). In 'Coming to Writing',[15] Cixous describes the process of feminine writing:

> life becomes text starting out from my body. . . . History, love, violence, time, work, desire inscribe it in my body, I go where the 'fundamental language' is spoken, the body language into which all the tongues of things, acts, and beings translate themselves, in my own breast, the whole of reality worked upon in my flesh, intercepted by my nerves, by my senses, by the labor of all my cells, projected, analyzed, recomposed into a book . . .
>
> It is impossible to say in advance what this being of air and flesh in me that has made itself . . . will be. . . . It takes on the form . . . that suits the part of it that wants to be expressed. (pp. 52–3)

Accompanying this insistence on the ongoing impact of the pre-Oedipal in adult life, Cixous stresses the role of the mother's body in (feminine) writing. She suggests that the rhythms and articulations of the mother's body have a continuing effect, and she believes the inscription of these rhythms is important in preventing the codes of the patriarchal symbolic from becoming rigidified and all-powerful.[16] Cixous gives an illustration of this in relation to her own writing in her essay 'Coming to Writing'. Here she explains how the rhythms and expressions of the German language – the language of her mother[17] – which she did not, in the context of a French colonial culture, learn the rules of, inform and unsettle the languages she speaks, and particularly her 'official' language of French. She writes:

> languages pass into my tongue, understand one another, call to one another, touch and alter one another, tenderly, timidly, sensually; blend their personal pronouns together, in the effervescence of differences. Prevent 'my language' from taking itself for my own; worry it and enchant it. Necessity, in the bosom of my language, for games and migrations of words, of letters, of sounds; my texts will never adequately tell its boons: the agitation that will not allow any law to impose itself; the opening that lets infinity pour out.
>
> In the language I speak, the mother tongue resonates, tongue of my mother, less language than music, less syntax than song of words. . . . Mother German is the body that swims in the current, between my tongue's border, the maternal loversoul, the wild tongue that gives form to the oldest the youngest of passions, that makes milky night in the French day. Isn't written: traverses me, makes love

> to me, makes me love, speak, laugh from feeling its air caressing my throat.
>
> My German mother in my mouth, in my larynx, rhythms me. (pp. 21–2)

Cixous suggests that the continuing impact of the rhythms and articulations of the mother's body – figured here in her own mother's foreign tongue – affects the otherwise omnipotent hierarchy and classifications of the (masculine) symbolic, challenging its constitution and definitions, and hence the subject's relation to language, *him*self and the world. In *The Newly Born Woman*, she stresses that the non-repression and inclusion of the maternal body in writing presents a link with the pre-symbolic relation between self and m/other, and thus a way through the loss, separation and perpetual alienation of a masculine schema. She describes this m/other language as a 'singing from a time before the law, before the Symbolic took one's breath away and reappropriated it into language under its authority of separation' (p. 93, translation amended): a language that will 'run the codes ragged' (p. 93) and 'make all metaphors . . . possible and desirable' (p. 93).

For Cixous, the (feminine) motivations of mother-love offer the model for a radically different relation to the other, and hence the possibility for an 'other' – feminine – economy and language: 'contrary to the self-absorbed, masculine narcissism, making sure of its image, of being seen, of seeing itself, of assembling its glories, of pocketing itself again' (p. 94). Cixous believes that the inscription of this m/other relation in writing will furnish a blueprint for revolutionary change.[18]

One of the questions raised by Cixous' description here is the material form such a language might take. This question is raised not only for those women – and men – who have no 'other' language, but also – if we interpret this language as a primarily physical mode of communication expressed through the holding, touching, caressing, singing and babbling exchanges between mother and child – in a more general sense as to how such expression might be embodied in the language system we have inherited. The rhythmical breathing Cixous refers to in *The Newly Born Woman*, for example, can be translated into a corresponding linguistic rhythm, employing a fluid sentence structure and the repetition of certain key sounds and stresses (see p. 93), but is nowhere given an alternative, concrete and therefore directly challenging form.

A second difficulty relating to this point concerns Cixous' insistence on the inclusion of the body in writing. While Cixous' arguments – that writing is itself a body activity and that our bodies act as an important source of imagery for the way we symbolize the world to ourselves – appear accurate, her corresponding premise that women's bodies have been appropriated by men does not necessarily entail the possibility that we might thus write differently. To put this another way: how can we prevent our writing from reproducing the ways we have been taught to see and experience ourselves and the world? Even if we could block our receptive faculties and memories and live our body experiences without disturbance from the numerous taboos, descriptions and images that surround us, how might it be possible to write this experience without recourse to the language system in which such definitions are embedded? A tentative answer to the first part of this question seems to lie in a link between the body and the unconscious. If the unconscious is viewed as the site of repression – the arena where excluded feelings and perceptions are stored – then it might be possible to draw on this source in writing. This correlation between the body and the unconscious does not, however, answer the more general problem of recuperation as soon as this difference is expressed in linguistic form.

Cixous suggests that women find it easier than men to acknowledge the continuing impact of the m/other-bond, partly as a result of our sex-specific potential to become mothers ourselves, and partly because of our marginalized position in relation to the prevailing schema. She believes that women's sex-specific potential physically to nurture and give birth to an other makes it easier for women to accept the disruptions (to the self) that an encounter with the other can bring. She writes in *The Newly Born Woman*: 'it is much harder for man to let the other come through him' (p. 85), and cites, as evidence, the way men generally conform to the codes of the patriarchal order.[19] She argues that women's relegation to the fringes of this order makes it easier for women to risk its decrees and experiment with and challenge its law.[20]

In 'Coming to Writing', Cixous suggests that, in contrast to a masculine approach, with its determined tendency 'to master. To demonstrate, explain, grasp. And then to lock away in a strongbox' (p. 57), the feminine writer is:

> she who looks with the look that recognizes, that studies, respects, doesn't take, doesn't claw, but attentively, with gentle relentlessness, contemplates and reads, caresses, bathes, makes the other gleam.

> Brings back to light the life that's been buried, fugitive, made too prudent. Illuminates it and sings it its names. (p. 51)

For Cixous this willingness to enable and sing the other, rather than appropriate the other's difference in order to construct and glorify the self in accordance with masculine law, is the keynote of *écriture féminine*. In *The Newly Born Woman* she writes:

> writing is the passageway, the entrance, the exit, the dwelling place of the other in me – the other that I am and am not, that I don't know how to be, but that I feel passing, that makes me live – that tears me apart, disturbs me, changes me, who? – a feminine one, a masculine one, some? – several, some unknown, which is indeed what gives me the desire to know and from which all life soars. This peopling gives neither rest nor security, always disturbs the relationship to 'reality', produces an uncertainty that gets in the way of the subject's socialization. (pp. 85–6)

Like the enabling mother, the feminine writer adopts this position of openness and predisposition to risk:[21] her body is the 'flesh that lets strangeness come through, defenseless being, without resistance, without batten' ('Coming to Writing', p. 39).

Cixous' account of the feminine writer's willingness to abandon constructions of the self which require the other's murder (*The Newly Born Woman*, p. 70) and formulate new modes of relations is developed in both the Verena Andermatt Conley compilation *Readings*[22] and *Writing Differences*. In *Readings*, Cixous compares what she describes as 'an economy of love' involving the 'displacement of a self toward a *you*' (p. 28) with conventional relations, which utilize the other in order to create the self: 'generally, we mirror ourselves in the eyes of the other' (p. 55). In 'Conversations' in *Writing Differences* she defines this 'economy of love' as:

> comparable to the work of love that can take place between two human beings. To understand the other, it is necessary to go in their language, to make the journey through the other's imaginary. For you are strange to me. In the effort to understand, I bring you back to me, compare you to me. I translate you in me. And what I note is your difference, your strangeness. At that moment, perhaps, through recognition of my own differences, I might perceive something of you. (p. 146)

This emphasis on knowledge of the self as a precursor to knowing the other is noteworthy in terms of the development of Cixous' own writing. In 'Coming to Writing', Cixous explicitly links this work of loving with feminine writing – 'writing is a gesture of love' (p. 42) – and in 'Extreme Fidelity' she describes Lispector's work, which she sees as the most complete illustration to date of *écriture féminine*, as 'an immense *book of respect*, a *book of the right distance*' (p. 19) continually striving against 'the movement of appropriation' that marks conventional love relations.

As in her delineation of femininity, Cixous insists that *écriture féminine* is not tied to sexuality. In 'Coming to Writing' she explains: 'woman, for me, is she who kills no one in herself . . . woman is always in a certain way "mother" for herself and for the other' (p. 50); and although she reiterates her belief that women's closeness to the maternal origin, willingness to include the disorders of the body and the unconscious and to risk the prohibitions of the law predisposes women to a feminine position, she does not preclude the possibility of men writing in this mode. Indeed in 'Extreme Fidelity' she suggests that many women writers have deliberately adopted a masculine approach in order 'to hoist themselves on to the scene of sociopolitical legitimization' (p. 25). In *The Newly Born Woman*, she cites as illustrations of *écriture féminine* the works of William Shakespeare, the French playwright Jean Genet and the German dramatist Heinrich von Kleist: 'beings who are complex, mobile, open' (p. 84) and in whose writings there is 'an abundance of the other' (p. 84). The incessant movement in Genet's writing, Cixous argues, means that his plays constantly change shape so that they are never arbitrarily fixed to represent (only) one viewpoint. Kleist, she continues, is similarly capable of such 'transformations' (p. 112): he 'insists on passing through the bodies and souls of those who are stretched to the limit, those closest to the lifesprings and, therefore, closest to life's origins, which is to say, to body, flesh, desire' (p. 112). Cixous' research seminar, as the Verena Andermatt Conley compilation and *Writing Differences* demonstrate, has studied the works of numerous male theoreticians and writers since its inception in 1974.

The process and purpose of feminine writing

In addition to the writer's position, Cixous' vision of *écriture féminine* also has implications for the process and purpose of writing. For Cixous, *écriture féminine* is the endeavour to write the other in ways which refuse to appropriate or annihilate the other's difference in order to create and glorify the self in a masculine position of mastery. In *The Newly Born Woman*, she compares the male discourse of 'classical fiction' (p. 97), which she describes as 'a signifier referring always to the opposing signifier that annihilates its particular energy, puts down or stifles its very different sounds' (p. 95),[23] with a writing 'freed from law' (p. 86), in which there would be:

> on the contrary . . . a recognition of each other, and this grateful acknowledgement would come about thanks to the intense and passionate work of knowing. Finally, each would take the risk of *other*, of difference. (p. 78)

Such a writing, Cixous continues, might thus bring into being a new 'type of exchange in which each one would keep the *other* alive and different' (p. 79). It would entail relinquishing the desire for power and approval (p. 87), and attending to both the purpose and process of writing, including the impact of the body, one's sexuality and unconscious drives. In 'Coming to Writing', Cixous contrasts the prevailing discourse with a language of the m/other (p. 54). Abandoning the unitary subject position required by phallic authority, the feminine writer, Cixous suggests, adopts a number of places simultaneously (p. 47).

In the Andermatt Conley volume *Readings*, Cixous compares what she describes as an illustration of masculine writing with *écriture féminine*. Reading Maurice Blanchot's *The Madness of the Day* she writes: 'Blanchot completely masters his text. Not the slightest trace of an effect of meaning escapes him' (p. 96). As a result, Cixous argues, the reader is prevented access to the text (p. 96). The reader 'stays outside' (p. 96). Since Blanchot refuses his madness a life of its own within the text, he prohibits the reader from experiencing it other than as he decrees (p. 96). In consequence, Cixous concludes, his text functions as a reflection and reinforcement of the law.

In her essay 'The Last Painting or the Portrait of God',[24] Cixous gives a parallel example from painting. She draws a distinction between what she terms 'works of art' and 'works of being', describing the former as 'works of seduction' (p. 116). She compares this type of painting to 'works of being' which, she suggests, 'no longer need to proclaim their glory, or their magisterial origin, to be signed, to return, to make a return to celebrate the author' (p. 116).

One of the paradoxes that my reading of Cixous in the light of her essay 'From the Scene of the Unconscious' raises is the extent to which the early texts – while they explore the experiences of the self in ways which correspond to Cixous' delineation of feminine writing (see Chapter 1 below) – arguably convey this experience less effectively than, say, the later *The Book of Promethea*, in which there are distinguishable 'characters' and a more traditional form of narration, or the later plays (see Chapters 3 and 4 below). This paradox reveals a tension between the purpose and form of *écriture féminine* in Cixous' work. It is similarly noteworthy that the writer Cixous sees as coming closest to *écriture féminine*, Clarice Lispector, employs many conventional procedures of literary composition.

For Cixous, *écriture féminine* also involves the inscription of that which is repressed within history and culture. In 'Coming to Writing', she describes writing as 'a way of leaving no space for death, of pushing back forgetfulness' (p. 3), and she suggests that this is vital both in terms of our need to put something in place of the 'abyss' (p. 3) opened up by the prospect of death, and as a condition of our duty to 'keep alive' (p. 2) those others obliterated by history. She argues that in this way feminine writing might formulate an 'order' in which the other's 'murder' (*The Newly Born Woman*, p. 70) would no longer be the principle on which relations are founded. One of the issues I shall be exploring in this study is the extent to which Cixous' early fiction can be seen as the endeavour to come to terms with human mortality as a result of her personal experience of death, while the later writing – particularly the two historical plays *L'Histoire terrible mais inachevée de Norodom Sihanouk roi du Cambodge* ('The Terrible but Unfinished Story of Norodom Sihanouk King of Cambodia') and *L'Indiade ou l'Inde de leurs rêves* ('Indiada or the India of their Dreams'), *Manne aux Mandelstams aux Mandelas* ('Manna to the Mandelstams to the Mandelas') and her most recent 'critical' writing – deals with the annihilation of the other in history.

Cixous gives a number of indications as to how this writing of the other may be achieved. In 'Coming to Writing', she contrasts those procedures of naming which function to perpetuate the patriarchal schema with a naming that is akin to loving (p. 2) and which enables the other to live.[25] In the Danish writer Karen Blixen's novel *Out of Africa*, one of the characters, Count Schimmelmann, argues that things only begin to exist in the world once they have been named by man:

> 'The wild animals,' continued the Count, 'which run in a wild landscape, do not really exist. This one, now, exists, we have got a name

> for it, we know what it is like. The others might as well not have been, still they are the large majority. Nature is extravagant'. (p. 260)[26]

Cixous, in her work on Clarice Lispector, compares such colonizing attitudes with Lispector's very different approach, and she quotes, as an illustration, the following passage from Lispector's *A Paixão segundo G.H.* ('The Passion according to G.H.'):

> I have avidity for the world, I have strong and definite desires, tonight I'll go down and eat, I won't use the blue dress but the black one. But at the same time I don't need anything. I don't even need a tree to exist. I don't impose my need on things, they exist without my asking them, demanding them to be there.[27]

The endeavour to write the other also entails attention to the process of writing. Writing, Cixous argues, creates its own others and body of meanings; she suggests in 'Coming to Writing':

> as soon as you let yourself be led beyond codes, your body filled with fear and with joy, the words diverge, you are no longer enclosed in the maps of social constructions, you no longer walk between walls, meanings flow. (pp. 49–50)

The (masculine) desire to limit and control meaning is both reductive and serves to corroborate the patriarchal status quo. In 'Coming to Writing', Cixous warns of the dangers of a language that works to uphold the dominant hegemony: 'rigid concepts, little cages of meaning assigned . . . to keep us from getting mixed up with each other, without which the Society of Cacapitalist Siphoning would collapse' (p. 49); and she urges writers to incorporate the myriad rhythms, sound patterns and signifying possibilities generated by the writing process itself. In 'The Last Painting or the Portrait of God' she stresses: 'words are our accomplices, our traitors, our allies. We have to make use of them, spy on them, we should be able to purify them' (p. 127). In 'Clarice Lispector: The Approach',[28] Cixous suggests that 'there is a way of saying "tulip" that kills every tulip' (p. 72), an approach she compares with Lispector's 'way of making-the-tulip' (p. 72). In 'The Last Painting or the Portrait of God', Cixous illustrates this last point with reference to painting. Since she is a writer and not a painter, she argues that she can only hope to give her reader/listener the experience of mimosa by singing 'the *word* "mimosa"' (p. 107, my emphasis). Describing her own writing process in 'Listening to the Truth' in

Delighting the Heart, Cixous asserts: 'language . . . has its own song, its own system of signifiers and phonic associations, its own cultural and poetic memory, its own treasure, its own patterns and harmonies, which work together as I write' (p. 69). The French title of *The Newly Born Woman – La Jeune Née* – exemplifies how such associations and possibilities may be reinscribed to prevent closure, since it includes a number of meanings which Cixous picks up and plays on in the text. A French reader also hears 'Là je n'est' ('There I am not')[29] in 'la jeune née', and this reflects the text's insistence that woman is not where the (masculine) symbolic wishes to define her.[30] 'Jeune' can also be divided into 'Je une' ('I [feminine] one'), and this stress on the feminine self is similarly worked on in the text. This attentiveness to the ways in which language contributes other possibilites that disrupt and extend the signifying procedure is an important component of Cixous' vision of *écriture féminine* and her own writing.[31]

In addition to the active incorporation of other possibilities generated by the writing process, Cixous stresses the role of the unconscious in preventing the movement towards closure. In 'Coming to Writing', Cixous describes the unconscious as a 'magic book by more than one author' (p. 55), contributing other voices that disrupt any tendency to mastery or the institution of a single truth, and as a 'jewelry box' (p. 46) of other meanings and possibilities for the writer to try.[32] In *The Newly Born Woman*, she completes this depiction with an account of the unconscious as 'the other country without boundaries . . . where the repressed survive' (p. 98). This last view of the unconscious as the site of repression is particularly noteworthy in terms of Cixous' exploration of the emerging subject in her early work.

Cixous sees the type of textual composition woven from the multiple and heterogeneous possibilities generated by the writing process as challenging the rules of binary logic, objective meaning and the single, self-referential viewpoint decreed by masculine law. She believes feminine writing has the potential to undermine and present an alternative to this law, and the hierarchy of linguistic, social and political relations the law creates. In *The Newly Born Woman* she asks: 'What happens to the subject, to the personal pronoun, to its possessives when, suddenly, gaily daring her metamorphoses . . . she makes another way of knowing circulate' (p. 96), and she highlights the revolutionary potential of feminine writing's capacity 'to spend, to valorize the appropriated, to think what is not-the-same' (p. 86, translation corrected).[33]

For Cixous, one of the ways in which the feminine writer – and the text's eventual reader – can work to prevent constructing the self in a position of mastery is by attending to the gaps – to what is repressed or marginalized – in the text. In *Readings* she describes language as a 'mortal mechanism' (p. 94), functioning to recuperate and express our lived experience in terms of its own strictures. Language, she writes, prompts us to 'organize, hierarchize and introduce an order' (p. 101). In *The Newly Born Woman*, she cites her reading of Freud's case study of Dora as an example of the way marginalized or unintended meanings can disrupt and even negate the writer's intended meaning.[34] Cixous suggests that time is a key factor in this process, and she urges the writer – and reader – not to hurry over any of the stages which might lead to an/other insight, knowledge, or means of expressing these, in the fallacious struggle for greater achievement. Once again, the work of Clarice Lispector provides the key example, and Cixous stresses Lispector's refusal to shy away from the difficult, the painful or the ugly in her work, allowing herself, instead, the time she needs to confront such feelings and comprehend and learn from her reactions.

Cixous develops this last point in 'Clarice Lispector: The Approach':

> at the school of Clarice Lispector, we learn the approach. We take lessons of things. The lessons of calling, letting ourselves be called. The lessons of letting come, receiving. The two great lessons of living: *slowness and ugliness*. (pp. 60–1)

She suggests that Clarice Lispector's writing, in contrast to the present 'time of the flat thought-screen . . . which does not leave time to think the littlest thing according to its living mode' (p. 62), seeks 'the approach that opens and leaves space for *the other*' (p. 62), and she cites Lispector's description of her role as writer as 'a means, and not an end' (p. 64).

As will be developed in Chapter 1 below, Cixous' early writing fulfils her delineations of *écriture féminine* in its attention to the multifarious possibilities generated by the signifying operation, and in its refusal to avoid difficult or apparently tangential subject matter in the interests of conventional narrational structures. This, however, creates a problem for the reader, and the experience of reading the early texts can be a bewildering and even alienating one. Time and energy must be invested in unravelling the text's meanings, and it is consequently difficult to return to the text with the freshness and desire that arguably produce the type of textual engagement Cixous is concerned with. The experience of reading some of the early texts can be compared to reading in a foreign language one only imperfectly understands: the text remains scarred by the frustrations and fatigues of the initial reading. This difficulty masks a more serious problem. If a new, feminine 'order' is to be achieved, then feminine writing has to engage with the general consciousness and not only with those individuals whose privileged situation affords time and access to education. Although Cixous is now considered an important figure in academic and literary circles, her work remains largely unknown to the general public.

Writing and its subject

In 'Extreme Fidelity', Cixous reads a scene from Lispector's *A Paixão segundo G.H.* in which the protagonist, G.H., encounters a cockroach. Cixous insists that G.H.'s first attempt merely to overcome her disgust for the cockroach by feigning the encounter is an error. The real encounter, she stresses, comes only after a considerable delay:

> She travels a hundred thousand years . . . before coming to the end of this painstaking journey from which not a single step can be omitted otherwise it would all be over, she would have skipped a stage in this step-by-step process. (p. 29)

This discussion of the confrontation with the cockroach broaches a further element crucial to Cixous' delineation of *écriture féminine*, namely, the relationship between writing and its subject. In the scene from *A Paixão segundo G.H.*, Cixous suggests that the reason G.H.'s initial attempt to approach the cockroach fails is that:

> she did not leave room for the other, and . . . in the immoderateness of love, she told herself, I am going to dominate my disgust, and I am going to go as far as the gesture of supreme communion, 'I am going to embrace the leper'. It is a mistake. The embrace with the leper transformed into metaphor has lost its truth. G.H. makes the gesture, which she does not analyse at the time, of incorporation. (p. 29)

G.H.'s exaggerated gesture did not, Cixous argues, derive from respect for the other. Her approach was part identification, part appropriation: the encounter 'transformed into metaphor has lost its truth'. Cixous writes:

> the most difficult thing to do is to arrive at the most extreme proximity while guarding against the trap of projection, of identification. The other must remain in all its extreme strangeness within the greatest possible proximity. (p. 29)

This search to encounter the other, in all its various forms, *as other* is, Cixous insists, a quest fundamentally at odds with the self-defence mechanisms necessitated by the (illusory) struggle for masculine meaning. In 'The Last Painting or the Portrait of God', she suggests that the purpose of feminine writing is 'not to submit the subject . . . to the laws of cultural cowardice and habit' (p. 118) but, on the contrary, entails 'the need . . . not to make things pretty, not to make things clean, when they are not; not to do the right thing' (p. 118). Feminine writing is a 'fidelity to life such as it is': 'and fidelity is equal respect for what *seems* beautiful to us and what *seems* ugly to us' (p. 119). The feminine writer's task, Cixous stresses, is 'to create without commentary, without condemnation, without interpretation' (p. 122).

In *The Newly Born Woman*, Cixous describes the feminine writer as a:

> traveler in unexplored places; she does not refuse, she approaches, not to do away with the space between, but to see it, to experience what she is not, what she is, what she can be. (p. 86)

As this last quotation illustrates, Cixous also highlights the feminine writer's need to acknowledge herself (sic) in the encounter with the other. A feminine economy and writing does not, Cixous insists, mean the negation or obliteration of the self since this would merely reverse the dialectic between self and other. On the contrary, it involves respect for the other *and* an honest appraisal of the self's own needs – including our desires, prejudices, predilections, questions, blind-spots and fears. This insistence on self-knowledge in relation to others is noteworthy in terms of the self-preoccupation of Cixous' early writing.

Cixous also touches on the importance of self-knowledge in *Readings*. Here she cites Franz Kafka's *Metamorphosis*, suggesting that Samsa's transformation into an insect is a consequence of his own self-doubt: 'he is the way he is seen . . . an insect . . . and he cannot negate it because the look of the other has its power. But who is he for himself?' (p. 103). Femininity, Cixous argues, is the difficult balancing act between relinquishing subject positions that threaten and prevent the other[35] while, at the same time, not investing the other with power over the self (p. 103). Feminine writing means embarking on 'the passage toward more than the self, toward another than the self, *toward* the other' (p. 112, my emphasis).

An interesting illustration of this last point can be found in Cixous' reading of Clarice Lispector's *The Hour of the Star* in 'Extreme Fidelity'. To attain 'the right distance' in order to write the character of Macabea, Cixous explains, Lispector was forced to adopt the subject position of a man:

> in order to speak in the most intimate way possible about this woman that she is not . . . it was necessary for Clarice to undergo a superhuman exercise of transferal of all her being, of transformation, of self-estrangement, in order to try to approach such a minute and transparent being. And what did she do to become sufficiently self-estranged? What she did was to be the most other possible from herself, which gave rise to something absolutely remarkable: for the thing the most other possible, was to go into the masculine, *to pass by way of a man.* (p. 12)

This issue of the feminine writer's relation to her subject becomes increasingly important in Cixous' own work (see, in particular, Chapter 3 below).

Feminine meanings

Cixous insists that feminine writing must refuse to prioritize and select from the range of possible meanings and work, instead, to be all-inclusive. She believes this is especially true of those significations that threaten or contradict the design the writer hopes they have achieved and wishes to impose on the reader. For Cixous, the meanings of feminine writing span the unexpected possibilities generated by the writer's attention to (her)self – including the motivations of the body and the unconscious – language, the promptings of the writing's subject, and those meanings marginalized, distorted or silenced by the masculine schema. In the bilingual French/English *Vivre l'orange/To Live the Orange*,[36] Cixous gives, as an example, her sudden sense of the magnificence of an orange as she is writing. Her realization is informed by a passage from Clarice Lispector she had previously been reading, and is interrupted by a telephone call reminding her of a demonstration in Paris in support of women in Iran. This interruption leads Cixous to remember the Nazi concentration camps. This, she suggests, is precisely the writer's dilemma: how can writers incorporate *all* these elements in their work:

> to be able to arrive alive a woman in front of an orange full of life, we must be able to think six million cadavers, three thousand nuclear heads, not forget, a billion enchained, walled up, in order to measure the worldwide force of a smile. (pp. 77–9)

Cixous stresses that this endeavour to include *all* meanings – those derived from and contributing pleasure as well as those which are painful or difficult – is crucial to *écriture féminine* in its struggle to comprehend and learn from the various forces that comprise life and in its undertaking to prevent the forces of holocaust from happening again.

In 'The Last Painting or the Portrait of God', Cixous argues that feminine writing – like feminine painting – has no subject (p. 124). Feminine art, she writes, involves neither the invention nor the telling of 'facts', but 'fidelity to what one feels' (p. 127). In order to achieve this, Cixous suggests, the feminine writer must 'give herself entirely to rediscovery' (p. 127, translation corrected), experiencing and inscribing 'what escapes us and makes us wonder . . . what we do not know but feel . . . what makes us live' (p. 129).

The insistence on a plurality of meaning has implications for the way writing is read. As Cixous explains in 'Coming to Writing', not only is 'writing . . . never read' – 'it always remains to be read, studied, sought, invented' – but it requires a corresponding position of femininity from the reader: 'reading: writing the ten thousand pages of every page, bringing them to light . . . *reading*: making love to the text' (p. 24). Such an approach is crucial, since it is this reception and interaction that gives writing life. Describing her attempt to write fire in 'The Last Painting or the Portrait of God', Cixous stresses:

> I gather words to make a great straw-yellow fire, but if you don't put in your own flame, my fire won't take, my words won't burst into pale yellow sparks. My words will remain dead words. (p. 107)

Feminine genre

Finally, as Cixous' own writing demonstrates, this openness has an impact on literary genre. The attempt to create a new relation between self and other has radical implications for characterization, while the endeavour to inscribe all the various elements of a situation – including those possibilities generated by the signifying operation – militates against the traditional structures of narrative. Cixous' insistence on time similarly disrupts notions of form. In 'The Last Painting or the Portrait of God', she stresses that the time of writing is necessarily the present.[37] This regaining of the present in writing – which, as is indicated in the reference to *Vivre l'orange/ To Live the Orange* (see above), *includes* the past and future – is a key theme of Cixous' work.

As has already been suggested, there is a tension between Cixous' insistence on a break with traditional forms and the fact that what may be considered her most effective feminine writing entails a partial return to established literary conventions. Cixous herself has documented how she had to change her writing practice in order to meet the requirements of the theatre (see Chapter 4 below), while fictions like *The Book of Promethea* employ narrative and 'characters' in a way the early texts do not.

In the Andermatt Conley compilation of extracts from Cixous' seminar, there is an exposition of the way feminine writing may subvert the law that structures our view of ourselves and the world in relation to more masculine forms of writing.[38] Cixous reads a novel by Clarice Lispector – the English title of which translates as *Near to the Wild Heart* – in conjunction with James Joyce's *Portrait of the Artist as a Young Man*, to argue that, unlike Joyce's work, Lispector's text is written from 'within' (p. 1).[39] Cixous suggests that *Near to the Wild Heart* has 'the audacity to let itself be written close to the very drive to write'; it is 'at the *écoute* of writing, of something that happens between the body and the world' and 'does not display a mastery of form or language' (p. 1). Lispector's novel, Cixous writes, as the title suggests, is 'near to the wild heart'. She emphasizes that the 'subject' of Joyce's work is ostensibly the same since it focuses on the artist's formation – though 'as a young man'. In the opening sequences of the novel, Cixous argues, 'we go . . . rapidly to the formation of the subject through the intervention of a third term. We go through the history of the mirror stage and of . . . cleavage' (p. 4).[40] The scene begins with the mother who represents both 'rhythm and music' (p. 7) to the young Stephen, and culminates in a terrifying physical threat – the intervention of an incomprehensible and castrating law: if Stephen will not apologize 'the eagles will come and pull out his eyes' (p. 7). Stephen's response, Cixous continues, is to compose a poem:

Pull out his eyes,
Apologise
Apologise
Pull out his eyes,

Apologise,
Pull out his eyes,
Pull out his eyes,
Apologise.

Cixous comments: 'the law that horrifies [Stephen] also gives him pleasure. The name of the law frightens, but "apologise" has a nice sound' (p. 7). She contrasts Joyce's transgressive relation to the law which, she suggests, necessarily has more impact on men than on women,[41] with Lispector's refusal to respond to its calling (p. 12). Joyce's achievement as an artist is to produce a transgressive pleasure from the law by playing with the signifiers and words through which it is transmitted, while Lispector's creation, Cixous insists, does not derive from the law at all.

Cixous develops her thoughts on writing and the law further in her reading of Blanchot's *The Madness of the Day*. She suggests that in order for society to function some form of 'civilization, limits and laws' are necessary (p. 23). The problem, she writes, is that the law we have inherited has been pre-defined according to a hierarchical and disabling schema (p. 24). The force of Lispector's writing, Cixous continues, is that she positions herself:

> at the origin of what could be the law. She herself decides the value of such and such a gesture. She had the incredible strength to resist the ready-made in the world with its finished laws ordered by a system of moral values, hierarchized into good and bad. (pp. 24–5)

'Nothing prevents me', Cixous stresses, 'except the law transformed into the self. *I*, the law' (p. 18). Lispector's genius is to have understood that the law depends on our investment (p. 25) and that 'one can have recourse to another logic altogether . . . reason did not fall from the sky. It is the very discourse of half of humanity. But one can have another reason, another logic' (p. 26). She concludes: 'one can think loss other than in the negative' (p. 67). This highlighting of the need to work through our internalization of the law's prohibitions and commands in order to achieve 'another logic' offers a fruitful context for reading the preoccupation with formations of the self in Cixous' early work.

In a later section of *Readings*, Cixous continues her account of how feminine writing may inscribe what is repressed by the patriarchal schema with reference, once again, to the work of Clarice Lispector. Cixous stresses that this inscription can only be achieved 'poetically', and she compares the way 'philosophical discourse' inscribes its subject as 'object' with Lispector's approach (p. 91). The difference, she suggests, is that whereas Lispector becomes her subject:

> philosophy has always wanted to think its other, to interiorize, incorporate it. From the moment it thinks its other, the other is no longer the other but becomes the same. (p. 90)

This quest for the other, Cixous goes on, entails abandoning those forms of perception and expression handed down to us (p. 138) – 'we need to abandon our old ways of looking so as to find again a space that would be the realm of the possible' – and the formulation of new modes in which 'death' will no longer predominate (p. 113). Feminine writing is the medium of this inscription which, like the mirror in Lewis Carroll's *Through the Looking-glass*, 'does not simply refer to the side of the same, but opens onto the infinite registers of the other' (p. 135).[42]

1
The Early Texts

> Ecrire? Mais si j'écrivais 'JE' qui serais-je? Je pouvais bien passer sous 'JE' dans le quotidien sans en savoir plus long, mais écrire sans *savoir qui-je*, comment l'aurais-je fait?
>
> 'La Venue à l'écriture', p. 39
>
> Write? But if I wrote 'I', who would I be? I could pass for 'I' in daily life without knowing anything more about it, but write without *knowing I-Who*, how could I have done that?
>
> 'Coming to Writing', p. 29

My reading in this chapter will focus on Hélène Cixous' *Dedans*[1] – *Inside* – as illustrative of her early writing, though reference will also be made to the other fictional texts written between 1967 and 1973. *Inside* was published in 1969, two years after the collection of stories *Le Prénom de Dieu*[2] ('The First Name of God') and in the same year as Cixous' doctoral thesis *L'Exil de James Joyce ou l'art du remplacement* (*The Exile of James Joyce*).[3] *Inside* concerns the nascent subject, in relation to the experiences of loss and death which I suggest mark this first period of Cixous' writing, and it is the text Cixous herself singles out as exemplary in terms of her writing biography in her article 'From the Scene of the Unconscious'.[4] My reading of *Inside* will involve detailed analysis of the text in the light of Cixous' account of her writing apprenticeship and delineations of *écriture féminine*,[5] drawing, for its wider theoretical frame, on psychoanalytic descriptions of the self's formation.

Inside is the story of the father's death. As Cixous stresses in 'From the Scene of the Unconscious' it was the experience of her own father's death that prompted her to write,[6] a point she reiterates in 'Coming to Writing': 'at first I really wrote to bar death. Because of a death' (p. 5). Writing, Cixous suggests, was initially a means of postponing the work of mourning – 'writing is always first a way of not being able to go through with mourning for death' (p. 38) – but then became a medium in which it was possible to recreate – and hence move beyond – loss (p. 8).

It is this process that is the subject of *Inside*. In 'Coming to Writing' Cixous asserts that it was the 'hell' (p. 38) of abandonment and bereavement that provided the motivation for *Inside*: 'its body,' she writes, 'is sobbing, stifled breath, blanks and crises' (p. 53). 'Hell' is at once the chasm of primary loss, and the ongoing agony of the feminine subject's struggle to locate herself within an alien order. Exploration of this 'hell' is both necessary and (necessarily) painful if the self is to succeed in emerging from it. As Cixous states in 'From the Scene of the Unconscious', it involves working through one's own primal scene of separation and understanding how the issue of origin has been culturally determined:

> first of all *inside*, the place where one makes acquaintance with mythologies, where one learns the secrets of narratives by way of dreams, where one collides with drives, which Freud called our Titans. One must go and see what is taking place deep down, what is repressed, what prevents us from living or from thinking and which is always on an epic scale, though these are unformed and dangerous epics. One must go back to the origins, work on the mystery of origins, for this is how one comes to work on the mysteries of the end. Going to work on the question of *where, where from*, in order to work next on *next*. (pp. 24–5)

Inside opens with an image of enclosure:

> MY HOUSE IS SURROUNDED. IT IS ENCIRCLED BY THE IRON GRATING. INSIDE, we live. Outside, they are fifty thousand, they surround us. (p. 7)

The positioning of 'inside' in the block capitals used to reinforce the image of enclosure immediately alerts the reader to its paradoxical status within the text. 'Inside' is both safe and imprisoning. The 'we' of the opening lines gives place to 'I', as an imagined struggle between the 'I' and 'the fifty thousand others' brings death 'inside' the enclosure. 'Inside' is described as a place the I must – but also need never – leave:

> I must go out. It isn't a duty imposed on me by the others however. I could stay here without ever opening the gate, the house would make it easy. I could grow up, grow old, reach the very end without ever going out. (p. 8)

Inside can be read as a metaphor for the state prior to separation in which the distinction between self and other has still to be figured. *Inside* is both 'inside' the pre-Oedipal body in which there is, as yet, no division and 'inside' the primary loss caused by the father's death.[7]

Language plays a vital role in the I's emergence from this 'inside'. The I reworks the proposition that 'my father was dead, because he was the best' by removing the conjunction and transposing the sentence into the present tense: 'then I made some progress in the art of defending myself and declared: "my father is dead. He *is* the best"' (p. 8). The suppression of the 'because' and substitution of the present tense in the second part of the phrase now enunciated as a separate sentence bring the father (back) to life.

Language's role as a medium in which it becomes possible to combat death is developed in the text. In the final section of *Inside,* language is imaged as providing the self with power over 'life and death, love and law' (p. 103). This function of language is also a theme of the short story collection *Le Prénom de Dieu*. In 'L'Outre Vide' ('The Beyond Void') the acquisition of language enables emergence from the womb of death (see p. 12); in 'Le Lac' ('The Lake') the father's last letter orders the telling of our lives: 'only what we tell ourselves is immortal' (p. 153).

One of the questions raised by *Inside* in the light of Cixous' depictions of *écriture féminine* is the extent to which the text moves beyond a personal exploration of loss and death. In her writing on Blanchot's *The Madness of the Day* (see the Introduction above), Cixous suggests that Blanchot's madness is refused a life of its own within the text as Blanchot struggles to comprehend and control his experience. A similar question is broached here.

In *Inside,* it is the father's gift of language that provides the central focus (p. 19).[8] To begin with it is the sound of the word that attracts – 'first, I'd listen to the sound of the new word my father pronounced' – while its meaning divides and organizes the world (p. 32).[9] This division involves the severance of self and other. The body is no longer whole and co-extensive with its environment but identified as separate 'inside' an already determined order: 'my fingers were chopped up into joints, my hand, which to me was beautiful and alive, was carved up, jointed, far away' (p. 33).[10]

The father's death coincides with separation from the mother (see, for example, p. 9).[11] The Oedipal triangle of father, mother and self is imaged as 'three forces, three kinds of matter, three sorts of space' (p. 17)[12] in which the self is the unknown: 'in the center there was me and what I could see, I was alone, barely knowing myself' (pp. 17–18). Division propels the I into language and the 'real' of time and history:

> yesterday I was little. Today I was somewhere else and someone else. Yesterday time, world, History, life, all forms of knowledge were in my father's head, and I was in his hands, and there was nothing I needed. . . . I heard the rumblings of the world that I would enter later on. . . . I had the right to rule in a world created for my pleasure, which was enough for me. What was real interested me not at all for it did not burden me. (p. 17)

The process of separation is also figured in the text through the image of a large, disembodied mouth (pp. 63–5). The mouth is speaking and the proximity of the lips makes them appear immense (p. 63). The mouth is both 'inside' – talking from as well as to the self – and outside: it is what the I sees. The words spoken by the mouth animate the self, a propulsion depicted in terms of heat and cold:

> la fermeté du discours frotte, frotte, pétrit la pâte, m'échauffe, je me creuse, pivote plus vite, vire, je me ramasse vers les commissures, elle m'aspire, je me gonfle en réponse, je brûle, ah! je me déchire, je m'ouvre, ah! je gèle au milieu là, fermons, resserrons, je préfère le chaud, la trace du trou au centre est un peu raide, mais j'en profite pour résister au froid: on me frappe du dehors, coups brefs, je laisse rentrer l'écho du bruit, pas plus, dehors le froid! (p. 98)
>
> [the firmness of the speech rubbing, rubbing kneads my pasty mass, firing me up, I hollow myself out, going round faster and faster, turning round, I pick myself up and make for the corners of the mouth, it sucks me in, I swell up in reply, I'm burning, ah! I'm being torn apart, I'm opening up, ah! I'm freezing in the middle there, let's close up, tighten up, I'd rather have the heat, the path made by the hole in the center is a little steep, but I'm using it to resist the cold: on the outside someone is knocking at me with quick short strokes, I let the echo of the noise come in, no more, out with the cold! (pp. 63–4)]

This passage, in its endeavour to convey the experiences of the body by repeating key words and sounds, its use of punctuation and accumulation of short phrases within an open sentence structure, presents an interesting illustration of Cixous' own feminine writing.

The pulsion towards the outside, towards birth of the self, which is at first resisted, is finally acceded to. The image of the mouth and lips, with the hole between, with its evocation of the female sex, underscores the self's separation as a form of birth:

> I concentrate myself around the lips. I am convinced, closed. . . . I pull myself together; it's all done, I make a sign, the mouth says not one word more, we understand each other, but that makes my grief explode: I'm left so alone and black when it vanishes. (p. 64)

The mouth's disappearance, its lack, is the necessary condition for birth. Evoking psychoanalytic accounts of the self's formation in relation to the mother – who is ultimately perceived as separate since her comings and goings are recognized by the child as beyond its control – the fusion of mouth, language and self (see p. 64) divides and becomes a memory:

> I am there, no doubt about it, but I miss it. Later on I miss the mouth and remember, I still miss it, I stay on reaching out toward the space that embraced it, maybe it will speak to me again, I start waiting for it, facing its absence, my smooth bearing, my taut substance, mesmerizing my fibers to the left, I stay on, so I'm the one who stays and it's the mouth that comes and goes. (p. 64)

The emphasis on the feminine, unfortunately lost in the English translation, reinforces the link between mouth and mother (both mouth and mother take the feminine gender in French).

The mouth's disappearance brings into focus a hand. This hand recalls the hand brought into being by language on page 33 of the text (cited above), the hand extended by the lover in Part Two (p. 109), and the I's severing of her finger on pages 124–5 – an incident graphically depicting the I's castration by the father-lover. Here, the mouth's removal brings the hand into existence: 'a blue hand stretches out palm down, on the left, below. The fingers appear' (p. 64). The hand's function is not, however, to replace the mouth, but to explore the newly perceived boundaries of the self:

> the blue hand hesitates or rather floats, resting on the moving surface that is me, or rather slides over my congealed surface, but where is it going? how far? fine hand long blue fingers sliding up to where I am and then am no more, and suppose it were to go all the way to the edges? (p. 64)

This exploration is linked to the self's desire for the lost mouth, in a passage which again employs a striking use of language:

la masse d'espoir se métallise, rivée à la cicatrice du trou sans cesse tac tapé toc à pe/toc-tits coups toc/de froid, toc, et hop, d'un bond se colle au creux de la paume et nous voilà partis vers les bords. (p. 99)

[the thickness of my hope turns to metal, riveted to the hole's wound knocked over and over again tick tock knock by lit-le/knocks cold/ knock, knock, and hop, my thickness clings to the hollow of the palm, and off we go in one leap toward the edges. (p. 65)]

The I's desire marks a progression, since the self now exists 'inside' (an) order:

I a soft amorphous shape without even a center before there was a wound, I trembled, you could have said I barely existed. So there has been progress: I remember, I am extensible, and no doubt prehensible, I can distinguish between large and small, black and blue, form and myself. . . . Things fall into place, there is progress. (p. 65)

Progress involves 'contradiction', since the I now has boundaries distinguishing her from the infinity of the world (p. 65). She is 'inside' a body demarcated by physical limits: 'skin I am inside that skin, stretched out between its lips and fingers' (p. 65). This insistence on the physical limits of the body is present in an earlier episode in which the I discusses with her brother whether or not there is a 'master' beyond our fear (p. 24). The conversation ends with the recognition that our capacities – to dream, move beyond interdiction, 'fly' (p. 25) – are bound only by the limitations of the body. One is 'inside' the human body; 'inside' human mortality.[13]

The mother, taking over from the father, plays a vital role in the self's construction:

I owe her . . . my discovery of social laws. . . . Shame upon shame, they put me together thus.

. . . Thus I learned that there was me and there was you, and that I could be one or the other. (p. 15)

The father is imaged retrospectively as the primary symbiotic relation. His death initiates separation (p. 20),[14] and memory of him becomes one of union:

in the space of his arms, rivers rolled me round without making a sound to the polished curves of his bones, I experienced every kind of giddiness and the universe was made of the flesh of my flesh.

I forgot the limits, I forgot the beginning, I mixed up the end with

> the curve of his arms, thinking I was in the inalterable center. (pp. 20–1, translation amended)

The world into which the father's death plummets the self is a world of terror and confusion:

> He wasn't holding me anymore. I was huddled in the right angle of a room, in the center of a gaping world full of disorder and noise. (p. 22)

It is a world the I resists:

> I had no urge to know, and no desire to remain, nor to return to a world where there was no place for me, nor to be thrown into a life where every object hurt and everyone was frightening. In my corner, my soul furiously fought off the intrusion of facts and my body helped by making ugly faces and lurching forward, which drove off the intruders. (p. 22)

'Inside' this world vacated by the father, it is the mother who lays down the law, imposing the negative[15] and teaching the I to 'stand up straight' (p. 31).[16] Dreams of merger with the mother are imaged through the grand/mother (pp. 42–5, 77–83). There is a change in sex paralleling Freudian accounts of the child's desire to be the mother's lover, though the I also fantasizes that it is s/he who gives birth (p. 81). Union with the grand/mother is blissful (p. 80) but also terrifying, since her presence is not guaranteed:

> I'm a hard shapeless blob blue or red in all her whiteness, maybe she's forgotten me, she's had so many others. . . . I'm getting smaller and darker . . . nearly dead. From loneliness. Then I burst with fear. (p. 82)

A major preoccupation of Cixous' work is the extent to which we accept or reject the laws that govern the prevailing schema. The themes of separation and (re)constitution recur repeatedly in the text. For example, the I declares:

> for the first time I separated myself from everyone else, and decided to change everything. . . . I would have neither model nor purpose. I would try only to be never stopped. (p. 11)

The I's refusal of the codes that institute social, sexual and linguistic law is depicted in the early sections of the text in Cixous' substitution of her (dead) father for God (p. 11). The replacement not only enables her to maintain a bond with the father who is thus reinstated in the present (p. 12), but also allows her to invent her own (his)tory (p. 12).[17] This (his)tory involves a number of elements that contradict what she has been taught, including the abolition of sexual differences (pp. 11–12). The only limits are the physical ones of the body (p. 26) and death.[18] In Part Two of the text, transgression of the law is figured in terms of a theft (see p. 101). Temptation is an object out of reach (see pp. 98–100, 101), which the self is unable to resist (p. 101). This transgression is framed in the text by the story of the archaeologist who collects beetles (p. 100). The collection is provision against the archaeologist's own extinction, but paradoxically takes him closer to death as the beetles become more important to him than his life. Positive transgression of the law and negation of the facts of existence are thus pitted against each other: life and love are equated with 'wisdom' while unhealthy adherence to death and the law lead to madness (pp. 102–3). This theme is reiterated in a later exchange between the I and her lover in which the static nature of death and the law are contrasted with the mobility and openness of life (pp. 105–6). The I's childhood perception of others' identity as fixed and as something for which she too must strive now gives way to recognition that – 'within the limits of what 's possible' (p. 110) – one can contravene the law (here symbolized by money) and be anything one wants to be. This emphasis on a law deriving from the self echoes Cixous' descriptions of the feminine nature of Clarice Lispector's writing (see pp. 21–3 above).

In the early sections of *Inside*, death is negated (p. 12). The I refuses to accept that the father is dead, taking refuge 'inside' her memory of union[19] and rejecting entry into the real (pp. 17–18, 33). This fantasy of 'inside', in which there is no division (p. 53) and in which the father is recreated as not dead (see p. 54), is also death of the self. There is no loss, no separation, no language – and hence no means of engaging with the world:

> every night . . . I would go back to my father in our private silent space, within our wordless immortality. Body to body, all losses, all dangers were abolished; in the moment he held me in his arms and I kissed him, I no longer wanted anything but death. (p. 54)

Symbiosis with the father is tantamount to death – 'as long as we were inside the closed circle, we were immortal, or else dead, it made no difference, since this way we were out of danger' (p. 54) –

or, as is imaged in the text's opening, a prison sentence (see p. 49). This view of 'inside' as a prison is repeated in the final section of the text. Here the scene from Shakespeare's *King Lear* in which Lear imagines a blissful life in prison with his daughter Cordelia is reworked, so that the dream appears as both desirable and dangerous in its repudiation of the world (see pp. 126–8, 138).[20] Separation, negated because it came too early, is finally acknowledged as essential to the self's survival.

The twin themes of death and separation in relation to life and love are evoked in Part Two of *Inside*. Here the hand which in the first section figured severance is depicted as the lover's gift (p. 109). The lover's hand is both other – outside the self – and alive. Recalling the object of desire imaged in the white iris on pages 98–101, the disappearance of the hand prompts both its replacement ('BECAUSE I CANNOT LIVE WITHOUT HIS HAND, I take a . . . lover', p. 115) and the I's castration: she cuts off her finger, signalling her decision to abandon her father and enter the world (pp. 124–5).[21]

The self's evolution in *Inside* can be fruitfully compared with other texts written during this period. In *Les Commencements* ('The Beginnings'), the self is given no choice but to move forward: 'in order not to fall one has to advance, if I don't advance I plummet' (p. 169). Here progression is advancement *through* uncertainty:

> in order not to fall I must *walk* in this void which is imposed on me as ground, walk in the way of men . . . a relation of demented mastery in which I kill myself killing the non-existence of the place to put my feet. . . . I am never sure of the next move. (p. 169)

Even the newly constructed self, with her apparent certainty that 'here I am one' (*'j'y suis une'*) (p. 170), is beset by doubt:

> something confuses it, very softly and subtly but it raises in me a violent distress . . .
>
> and then I am no longer one, there I was one. . . . This would have been Me would have been One . . . but at the same moment there was slippage from This to Nothing. (p. 170)

The scene of castration is figured in Uccello's painting of Saint George and the dragon:

> then Saint George leans forward on the lofty horse with the aphrodisiac curves, and bars the entry of the Plutonian mouth with his drawn lance set through the dragon's tongue, thus in a stroke,

> he bars: the vanishing hole, the Great Greedy Gullet, the Phallus with the poisonous teeth, with a single piercing which separates his warmth from mine. (pp. 179–81)

The voice of the castrator – the 'father-mother' ('*père-mère*') – is the voice of love (p. 181); it enables the self to live. The gift of language, with its capacity for invention, aids the self to replenish 'Nothing' (p. 182). A major theme in Cixous' work is the self's relation to others, and this is explored in *Les Commencements* through the figures of Saint George and the dragon. The two are imagined substituting for each other: 'without one absorbing the other and without one denying or mutilating the other' (p. 240). In *Neutre* ('Neutral'), the reply to the question 'Who am I?' comes through the relation with others (see for example p. 20).[22] The reply is partly linguistic, as is suggested by the opening 'exergue' from Saussure, in which meaning is shown to derive from the relationship between the elements of language.

The subject of *Inside* is feminine, though the I's socialization entails a shift in gender as a masculine response is enjoined on the self:

> they told me: you are, you have, you will be, look how handsome he is, this little boy in the mirror, who is he? I knew him, I used to see him every day. He was there. They tell me: peekaboo, it's you. (p. 14)

The movement between feminine and masculine gender continues throughout the text. The sections in which the I's story merges with the father's and grand/father's are written in the masculine (see for example pp. 66–72), and the masculine is also used in relation to the grand/mother (pp. 77–83). At times the gender is undetermined, as in the formulation 'Je fus frappé (ée)' – 'I ([wo]man) was struck' (French text, p. 122). These shifts in gender echo Cixous' insistence that gender is not tied to biological sex and is constantly changing.[23] Reflecting on her origin, the I concludes here:

> sex was determined independently of anatomical and physiological requirements, whence the conflicts or contradictions that often follow, after coming out into the world. (p. 79)

Despite this insistence and the shifts in gender, the I of the text refers to a body that is clearly female. Thinking of the dead father, the I writes: 'my womb dreamed a thousand times that it was full of him' (p. 101). Although this can be read as metaphor, especially in the light of Cixous' own delineation of 'woman' as she who gives birth to another,[24] the emphasis on a female body in *Inside* strongly marks the I as feminine-female.

The question of 'who I am' (p. 42)[25] voiced in *Inside* involves not only the relation to others but also the question of origin.[26] As has already been noted, the grand/mother has a central place in the text and prompts the I's fantasized imagining: 'how was it in you?' (p. 45). The speculation extends to the father, as the I dreams she is born from him (p. 62). The question of origin embraces the father's story (see pp. 66–76), which connects back through the lives of his parents and grandparents to past generations (p. 67).[27] These inherited tales disrupt the present, and impose an obligation on the I:

> under the voices of all my fathers, I hear the sound of words . . . the blowing reverberates in huge distinct sounds . . . claimed by their blood, purple and boiling I throb in tiny beats . . . how ancient we are! – surpassed by the curved lines of sound which turn into words on the horizon, I want to seize them, so I give up resisting the voices, I stop tensing myself around the hinged portals of my little bones, I surrender, ear . . . ear of the last generation, I surrender to the knowledge of my fathers, attached to the obscure head of my race, memory open to what they have lived. (p. 78)

The issue of the I's identity in *Inside* includes the relation to God. At first God is synonymous with the father (see p. 21), though later comes to represent life in the struggle between life and death (p. 53). As the link with the father is externalized and memory of him fades, the I's view of God alters and she seeks positive proof of his existence: 'I'm screaming I am, prove to me that you are' (p. 57, translation amended).

In Part Two of *Inside*, the impact of the father's death on the self's development is explored from the standpoint of the adult. Whereas Part One moves back and forth between the child's perspective and that of an older writer recounting the child's story, the second section is written in the present from the viewpoint of the I following a gap of twenty years (p. 91). The fantasy of a pre-Oedipal union with the father here gives place to the realization that all the I's subsequent lovers have been substitutes for this first relation (p. 104). As the bond with the father diminishes, the question of the I's identity is posed in relation to the lover as other. A lover's affectionate attribution of animal names (p. 110), for example, prompts the question:

> for several days now my last lover has been saying that . . . for him I am everything, everything for him, I for him everything, everything

> for him am I, I-everything; for him. Is there a way to measure my anxiety? . . . Am I everything. . . . Or am I everything he wants and nothing more than that, only the everything he wants, and then what and where? Or am I just his solitude in the total scheme of things, all alone and still everything between him and them and then am I perhaps nothing at all? (p. 111)

With a later lover, the question re-emerges through the impact on the self of another's desire: 'he'd been concocting corrupted effigies which bore little resemblance to me' (p. 116).[28] The relinquishing of the bond with the father entails a move into the present time: 'to be? I had not been (had been) (am) (to be). . . . It's the kind of accomplishment that makes the present eternal' (p. 125, translation corrected). The bond with the father is none the less acknowledged as having been instrumental in creating this 'inside' (p. 129). Entry into the present, signalled by the transition from a preoccupation with death to focus on love, involves the I's recognition: 'better a living lover than for love to be dead' (p. 129). Writing plays a role in realizing this new relation, and the attendant (re)formation of the self:

> I'm writing. It's not easy.
>
> What then? The truth. I write: my dear tree, he has returned. . . . I have to go but I shall return . . .
>
> How do you know? says his voice inside me.
>
> Because I know who you are. Because I know who you are not. And who I am and who he is and who we are, youmeyou, and who we are meheme. (p. 128)

The self's (re)definition takes place in language. The word 'love', for example, which had been appropriated by the father, is now returned to her (p. 129). The acquisition of language, in conjunction with the powers of the imagination, has the potential to vanquish death (p. 130).[29]

The text ends with a vision of 'inside' 'beyond walls and time' (p. 136). Transcending the confines of the law, this new 'inside' is imaged as a place of creation of 'new tales' (*'nouvelles histoires'* – the emphasis on the feminine is noteworthy), in which both self and other can exist (p. 136) and in which language presents a means to combat death: 'I rejoice in my power to speak . . . and that I can say kiss off kiss off kiss off to death' (p. 135, see also p. 65).[30]

In addition to the novel's conclusion, which, in its affirmation of life, language and a relation to others in which both self and other are free, echoes Cixous' depiction of *écriture féminine*, the form and composition of *Inside* include a number of elements that can be seen as illustrative of feminine writing. There are no characters in the novel beyond those given voice by the central I. This I changes, altering gender and viewpoint. There is no story in the conventional sense of the word, though there is a sense of something having been worked through. The text comprises a series of meditations, some of which – while they are recounted by the I – are those of others (see pp. 38–9). Language has a central role in expressing, guiding and accompanying the various reflections: the mother's 'NOTHING', uttered as she turns the pages of a book on anatomy (p. 30), affects the I's image of her dead father (p. 30), while her brother's dialogue with God/the father is registered as a series of sounds (p. 59).[31] The title has numerous echoes in the text, ranging from those of non-separation, death and the law to the enclosure 'inside' time figured in the town to which the adult self returns (p. 95).[32] There is inclusion of dreams (see pp. 35–9), fantasies and desires (see, for example, the I's fantasy of giving birth as the son to the grand/mother p. 81), together with the contradictory and unflattering pictures of the author these give. There is also a strong emphasis on the body (see pp. 77–8). Experimentation with the form of writing, as in the use of block capitals to distinguish certain sections of the text (see for example p. 7), the exchanges written in theatrical form (see pp. 71–2), and the inventive use of punctuation and textual spacing, is an important feature of the novel. However, there is a sense of organization and control in *Inside*,[33] manifested in such arrangements as the division of the text into two sections representing past and present time, and the author's intervening commentary on the significance of what is happening.[34] Despite the innovations described above, the novel is on the whole conventionally written, without the radical formal experiments undertaken in a number of the texts produced during this period.

Neutre, for example, represents a definite break with traditional literary forms. The author suggests in *Neutre* that 'The Narrative' (*'Le Récit'*) – identified as one of the principal components in the list of 'PLAYERS, PIECES AND RETURNERS' – is to be pursued as one pursues and works on the meaning of a dream (p. 22). There is insistence that *Neutre*'s 'tale' (*'histoire'*) is 'like a woman' (p. 25, see also its comparison to the female sex, p. 33) and that its form is 'a polysemous cake' (p. 26), its various layers deriving from different times and perspectives (p. 26, see also: *'Dieses Buch*, delivers/books itself [*"se livre"*], excels in joining the opposites by representing them in a single object', p. 33). The 'hero' of 'The Narrative' is figured in the masculine as a bird (p. 27) who 'resembles everything that one (The Narrative, as universal desire) wants' (p. 27). 'The Narrative' gives the reader no guarantees – 'nothing assures us it will lead us to the closest . . . by the shortest path' (p. 28, see also p. 32) – but on the contrary 'ventures us' (*'il nous risque'*) (p. 28, see also the warning of the uncertainty of the text's gender p. 68). The work of polysemy in *Neutre* – the purpose of the 'game' played by the text is at one point described as moving from one to the other 'without regard for semantics but in accord . . . with the music of grammar' (p. 100) – is exemplified in the plural connotations of the title and in the textual transfigurations of another of the 'PLAYERS, PIECES AND RETURNERS': 'Hazard' (*'Le Hasard'* – it also figures in the text as *'le hasart'*: hazard, art). This is translated, via the Spanish and Arabic, as a 'lucky throw of the dice' (p. 30). These meanings – of a game, a throw of the dice, good fortune – recur throughout *Neutre,* as do the signifiers and meanings contained within 'le hasart': 'hazard', 'art', 'Mozart' (who is described as entering the text 'polysemously' [p. 39] 'by the second half of the name . . . by the rhyme with *Hasart*' [p. 361]). The I is described as proceeding here 'by semantic subversion and spelling mistakes' (p. 126); the I's cry for example – 'I scream' – is transposed via the English to 'ice cream' (p. 149, see also the transformation to 'sorbet' p. 165, and the insistence: 'that the sorbet is not just a caprice of the author but an essential production . . . disseminated by the textual family', p. 68). The text is held together not by any 'suckling breast' but by 'artifice' (p. 130). The form of *Neutre* also presents a break with traditional narrative, as the following extract drawn from Milton's *Samson Agonistes* illustrates:

> l'on y verrait, même sans yeux, à la lumière de ce foyer secret
>   le même où, sans yeux, Samson tondu
> O darK dark dark amid the blaze of noon
> O a a a a a oo
> médite de tirer l'éternité du ventre de sa mort. (p. 34)
>
> [one would see there, even without eyes, in the light of this secret foyer
>   the same in which, eyeless, shorn Samson
> O darK dark dark amid the blaze of noon
> O a a a a a oo
> meditates on drawing eternity from the womb of his death. (p. 34)]

Words are crossed through (see p. 92), inverted (see p. 108), represented by a line of dots (see p. 93), written in different languages (see pp. 32–4). The role and participation of the reader in creating meaning is recognized and actively encouraged: 'so in forcing it a little, one could bring [the text] to recognition, and at times to making-itself figure, in the eyes of whosoever desires to see it, a head, limb, or sex' (p. 35, see also p. 41 and the notes to the reader pp. 81–3). There is also insistence in *Neutre* that the text does not contain (a) truth, figured in the writer's attempted demasking (of the hero?): 'it was a trap, and this mask a mask for another mask' (p. 41, see also p. 70 where meaning is described as 'the text's opium'). Echoing Cixous' delineations of femininity, there is also emphasis that others must be allowed their existence (p. 46), and that a variety of viewpoints is needed in order to create a '*composite* meaning' that would be 'a plural meaning, a system of *simultaneous* perceptions . . . in perpetual motion, independent of all judgement' (p. 88, see also p. 58). The author's role, which ranges from secretary to dreamer to analyst to criminal (p. 111), is linked to this multiperspective, and to the plurality of 'The Subject' who is both *bi*sexual (p. 56) and 'the seat' ('*siège*') of several' (p. 52).[35]

The formal innovations of texts like *Neutre*, however, do not in themselves qualify the writing as feminine. While the polysemy of the language and structure points towards the prevention of closure and establishment of any single truth, it can be argued that the very difficulty of such texts impels organization by the reader in a way more ordered texts do not. In this sense the propositions might almost be reversed: a simple form inviting multiple interpretations and the layerings of possible meanings activating a desire for control. *Inside* would seem to fall somewhere between the two. Its internal organization can be oppressive; yet its textual density can also prevent a feminine response. There are other senses too in which *Inside* does not adhere to Cixous' depiction of *écriture féminine*. The text focuses exclusively on the I, and those others who are given voice are done so only through the I. There is little sense of any engagement with a larger history beyond the intensely personal arena of the I's struggle despite the story of the father's origins and the lovers' dealings with the world.[36] The claustrophobia of this 'inside' can be overwhelming. Even the incorporation of dream scenarios, far from being liberatory for the reader, can be alienating: their intensely personal references often leave the reader *outside*. Despite the exploration of femininity and final movement towards a space in which both self and other can be affirmed, no alternative pattern of relations is envisaged. The I's decision to (re)create her own law is nowhere explored. Although it will be my argument here that the obsessive investigation of 'who am I?' undertaken in texts like *Inside* is the necessary prerequisite for an/other writing, the actual experience of reading may be laborious and confining. While *Inside* is clearly not a 'work of seduction' in that it deals with subject matter often regarded as taboo, it is also not yet, for the reasons outlined above, a 'work of being' in the sense Cixous intends.

2

Creating a Feminine Subject

Où commence une femme?
La, p. 129

Where does a woman begin?

In the group of texts written between 1974 and 1978[1] the focus shifts from the impact of the father's death to an exploration of loss in connection with the mother and attendant creation of an I that is both feminine and female. This exploration of the feminine I's formation in relation to the m/other, language and the social schema is the subject of *Angst*.[2]

In 'Coming to Writing', written concurrently with and published in the same year as *Angst*, Cixous outlines the complex bond between father, mother and nascent self in terms of her own childhood experience:

> I adored God my mother. Love me! Don't abandon me! He who abandons me is my mother. My father dies: thus father you are my mother. My mother remains. In me forever the fighting mother, the enemy of death. My father falls. In me, forever, the father is afraid, the mother resists. (pp. 19–20)

It is this double role of the mother in initiating separation and safeguarding life that is the concern of *Angst*.

Angst opens with a scene of division:

> during this scene the impossible takes place: my death attacks me, life panics and splits in two. . . . The body breaks, the sky shatters, the scene bursts into flames. You fall and the earth is no longer there. (p. 7)

Evoking psychoanalytic accounts of the self's formation, severance here entails the acquisition of subjectivity in language: 'cut. You say

I. And I bleed. I am outside' (p. 7).[3] The image of castration figured in the words 'cut' and 'I bleed', its recompense through the saying of 'I' and consequent realization 'I am outside'[4] create a starting point that at once echoes and moves beyond the concerns of *Inside*. The subject depicted in the opening lines of *Angst* is still without form – 'formless, helpless, almost bodiless' (p. 7, see also p. 19) – and it is this acquiring of 'form' that the text will explore.[5]

In *Angst*, the possibility of 'inside' is no longer available: 'here, I no longer have what I once had' (p. 7). The opening pages present the division between the 'inside' (p. 8) from which the I now perceives herself to have been banished and the outside (p. 8) within which she must find a place. 'Inside' is imagined retrospectively as containing both wholeness and meaning, while 'outside' is the 'nowhere' (p. 8) from which 'there is no way out' (p. 8, see also p. 15).

Other texts written concurrently with *Angst* similarly explore the I's formation in relation to 'outside'. In *Révolutions pour plus d'un Faust* ('Revolutions for More than One Faust'),[6] the self's construction involves the examination and rejection of existing formulae and an opening to the other in the self (see pp. 23–4, 28, 193). Subjectivity is a correlation between the same, the other and the real (see p. 86), a simultaneous 'decomposition and composition' in relation to the world (p. 196). In *Souffles* ('Breaths') the voice that induces separation impels an opening to the other:

> 'blocking my return never did one so violently bring me to light.'
>
> It was needed: it is not to me, it is to you that I am led by this voice which passes through me and dislocates me. It is onto you that I open myself. (p. 23, see also p. 74)

Although this self-abandonment is necessary – 'I had to overcome myself . . . to come over myself towards you' (p. 23) – if the other is to be reached, there is also warning that this should not mean the self's negation: 'leave myself, eclipse the self and become you' (p. 23).[7]

In *Angst*, it is the mother who initiates division:

> my mother puts me down on the ground. The room closes in. 'Wait there for me. I'll be back straightaway.' My mother goes out. The ground closes in. I am outside. . . . Betrayed. Everything starts to die. (p. 8, see also p. 190)

Despite the feeling of betrayal conveyed here (see also p. 37), the emphasis in *Angst* is none the less on individuation as the product of mother-love (see, as an example, p. 17).

This role of the mother is also a theme of other texts of this period. In *Souffles*, the mother's role is figured in the slippage between mother (*mère*) and sea (*mer*). The I is forced by the sea (*mer*) into a château where: 'I enter with the feeling of leaving – of myself leaving myself thus accomplishing a destiny that is always awaiting me' (p. 79). This image of the sea-mother is repeated in *Préparatifs de noces au delà de l'abîme* ('Preparations for Marriage beyond the Abyss'), where it is her voice, with its gift of language, that enables the I to overcome the 'abyss' of separation.[8] The mother's role in the self's (re)birth is also a theme of *La* (see pp. 44, 147).

As the quotation from 'Coming to Writing' cited above suggests, the mother's role in *Angst* includes the father (see, for example, pp. 19, 84, 176). The conjunction of mother and father transforms the parents into 'God' (see pp. 22, 53, 57, 61, 202);[9] and the I's acceptance of severance forces her recognition: 'god does not exist' (p. 215).

The mother's role is none the less presented as the one the I must adopt if she is to succeed in giving herself birth:

> bring yourself into being. Give birth to yourself. Be love's belly. The second mother. Love yourself for she who went away. Mother is here, mother is there, she's still here, there, and everywhere, wherever you want to give yourself a body going to and fro, hopefully, between the wall and death. Be your mother, have the child. Try it: a door will open. (p. 19)[10]

This depiction of the mother's function offers an interesting divergence from classic psychoanalytic accounts of the parents' role in self-formation.

The violence of individuation is figured in *Angst* through the graphic image of the body being cut to pieces (p. 42).[11] The image recalls the episode in *Inside* where the I's hand is no longer viewed as part of a co-extensive whole but in terms of a predetermined order of separate parts (see Chapter 1 above).[12] As in *Inside*, the process is initially resisted by the I, and dreams of (re)union (see, for example, p. 39) continue to affect the adult self:

> when will I be able to rest on a breast with no scar? An absurd longing, from all points of view. An everlasting longing. (p. 134)

Recalling *Inside*, failure to overcome this desire for union and confront the real is depicted as death of the self (see, for example, p. 106, pp. 110–11).

The task of self-creation is one the I would willingly delegate to others (see, for example, p. 43). She searches for definition in the eyes of her lovers (see p. 50), with predictable results (see pp. 52, 58). The I's difficulties are compounded by the criteria and restrictions of the social and cultural order she now faces (see p. 42).[13] This order is characterized by its repression of the origin (see p. 45),[14] and refusal to acknowledge death (see p. 213). As in *Inside*, it is an order where the I must negotiate between different social and sexual positions (see pp. 40–1, 48–9).[15] This choice is humorously portrayed in a scene where the I imagines herself before two paths: 'the one that goes left as you go out. And the other' (p. 134). The difference between the paths is the difference between 'I-want' and 'I-must-not' (p. 134), and the I imagines herself: 'for both runners at once' (p. 134).

This image of a crossroads is present in *Révolutions pour plus d'un Faust*.[16] Describing the text (see the back cover of the Seuil 1975 edition), Cixous writes:

> s/he who wants to think herself and to think able to act, enjoy, transform, when s/he stands at the crossroads of the laws, of her desire, of the Real and the Imaginary, of Action and its Representation, who will s/he be?

This 'crossroads' is figured in the text as the place where the I and the world meet (p. 41). The law is characterized by its apparent ability to explain the world: 'the World invents kin, origins, an exterior for itself . . . through wanting to see it believes it sees, through believing it sees it sees the scene of sources' (p. 41). This explanation prevents individuals from carrying out their own experiments: 'why are you dallying with useless enquiries? I've already found everything. Listen to my song, learn it, that's sufficient for your knowledge' (p. 116). The Law's 'Mortal Reason' (p. 125) refuses 'the presence of illogical forces: love and art are forbidden there' (p. 125); its aim is the institution of 'Impotencies': 'accumulation, accomplishment, capitalism, acceleration, repetition, capitalism' (p. 143) and money (pp. 210–11).

In *Angst*, language plays a crucial role in the self's construction. It orders separation (see, for example, p. 19), and provides the I with a medium in which it becomes possible to (re)create and hence surmount loss (pp. 13, 14, see also pp. 190, 191–3). Words substitute for the body union, healing the split between self and m/other: 'today you are: a breast no longer speaking in flashes of lightning and blood, but in words' (pp. 133–4).

This role of language is explored in *Souffles*: 'the voice opens my eyes, her light opens my mouth, makes me cry out. And I am born from this' (p. 9). The voice, linked to the mother through the feminine gender in French, induces the I to birth:

> au travail! . . . Sa voix. Arrache les rideaux, démasque les abîmes, me dénude. . . . Sans sa voix rien n'est. Nécessaire – sa violente exigence, heureusement. Sans elle pas de genèse, pas de catastrophe. Rien d'écrit. (p. 12)
>
> [to work! . . . Her voice. Tears down the blinds, unmasks the depths, denudes me. . . . There is nothing without her voice. Necessary – her violent demand, happily. Without her no genesis, no catastrophe. Nothing written. (p. 12)]

The passage is framed by the italicized interjection of '*Fort!*' (p. 9) and '*Da!*' (p. 10), with their reference to Freud's study of language's role in childhood attempts to control and substitute for loss.[17] Cixous' insistence on the mother's gift of language in these texts marks a significant departure from the focus on the father in her earlier writing, and presents an interesting commentary and reworking of traditional psychoanalytic accounts of language acquisition.

In *Angst* language is linked to writing:

> isn't it time to part with the secret by writing it down; time to live and so get beyond it; time to tear yourself out of love's breast by opening your mouth and breaking the silence; time to get out of the room by protesting? (pp. 114–15)

In *Le Portrait du soleil* ('The Portrait of the Sun') writing has the power to fill in for loss:

> the breathless and black cavity which begs me to fill it, to stuff it with all possible names. – I try, I try – in the wake of the flood of Regret, exact and only source of my ink. (p. 54)

In *Souffles* it aids the I's (re)birth, since it precedes the self (see pp. 213, 220) and conveys other possibilities (pp. 213, 214). This view of writing is reiterated in *La*, where it presents the means 'to live again and differently' (p. 147).

As a consequence of its investment by the social and cultural schema, language none the less creates difficulties for the self. These are humorously figured in *Angst* in the I's inability to say three:

> believe. You count up to three, and at three you begin. You've got the belly and the love. Close your eyes and open your mouth and out

> pops the little child. One! Two! Mother says: One! Life say: Two! But when I wanted to say Three the word didn't come out. I couldn't say it. A voice seemed to be prompting me, but the word stuck in someone else's throat and the thing didn't happen. And yet I opened my mouth, but my tongue didn't move. (p. 21)[18]

Language transmits the law, evoked here in the impossibility of finding 'the names that recall life, confirm it, swear to love it' (p. 46, see also p. 55).[19] Language's capacity to construct and convey meanings that imprison the self is depicted in an episode in which the I imagines herself addressed:

> the black words. . . . He didn't 'say' them. He 'put them forward'. . . . Their power, craftiness – I was stung. Taken in. . . . Their web of metaphors, smothered innuendos. I was summoned, pressed, beseeched. . . . He was expecting me to join him in a quarrel whose origin I didn't know. . . . I was struggling in the web.
>
> I suspected him of wanting to fabricate a story for himself. To trap me in. I felt I was turning into his fly. His food . . .
>
> He was playing chess with himself. He didn't place a word until he had measured his chances of protecting it. On the defensive. All the sentences calculated with an enemy in mind. (pp. 127–8)

The masculine comportment of the he in this passage presents a vivid illustration of Cixous' definition of masculine gender, in the desire for the other's subjugation, combat and concomitant need for self-defence. It is a comportment that traps not only she but also he: 'he himself was buzzing, writhing in the web' (p. 127). The feminist implications of such positioning are depicted in a later episode recalling Cixous' analysis in *The Newly Born Woman*:

> I was crouching on the divan, in the corner with no shield, with no reason, my wings folded; there was a whole network of threads in the air. I saw him cheerfully moving to and fro weaving, making knots, his proposals getting madder and madder, nearer and nearer. It was a question of my whole life. He was pulling it to pieces, I wasn't living it. He separated, unwound, killed, cut, picked through, eliminated, re-made me other distant and solitary lives. As if he were making love to my life, in his way . . . crossing-out, rewriting, pages, extracts. And all in praise of his fictions he was annihilating my reality. (p. 131)[20]

Recalling Cixous' account of how men achieve their ego identity through projection on to women, the he admires:

> 'your strength, courage, beauty, your path, purity, youth, vigour, innocence.' He saw in me everything he claimed he didn't have; I didn't recognize myself. (p. 132)[21]

La similarly contains themes that evoke Cixous' feminist study in *The Newly Born Woman*. Woman is here 'incarcerated', 'her desires incarnated in a gaol that is much too small for her' (p. 225, see also pp. 223–29). The law is depicted as 'the violent intervention' that cuts short women's natural mode of proceeding, described here as 'without calculation, without measuring the abyss with her eyes, without preparation' (p. 232). There is investigation of women's abdication of responsibility and institution of men as gods:

> 'I am going to encounter myself', our soul petrified with fear cries out, 'quick, a god!'
>
> – A god? But of course, right away!
>
> At this moment, she is so tired . . . she forgets that a god by definition never presents himself. And he who presents himself as god, she still knew this the day before, can only be one of these diabolical left-over mothers, always there to protect you from seeing . . . from life! (p. 262, see also pp. 163, 258)

Men have a vested interest in perpetuating this institution (see p. 261), despite its destructive effects (p. 266). This insistence on men's and women's collusion in the construction and maintenance of the patriarchal status quo confirms the need for individuation: 'one has to go out. Tackle the real. Go facing up to solitude, take hold of one's void. And let him go. The most difficult task consists in separating oneself from the gods' (p. 267, see also p. 270). *La* none the less refutes the view, presented in the biblical version of Genesis, that emergence means the irretrievable loss of paradise (p. 268). This coward's reaction to birth is delineated as an excuse for inaction:

> you are not born. You let yourself fall, you reveal your hate in allowing yourself to fall, on the pretext that you are obeying the law of gravity. In this you are in perfect agreement with death.
>
> Your whole approach rests on the existence of the first Judgement. And what if you were not condemned? What a catastrophe for the lazy! All would not be lost. You would have to raise yourself up! Invent! No more excuses! (p. 269)

The way forward is depicted as the gradual relinquishing of the 'props' that prevent us from living:

> the true path of birth does not simply pass through the mother. Leaving our birth place, moving away from the port, from the bay, this is not enough. Above all we must rid ourselves of the dead, gods and men who play the mother. (p. 270)

The desire for a god who will substitute for the lost mother/father and stand in the place of truth is also a theme of *Préparatifs de noces au delà de l'abîme* (see p. 18). The feminine subject, composed of the slippage between a feminine 'I', 'you' and 'she', lacks the necessary courage to live:

> standing before the immense wall of air, I would so much like to cross, but no I, no courage, not enough. . . . She cannot allow herself to desire what you need to desire in order for I to come back to you. . . . Failure of I? (p. 18)

As in *La*, the I initially seeks to postpone the moment of choice by handing the question 'Who am I?' to a lover. This substitution – see 'the Course of Substitutions' (p. 104) – is described as the replacing of 'an object b for an object a' (p. 106). Unlike Lacan's analysis, however, from whom the term 'object a' derives, the concern in *Préparatifs de noces au delà de l'abîme* is not with the object but the impact of the loss of love on the developing self: *'could I love the lent-presence in the absence of love, the time to feel myself loved a little'* (p. 106). The problem with such a substitution is not simply that it depends on fantasy, but that the transient nature of projection and desire means the substitution cannot endure (p. 112). As in *Angst*, the way through lies in the mother the self must become:

> let the day come, at last, in which to look in the depths of the great mirror without closing one's eyes, without fearing oneself, without complaining, without dissolving into anyone . . .
>
> the world will begin this morning, in which able to shout out: *there will be no one. I will be alone. I will be able to comprehend myself as a daughter comprehends her mother*. (p. 74, see also the imagined sojourn in 'the good sea/mother' [*'la bonne mer'*] p. 30)

Such self-knowledge – 'I made my acquaintance' (p. 77) – is the starting point for life:

> and on one side I saw seated all those I had been when I believed love was going to come, had come, would come, for the last same time under the guise of a god more or less *a*; on the other I saw all the

> young women rise up I had never been only in dreams dreamed from afar, from very far, by my souls before the law. (p. 159)

In *Angst*, writing plays a major role in the self's formation (see for example the series of metaphors linking the I to the text [pp. 10, 11, 24, 57, 96, 97]). This function of writing is also explored in other texts written during this period. In *Révolutions pour plus d'un Faust*, writing is itself one of the text's subjects. There are numerous reflections on the process and purpose of writing (see, for example, p. 15), and on the writer's role (see, for example, p. 21). The importance of creativity in art is highlighted in the comparison between 'those who make effigies from the living model' (p. 74) and the philosophers whose ambition is understanding (see p. 67).[22] Unlike the philosophers, creators give birth to life (p. 74), a difference figured in the contrast between the creative 'mother-man' (p. 100) and the 'war-man': 'he who destroys and does not create' (p. 101). Like the creators, writers are attributed with the potential to initiate change (p. 94).

In *Angst*, the point of separation is the point at which writing begins:

> the unique moment arrives when you come in sight of the parting of the ways. A pitiless moment. When at last what had to happen is going to be decided; to be written. (p. 134, translation corrected)

The 'way' is imaged as a page, and the I's struggle to locate a position for herself is depicted in terms of writing:

> every morning it's the same old story: you struggle, overcome, stretch out the other, get through and writing crosses to the other side. You are going to enrich the universe. (pp. 23–4, translation corrected)

The power of imagination joins with the possibilities of writing to produce a means of new creation:

> set off, any way. . . . If there's no earth, invent it, if the earth doesn't go fast enough, leave it behind, take off, if there's no road, make one, invent it with feet, hands, arms, passion, necessity. (p. 54)[23]

Writing, thus invested, becomes a way of warding off the forces of death:

> from line to line against the giddiness which is threatening the Letter who is putting death off from word to word, in order to give life, if it ['*elle*'] exists, the chance . . . the trembling of the paper strained by the thought's efforts to be newly embodied, to put a new face on things. (pp. 74–5)[24]

The author's vision of writing in *Angst* is none the less complicated by the difficulties of writing the truth (pp. 112, 167). Even if one were able to find the words to convey truth (see pp. 116, 146), the very act of writing would mean they are no longer true:

> every time I have wanted to tell the truth I have lied. It couldn't come out. I chose to use analogies which I vaguely felt would save the truth. . . . If I did succeed it would mean I had failed. I would have brought it down to my level. (pp. 115–16)

This does not, however, mean the abandoning of the endeavour (see pp. 144–5).

There is repeated insistence in *Angst* that while writing cannot prevent death, it can (re)inscribe loss and hence proffer a new 'order' based not on loss but on love:

> 'do you really think you can change what has already been done?' I didn't *think* anything, I *wished*. Love needed to. . . . With all my dreams to help me I tried to create another scene for love, ignoring the laws. . . . All my tears and anger turned to a few grains of sand and a little light – enough to sketch another space from which I could make up a better story. (p. 99)

This emphasis on writing's capacity to present an alternative to the loss that structures the current schema will become increasingly prominent in the texts that follow.

The difficulties of writing (in) an/other mode are comically portrayed in *Angst* in the attempted rewriting of the story of Tristan and Isolde. The account is interesting since it highlights the way the laws that govern the social order operate to prevent an/other writing:

> they wanted to live differently. . . . The world would do all it could to destroy them. . . . I decided to do all I could to free them. They were being watched. The tunnel was swarming with people who hated them. Not only the police but the whole of society, all its hypocritical jealous men and women. I projected them outside in one go. Two

> thunderclaps. Saved. As soon as they were in darkness there was a commotion while I invented their flight. A prisoner of these dark times, in the midst of preparations for repression. . . . I played the idiot while troops were massing at the openings, ridiculous armies with cross-bows which could nevertheless kill you if you came within reach. I turned base and mediocre like them, in order to invent in secret, beings who are not tolerated in reality, in order to get near the frontier without being stopped . . . To send them, in one movement of my soul, living into the light, into eternity. Imagine their journey. Work with feverish brain to give them the means to go where no one has ever been before, alive . . . once passed the limits of the possible, give them instructions for the future. Bring them to life, lead them, worship them, endow them with energies you yourself don't possess, give them all the virtues you could never have. Follow them to the end – beyond is the other life. (pp. 100–1)

This insistence that writing can surmount the forces of death and oblivion is also figured in *Angst* through the intervention of K:

> his way of conjuring up out of the earth, out of texts, those who had preceded him in his fight against darkness. His way of reviving them; loving them sorrowfully, in terror; of making the voice of their last agonies re-echo in his voice; of gathering to himself alone the vast sum of their loneliness; their stores of knowledge. (p. 142)

It is K who encourages I to write (pp. 178–80). That K is Kafka is hinted at in the text (for example on p. 143), a suggestion reinforced by the inclusion of phrases in German (see, for example, p. 142) and the picture of Kafka on the cover of the Des femmes 1977 edition.

The emphasis in *Angst* on the need to live – and love – in the knowledge of death is present in other texts of this period. In *Préparatifs de noces au delà de l'abîme* the I writes:

> I work hard at not-death. The wisdom of moving away from the traps of death. . . . *Not calling life by the names of death. To have the courage of each moment. . . . Live for life.* (p. 67, see also p. 94)

The way through is depicted as a love which, accepting separation and refusing to install the other in place of the lost M/other, defies the interventions of the law and gives birth (p. 141) – to the self as well as to others (see pp. 142–3). In *Révolutions pour plus d'un Faust* recognition of the fact of death is liberating for the I since it becomes a reason not to comply with the law's dictates.[25]

Madness is a major theme in *Angst*. It derives from the failure to achieve separation and engage with the world and, conversely, possesses the potential to disrupt the dominant schema.[26] As in *Inside*, the I initially resists separation, which here brings anguish:

> slip between the sheets, god the mother's dress smells so good; if only you could stop growing up, if only you could stop that night and not die, instead of waking up – mad. (p. 166)

Inside is security but also death of the self (see p. 166); outside is reality (p. 167) but also alienation (p. 168) and struggle as the I endeavours to negotiate between life and death, self and other, true and false (pp. 165–6). Refusing outside, by fantasizing the union of inside, is a way of avoiding anguish, though it bars the self from the possibility of production and exchange (p. 169).[27] Allegiance to the law is also portrayed as madness, since the I must conform to an order within which *she* has no place (pp. 170–1).[28] As in *Inside*, exploration of this 'hell' is none the less depicted as the starting point for its transcendence:

> wasn't I right to hide away in sleep, not to rest, but to bury with me the grave anxieties that are wearing me out? Right to go down into the dark with all my creatures and all the monsters created to stop me getting out? (p. 90)[29]

As in *Inside*, emergence from union entails a move into the present time (see pp. 159, 164, 176). This present, combined with the power of love, is posited against the forces of repression and death (see p. 102, also p. 279). Self-definition, acknowledged as the necessary precursor to living, is derived through a relation with others, including the others of history (p. 129).

More explicitly than in *Inside*, the femininity of the I that comes into being in *Angst* is explored in relation to a body that is portrayed as female. This is evidenced in the I's dreams of giving birth (see for example p. 21) and her investigation of her sex (pp. 180–1). This correlation between feminine and female is also present in other texts written during this period.[30] The femininity of the I in *La* is reinforced through the title with its reference to the feminine gender and place. Here the I's construction derives from the relationship with the mother (see pp. 44, 106–7, 116) and a feminine other (pp. 57, 86, 116, 205–6). There is emphasis in *La* on women's bodies (see p. 12, also p. 249), which contain the 'secret' of origin (see p. 58, also p. 133), and thus proffer a link to the period prior to the law's intervention with its annihilation of all but the socially constituted self (see

p. 59). Knowledge of this time – described as the knowledge of love (p. 59) – enables the I to circumvent the law with its institution of the masculine, to encounter others (p. 65, see also p. 142). Unlike masculinity, femininity is that which 'ignores the no, the name, negativity' (pp. 209, 211) and takes differences into account (p. 209). The keynote of femininity is openness – in order to arrive 'there (*là*): the pain, the love, the There (*Là*) of which we are undertaking the analysis does not constitute a rigid phenomaman (*phenomère*), but is always on the way, on the way on . . .' (p. 86) – its aim loving and enabling others (p. 234). This feminine position is linked to an/other vision of the world:

> she moves away from the deadmale state ['*l'état de mortmâle*'] . . . she quickly comes by an aural way to rise above . . . all the overurban pretension. With relish: for the love of what she could see if she managed to surmount the edifices that prevent her from contemplating her infinite. Her greedy desire gives her the voice that transports. The winds that breathe music. The pre-vision. (p. 223, see also p. 234)

In *Angst*, the issue of gender is explored in terms of the difference between a relation to others in which the self is concerned to protect his (sic) boundaries (see pp. 35, 36), and a more open, loving relation able to 'take pleasure in advance in the beauty awaiting you, the generosities of soul' (p. 36, translation corrected). Masculine subjectivity is depicted as capable of deceit and even assassination (see p. 32); feminine subjectivity is attained only with difficulty and requires constant work (see p. 36). The feminine subject is not single but multiple: 'don't our bodies change their names, depending on the time, the need, the anxiety? Depending on the questions?' (p. 27, see also pp. 45–6),[31] the various selves grouped for convenience under the appellation 'I' (p. 70). On page 69 this multiplicity is figured in terms of a choice between the right and left hands, a choice complicated by the fact that: 'you aren't just one other self, but you have as many selves as fingers on your two hands. Plus the thumb'. As in *Inside*, gender is presented as a matter of choice (see p. 64).[32] Echoing Cixous' delineation of a feminine subject position, the I is at times absent from the text: sentences are subjectless or, as on page 56, are transposed to 'you'.

Angst concludes with a short postscript by the author reviewing her work to date:

> and so, ten years to take a step, the first after god the death, ten years to wrest love from the contemplation of god the mad. Ten books to want to finish it with death. (p. 281)[33]

The summary is interesting in the light of Cixous' account of her writing biography. *Angst* is described as leading to an encounter with a woman: 'who does not die, who loves, who does not kill, who thinks' (p. 282).[34] The meeting occurs at the crossroads of 'my refusal to follow Death's long way round' (p. 282) and the other's refusal to accept the law as it is:

> a woman capable of confronting the Law and its mannequins, without letting herself be won over by their effects of gown, mirror, knowledge. . . . It exists, love without a fight, it is allowed the body without constraints, it exists pleasure without debt. It is possible, History without enslavement, there is ground for living without mutilation, it is (only) up to women to produce it together. (p. 282, see also p. 283)

As in Cixous' descriptions of feminine writing, there is, through this path 'beyond the little economy of death' (p. 283) and encounter with others,[35] the possibility of transformation: 'in the place where the dream gives way to the real' (p. 283). It is a place linked to writing, to the 'thought-body, this women's real' (p. 284):

> and if you reach there ['*là*'], where love does not separate, after the end of the non-life . . . there will be an other writing ['*une autre écriture*']. (p. 284)

The writing of *Angst*, in its highlighting of the mother's role, marks a progression from the early texts in terms of Cixous' delineation of *écriture féminine*. While the detailed investigation of the 'angst' the I undergoes as she endeavours to resist separation recalls the claustrophobia of *Inside*, this is offset by the proposition of an alternative vision and, to some extent, the style of writing. *Angst* includes a dramatization of the I's experiences and a number of stylistic features which evoke Cixous' descriptions of feminine writing. Although there is less formal innovation in *Angst* than in other texts written during this period,[36] there is repeated word-play, as in the play on 'l'être' (the being) and 'lettre' (letter), the slippage between 'l'homme au Sein' (the Breasted man) (French text p. 77) and 'le Grand Saint' (the Great Saint) (French text p. 83),[37] and in formulations such as 'trois jouïrs sans interruption' (three pleasure days with no interruption) (French text p. 32) and 'vint le 20 (pronounced *vint/vain*) ne vint pas, qui vaincra les vains jours'/'départ, levain, ou le 23' (French text p. 51).[38] There is inclusion of other languages illustrated in the use of English and German (see, for example, French text p. 199). The unconscious is given a prominent role as the

I explores her fantasies, and there is depiction of that which is taboo, shameful or ugly as in the imagined murder of the mother (p. 65, see also pp. 113–14) and the disgorging of the self (p. 170). More significantly than in *Inside*, there is also a sense of the body writing. The reader is given a pre-eminent role:[39] not only can the reader choose not to read (p. 97), but it is up to the reader to create meanings: 'letters have nothing to say to you; it's your decision' (p. 97, see also for example pp. 197–8 where it is left to the reader to organize and make sense of the material). However, despite the insistence on and final vision of a new model of relations in which love, and not death, will be paramount, there are few passages in which this is explored beyond the longings of the I. While the impact of the law's prohibitions and the various ways the self endeavours to overcome these are graphically portrayed, the question remains as to whether such descriptions qualify the writing as feminine. Although there are ways in which *Angst* moves beyond *Inside* in terms of Cixous' depiction of *écriture féminine*, it can be argued that the reader is left ultimately in the same place. It will be the task of the next group of texts to transform Cixous' descriptions of feminine writing into a practice which embodies an alternative for the reader.

3

Writing with the Voice of the Other

Comment approcher les quinze mille aspects de chaque 'tu'. Appeler 'tu' chaque chose. A se laisser appeler et rappeler, par chaque instant de vie.

Vivre l'orange/To Live the Orange, p. 103

How to approach the fifteen thousand aspects of each 'you'. To call each thing 'you' . . . bid it let itself be called and recalled, by each moment of life.

Ibid., p. 102

Whereas the texts discussed thus far can be viewed as stages towards an/other writing, their themes and form only partially fulfil Cixous' depiction of *écriture féminine*. The group of texts written between 1978 and 1983 – from Cixous' tribute to Clarice Lispector in *Vivre l'orange/To Live the Orange* to *The Book of Promethea*[1] – correspond more closely to Cixous' description. Of this group I have chosen to focus on *The Book of Promethea*, since its engagement with the others of Promethea and writing, and endeavour to articulate alternative modes of perception, relation and representation, extend beyond the preoccupations of the early work to illustrate the possibility of feminine writing. *The Book of Promethea* incorporates many of the elements of Cixous' delineation of *écriture féminine* (see the Introduction above). The process and purpose of writing are constantly questioned, as is the relationship between the writer and her subject. There is a movement away from the self-concern of the early writing, towards a dramatization of an/other type of relations in which love, and not death, becomes the key motivating element.

The writer's position is a topic of constant scrutiny in *The Book of*

Promethea. The opening pages discuss the writer's task, suggesting that this is one of scribe rather than Creator (pp. 5–8, see also pp. 208–9). 'The book' is 'of Promethea' not only because it is about her but because it is she who produces and dictates what it will say: 'in reality it is she who has already formed the whole text' (p. 5, translation corrected, see also pp. 7–8).[2] Cixous is not the Author but the author, a teller of the tale; a role requiring delicacy and application: 'I shake with a surgeon's terror. If I am not to damage the body's wonderful internal organization, the move must be as delicate as the Creator's. And I am not at all the Creator type. I am merely an author' (p. 5).[3] Writing involves opening to the other – including the myriad shifts such a relationship entails – and the courage to transgress, whenever necessary, social and literary convention.

The author's task is complicated in *The Book of Promethea* by the fact that the author is herself a participant in the story. This division is figured in the splitting of the writing self into I (*je* – sometimes also written *Je*) and H. The adoption of a second position aids the author in writing about herself (p. 175). The division is none the less arbitrary, and in the writing the two positions constantly merge and reoccur:

> I feel so close and yet know I am so different from H and from Promethea. . . . My aim is to slip as close as possible to the two real makers' ['*deux vraies faiseuses*'] being until I can marry the contour of these women's souls with mine, without, however, causing any confusion. But in the extreme closeness sometimes necessary, it is always possible that two I's will verge on each other. (p. 5)

This fragmentation of the writing subject also appears in other texts of this period.[4] *Illa* opens with a series of questions: 'who? Am? . . . I? Us?' (p. 7). As in *The Book of Promethea*, the source of writing is another:

> I received, with the most uncommon violence, the other's first strike in full indifference, in the chest . . . at the time of ignorance, without writing . . . nothing had yet happened, I was struck, with the most precious violence . . . by the other's flash, the door opened I threw myself out of me, adoration began, the narration, the quest, to write. (pp. 29–30, see also p. 12)

The I is variously signified as I, she and they (*elles*), subject to external constraints (see the comic descriptions on pp. 48, 50, 52), and in search of a writing in which 'she' might figure differently (see pp. 57, 58, also the notes on pp. 66–71). In *Ou l'art de l'innocence* ('Or the Art of Innocence'), the question 'I do not yet know in beginning what there is of me in I, who is there . . . who am who' (p. 24) is resolved by 'come who I can be' (p. 24, see also the use of 'I could be' as subject, p. 19) and the distribution of the writing among a number of voices. Although there are differences between the I and the other voices (see, for example, p. 76: 'Aura makes me question my relation . . . to the law of meaning in language'), there is also insistence that these collectively comprise the I (see, for example, p. 79) or aspects of her (see pp. 145, 229, 297). As in *Illa*, there is exploration of the I's formation in relation to others: 'I have learned: to travel alone is to not-travel. . . . I need you' (p. 20, see also pp. 25, 144, 157).

In *The Book of Promethea*, the division of the writing subject between I and H is given a number of justifications. The fact that 'I had reserved two places for myself in the text' (p. 12) means that the author can 'slip continually from one to the other' (p. 12), thereby circumventing the conventional position of mastery.[5] This slippage highlights changes in the I's position and reveals her uncertainty; it also marks a difference between the I who lives with Promethea and the I who is writing her story (p. 11). This is humorously figured in the passage on page 12 in which I imagines herself able to devote her energies to the task of living with Promethea while H, described here as 'my first person' (p. 12), writes: I can delegate to H the job of dealing with all the 'questioning by reporters and police' (p. 12). Recalling the paradox of inside featured in the early texts, this division provides an answer here to I's question: 'how can one manage to be simultaneously inside and outside?' (p. 16, see also p. 18). The distinction also figures the I's doubts as to which of her selves is in love with Promethea (see p. 209).[6] A single subject position would similarly be insufficient to render the complex reality of Promethea (see pp. 40–1), and the writing requires a number of perspectives if this reality is to be conveyed (see p. 49). The I involved in living with Promethea also imposes her need to remember and savour what has happened, and this inevitably shifts the focus away from Promethea (see pp. 40–1). The inclusion of other writing positions is an attempt to hold this egotistical pleasure in check (p. 41).[7] The splitting of the I also images the I's (re)creation *in* the relationship with Promethea (see p. 72, the insistence that Promethea gives birth to I pp. 76, 175). At the same time, it emphasizes the self-transformations that occur in the process of writing (see pp. 96, 128, 141). The fluid nature of the positions is signalled by the author's occasional difficulty in determining who is writing: for example: '(I no longer know if "she" is Promethea or me, in these notes)' (p. 139).

The division between I and H also allows the author to move away from any classification of the writing as autobiography (p. 19). The slippage between the two positions underscores the differences between the I writing and the I of the author (p. 19). The I writing undergoes changes during the course of the writing, a transformation imaged in the frequent disagreements with what has already been said (see p. 55).

The self-questioning and contradictions of the I in *The Book of Promethea* are radically different from the fragmentation and anguished preoccupation of the I of *Inside* and *Angst*. In contrast to the earlier texts, the fluctuating positions are here the result of the endeavour to live and write an/other form of relations. The dissensions and changes are the consequence of our own and the other's continually evolving viewpoints and the present deadly means of representing these. It is noteworthy that the three-way division of I, H and Promethea in *The Book of Promethea* recalls Cixous' insistence, in the early writing, on the need for a third term to break open the current symbiosis of self/other relations.

There is reference in the group of texts produced between 1978 and 1983 to a difference in the author's past and present attitudes to writing. *Anankè* opens with the statement: 'I had just arisen. It was the first October of my new life' (p. 9) and the suggestion that there is a chasm between the author's current and former self who lived only for writing: 'I was so much not me, she I knew at the time I lived for writing' (p. 10, see also pp. 46, 121). This previous self is described as writing in isolation without 'an Other to shine or illuminate the body' (p. 13, see also p. 31) and, in a reworking of the tale of Sleeping Beauty, viewed here as a regressive fairy story told to women to prevent our birth (p. 196), as vainly seeking 'the Promised Town' (p. 30). *Anankè* gives an account of the author's past life that offers an interesting commentary on the texts preceding *Vivre l'orange/To Live the Orange*:

> confine[d] . . . in the same room of repression, her libido well suspended, all her forces attached to one lone object, the lost one, the little o to be rediscovered, the only you or the last king. (p. 14)

'The only you or the last king' recalls the merging of the mother, father and (male) lovers in *Inside* and *Angst* (see also *Anankè*, p. 18, the figure of 'my mother K', pp. 19, 122). It is contrasted in the text with the I's encounter with 'the other than myself' (p. 40, see also p. 128 where the other is described as 'she who teaches you your differences'). A key theme in *Anankè* is the importance of journeying with others: 'if you set out alone . . . all the paths lead you back to me' (p. 134), resulting in the realization that identity is forged in relation to others and that the voyage of self-discovery is consequently never complete (p. 191, see also p. 199). As in all the texts written during this period,[8] the other in *Anankè* is a woman (see pp. 40, 121), and the language and imagery used to describe the I's (re)birth are emphatically female (see pp. 110, 190, 207–8). *Anankè* highlights all the difficulties of this birth. The 'departure' is surveyed by:

> a bloke from the symbolic police [who] looms from behind the unconscious, to throw at her: *'you conduct very badly'*. . . . There was . . . this censure around her and in her, against which she collided. (p. 49, see also pp. 50, 52, 53, 123, 183)

The difficulties are vividly depicted in an imagined play in which the I must adopt a role (see pp. 109, 110) without a god to dictate this to her (p. 150, see also pp. 170–1).

The fact that the writer is a woman is explored in *The Book of Promethea* (see p. 5). The author draws on her capacity to remember: 'as a woman' (p. 9). This capacity to remember what might otherwise be effaced is an important component of Cixous' vision of *écriture féminine* and is evoked in other texts written at this time. In *Le Nom d'Oedipe* ('The Name of Oedipus'), remembering is linked to the mystery of origin. Woman's intimate knowledge of the origin is contrasted with Oedipus' desire which perversely involves renouncing life: 'my whole life for the answer' (p. 26). The destructive nature of Oedipus' longing is underscored by the Chorus as 'the fervent desire for death' (p. 26). Ironically, knowledge is presented as within Oedipus' grasp if only he will 'hear it/Otherwise' (p. 27). It is Oedipus' obsession with the form of the oracle that prevents him from hearing its truth: 'you are just an ordinary man. You do not see the truth unless words have designated it' (p. 27). There is similar insistence on the disjunction between language, with its propensity to order, confine and eliminate, and meaning in *Illa* (see p. 56). This is imaged in the disastrous effects the grand narratives are shown to have on women, distorting our comprehension of the truth:[9]

> when they steal one towards the other outside the fiction realities slave to the principle of women's separation, in the mesh of words, without spice, without smell, without density, without mobility . . . escape from the dehydrated discourse, with the verb with no face, no body, no warmth, and find themselves again in the Great Language they travelled in perfect freedom . . . at the stage of their all-powerfulness. (p. 73, see also pp. 38, 125, the insistence 'a woman who does not forget does not surrender her soul to death' p. 84)

In *Illa* truth emanates from woman's body:

> she [truth] exists, she emanates from the skin of a mature young woman, whose soul has never allowed itself to be seduced or worried by the two fears . . . neither by the fear of love nor by the fear of death, – she is a woman who has never loved out of hate, out of poverty, or out of habit, this is why her body can express the essence of the truth, – what her smile wordlessly promises her body frankly gives, before words – and equally after words –
>
> so now saved, regathered, preserved from the past, all ready to enter into possession of the lost present. (p. 126)

In *Ou l'art de l'innocence*, the link between women, the origin, and new creation in language is also highlighted (see, for example, p. 53), as is the insistence on memory: 'the mystery is woman. . . . Listen from the depths of your body and know' (p. 200).

In *The Book of Promethea*, the fact that Promethea is a woman (see pp. 8–9) is important since it allows H 'to write as herself' (p. 8). As a woman, Promethea supports and encourages the other/author (p. 150).[10] The depiction of the author's female sex connects to the account of the love relation with Promethea to parallel Cixous' descriptions of feminine gender (see the Introduction above). The author's desire to win Promethea, for example, is portrayed as the desire to surround and enable the other through love. This representation of a love relation that aids the other to live and develop (see p. 106) recalls the emphasis on mother love in the preceding texts.

The opening pages of *The Book of Promethea* explore the purpose of writing and compare this with the motivations for the author's previous work.[11] Since H cannot decide where or how to begin the book, she tries a number of approaches at once:

> she no longer knows where to begin: singing, burning, liquidating, flowing, gushing; so she does it almost all at once in moist, glowing disarray. (p. 6)

The verbs – 'singing, burning, liquidating, flowing, gushing' – echo the fluidity, musicality and passion of Cixous' depiction of feminine writing. This is similarly evoked in the author's refusal to select or prioritize from amongst the various possibilities that present themselves.[12] The 'whole book is composed of first pages' (p. 15), each new page denoting an opening (p. 15) with no end (p. 14). The author's approach, deriving from the endeavour to convey Promethea and I/H's love for her (p. 6), involves a relinquishing of all previous methods:

> at the same time she is also busy burning old books, manuals, professional papers, theoretical volumes – because they keep her from doing the one thing that now seems urgent and right to her: shouting her loud hymn of ecstatic pleasure, breaching the hide of the old tongue's hard blare. (p. 6, see also p. 42)[13]

These former methods supported and confirmed H in her dealings with the world (p. 7). They have been 'the champion theories I have so carefully shaped' (p. 6), disguising their real nature as 'hypothesis and illusion' (p. 7) to provide her with a code by which to live (p. 7). Confronted with the 'reality' of Promethea (p. 6), these theories – the existence of which has depended on their confinement within 'symbolic fields' (p. 6) – are proved redundant, their reasoning and distinctions unworkable (p. 7). H must: 'writ[e] off a certain way of living with dictionaries, well-ordered intellectual drawers, high-heeled shoes, jewelry, badges, degrees, funds of knowledge, etc.' (p. 7, see also p. 24). The insistence on abandoning old positions is figured in the 'First notebook' (see p. 79) in terms of attitudes to living. The author realizes she can no longer write as she has done before:

> I am – or was until now – an author who has always worked hard to transform reality into fiction; out of equal respect for reality and for fiction, I felt obliged to be wary of any attempt at representation, and that made me always want to keep writing at some distance from life itself. (p. 12)

This previous approach is inappropriate given the author's aim of writing life with Promethea who precedes and exists outside the writing.[14] Not only is the author no longer the Author, but even her craft is obsolete:

> I have new problems with this book; because up to now I was the one who wrote my books for the most part, at least as far as form was

> concerned. . . . I did not impose a ready-made mold. But I let motifs, melodies, dimensions, colors, suggest themselves to me, like a good architect who considers all the geographical and historical features and the innermost requirements of the divinity that is to reveal itself, in the temple. (p. 13)

This sense of being without even the tools of her craft ('almost redundant' p. 13), waiting on Promethea,[15] recalls Cixous' description of *écriture féminine*. The author's declaration that her mode of proceeding is 'to put myself in Promethea's place' (p. 16) similarly evokes Cixous' depiction, as does her refusal to think or write philosophically: 'my guess is that I could very easily . . . take advantage of this to spare myself any questions thrusting too close to the heart, ones that might possibly ruin the agreeable portrait of myself from which I have derived so much strength and satisfaction' (p. 105).[16] The author defines her aim in writing as:

> the thing I would like to do: record Promethea's right-now, its mystery, the drastic nature of its pure violence.
>
> Write along with the present? I am right there with it. In hot pursuit.
>
> Write before it cools off? Before memory gets there, before it has begun its embalming and forgetting and storytelling.
>
> Welcome its violent strangeness with another strangeness, also violent, its skin peeled away. I would like everything to be written as if Promethea wrote herself alive before me. Suppose there were no paper! I am afraid it muffles our laughter a bit, I hope our cry will tear it.
>
> No rereading, scarcely jotting, quivering . . . (p. 91)

The delineation again evokes Cixous' description of feminine writing. The principal focus is Promethea, rather than any preformed narrative or intention the author may have. The author is not, however, the passive recipient of writing since she must work to accompany her subject and prevent the intrusion of anything that may obscure or alter its truth (see, for example, p. 111). This includes the author's own memories and desires as well as the distorting effects of the signifying process.

In *Ou l'art de l'innocence*, the task of writing present, living truth is depicted as requiring a fluid style, unlike conventional forms of narration to which such an endeavour is alien:

> for when one tells a story, the people who inhabit it remain motionless and alike beneath their name, they do not change their clothes

> throughout their whole lives, their names stay the same, and not only their names, but all their qualities. . . . Whereas living people are never alike for two hours, and even in an hour are completely different, through endless, natural variations. (p. 54)

This has implications for the writing, and the author must strive to create 'a plural, open' space for the text (p. 54). The multi-faceted and changing nature of truth is also figured in the different voices: 'the things Nuriel says are of her truth. This does not mean they are true for me' (p. 57). The author's role is likened to that of 'equilibrist' (p. 250) as she traverses the incessant fluctuations and evolutions of the work.

The author of *The Book of Promethea* must similarly abandon her desire to order and organize the writing in order to create a position for herself. Her task is one of listening (p. 91), of 'exposing myself to impressions as faithfully as I can' (p. 93). *The Book* is described as 'a book of love' (p. 13), 'a book about now' (p. 13); and the author's avowed aim to make Promethea's 'right – her reality, her presence, her grandeur – prevail' (p. 14) entails a double-edged relationship: writing is both the author's adversary (p. 14) since it has the capacity to carry her 'far from the truth' (p. 15, see also pp. 18, 21) and an invaluable aid (pp. 14, 101). Writing *The Book of Promethea* is deemed important as there is the possibility that through this means the love might be shared and 'others can see which way to venture' (p. 17, see also pp. 112, 114). This desire is given credence by the I's reluctance to emerge from the pleasures of the love relation in order to confront the task of writing (p. 18).

There are numerous reflections on the process of writing in *The Book of Promethea*. There is debate as to how the book should begin. This is imaged in the author's desire to reorder the first pages, a desire that clashes with Promethea's 'merciless' insistence that the book should be left as it is (p. 63). The outcome of this discussion is finally resolved by the tossing of a franc coin (p. 63). The debate is resumed over the text's title (pp. 210–11), as well as in the author's decision to leave the 'disorder' of the last notebooks 'in homage to Promethea' (p. 181).

The Book of Promethea also involves a meditation on the nature of love. Early in the text, there is recognition that love includes *being* loved, a situation the author admits she finds difficult (p. 20, see also pp. 105, 159). There is portrayal of feelings and behaviour that fall outside what is generally considered normal, such as the desire to eat (p. 60), wound (see pp. 66, 77, 94–5, 105–6) and possess the other (pp. 105, 118, 143).[17] There is constant reference to the work loving another requires, figured in the image of paradise, attainment of which depends on our incessant labour (p. 60, see also p. 153). The task of (re)creating paradise parallels the work of love since the relation must be continually (re)invented, nourished, nurtured and named (p. 61). Living this paradise, which necessarily lies outside the current schema, involves considerable risk (see p. 67). This is comically portrayed in the imagined fight between the self inebriated by love and the self moulded by the 'State and family gods' (p. 80). Loving is also depicted as dependent on locating and maintaining an appropriate distance to the other (see for example pp. 64–5) in which both self and other can live (see, for example, the discussion on pp. 69–70).[18] This is highlighted in the 'Notebook of Metamorphoses' (p. 138), where separation from the other engenders the other's (re)birth – 'I accept being separated from you . . . to separate you from me, to give you a birth' (p. 142, see also p. 154) – and where the I's own fears of obliteration within the couple are expressed (p. 147).[19]

As elsewhere in Cixous' work, the emphasis in *The Book of Promethea* is on a relation to others that involves equality, delicacy and respect (see pp. 81–2).[20] This relation derives strength from the physical contact between the lovers, which depends on a form of communication beyond words (p. 70). The fact that the lovers are women is also highlighted, and this is linked to a mode of living the love relationship that evokes Cixous' description of femininity (see the Introduction above). I's desire for Promethea is presented as a desire which – in contradistinction to any masculine attempt to conquer or render her same – delights in her differences: 'I do not want to win, if I were victorious I would be the one defeated. . . . I want to know you by means of every science and every art, but I want you to keep yourself intact' (p. 107).[21]

The love relationship with Promethea nevertheless includes a problem: how to live its paradise while at the same time remembering the plight of others (see p. 81). The admission that paradise must involve both (see p. 153) marks a significant departure from the self-preoccupations of *Inside* and *Angst*.[22]

The insistence on the present – on writing the present reality of Promethea (see p. 13) – is similarly a key concern,[23] echoing the emphasis of earlier texts. While the author must strive to relinquish past perspectives and techniques (and especially those which derive from her own history [see pp. 30–31], real, historical time none the less has a place in the writing. This is again figured in terms of interior and exterior – the 'inside' and 'outside' which are such consistent motifs of Cixous' work. Here the interior present of loving/living with Promethea (referred to on p. 33 as the 'Present Absolute') eclipses the exterior fact that it is 1982 (p. 30). This is most forcefully expressed on page 101 where advancement 'inside' Promethea entails a simultaneous abandoning of history (p. 101).

The need to remember what is happening beyond the interior of the couple is a consistent theme of this group of texts. In *Le Nom d'Oedipe,* the importance of 'keeping alive what is no more' (p. 58) is given as justification for Jocasta's actions, even though her inability to connect past and present (p. 64) precipitates her death. In *Illa,* there is the recognition that the labour of living the present (see p. 168) must incorporate whatever is painful or ugly (pp. 165–6, 170). In *Ou l'art de l'innocence,* the author reminds herself as she sits writing on her balcony: '"at this moment you are in luxury, and the essence of luxury is: peace. Do not forget the reality"' (p. 247, see also pp. 269, 292, 298). This reminder leads to a redefinition of 'happiness in History' (p. 294), as both 'prehistoric happiness, the happiness of living simply living' (p. 294) and 'the happiness of drawing life from death' (p. 294, see also p. 301).[24]

Recognition of human mortality is present in *The Book of Promethea* in the insistence that love encompass history. Acknowledgement of death is the prerequisite to greater participation in life (see p. 128). This is expressed on pages 196–200, where the author compares her past – a life 'not without its charms but lacking flesh and warmth and seasons, a life with nothing worth dying for' (p. 196) – with the day-to-day reality of living with Promethea (p. 197).

I suggested in the Introduction that for Cixous a feminine mode of writing centres on the other.[25] In *The Book of Promethea,* writing the other is the author's avowed aim. Here all the difficulties of 'putting life into words' (p. 21) are compounded by the fact that the purpose of the writing is 'translating someone else' (p. 21). The author must avoid the lie (p. 21, see also p. 28) of imputing words to Promethea if she is to achieve her goal. This nevertheless gives rise to a problem, since the obvious solution – 'take down Promethea's words under dictation' (p. 21) – fails to convey the nature of the author's relationship with Promethea and especially what is not said in words (p. 21).

The author of *The Book of Promethea* refers to the work of Clarice Lispector as inspirational in this regard (see p. 36). Cixous' response to the writing of Clarice Lispector is set out in detail in *Vivre l'orange/To Live the Orange*. Her homage to Lispector's work presents an interesting commentary on the texts of this period.[26] In *Vivre l'orange* Cixous outlines her suspicion of 'words that fall upon things and fix their quaverings and make them discordant and deafen them' (p. 8), citing by contrast:

> those [*'celles'*] whose speaking is so profound, so intense, whose voices pass gently behind things and lift them and gently bathe them, and take the words in their hands and lay them with infinite delicateness close by things, to call them and lull them without pulling them and rushing them. There are women who speak to watch over and save, not to catch. (p. 8)

This comparison, between a language the express purpose of which is to 'seize and mean' (p. 8, see also p. 74), and a language which attempts to 'remain near by things . . . to reflect and protect' (p. 8, see also p. 10), recalls Cixous' own writing during this period in its refusal to impose external categories and its concern to safeguard life (see, for example, p. 106). Central to *Vivre l'orange* is the notion that while our relation to others is also linguistic, this symbolic connection does not mean the severing of words from experience. This is figured in *Vivre l'orange* through the comparison of Cixous' own hitherto rather abstract writing with Lispector's written gift of the orange:

> my hand had no more the goodness of knowing the orange's goodness, the fruit's fullness, my writing was separated from the orange, didn't go to it, didn't call it, didn't carry the juice to my lips.
>
> . . . She put the orange back into the deserted hands of my writing. (p. 14)

For Lispector, Cixous suggests, language retains a link with the pre-symbolic experience of being in the world (p. 46), and thus is in contrast to 'these feeble and forgetful times, when we are far away from things, so far from each other, very far from ourselves' (p. 46). This bond between language and the body is expressed in *The Book of Promethea* through the author's desire to maintain an umbilical cord with both domains (see below). The orange of *Vivre l'orange* also figures the present time (see p. 18), and the insistence on 'saving the moment' (p. 18) recalls this theme in *The Book of Promethea*. There is repeated emphasis in *Vivre l'orange* that the present must include not only the present experiences of the self but also the wider present of history. This is exemplified in the telephone call reminding Cixous of the plight of women in Iran: 'one thing is not to forget the orange. Another to save oneself in the orange. But it's another thing not to forget Iran' (pp. 22–4, see also pp. 76, 80). There is reference to the self-transformations this other approach entails. Enabling others involves the self in a series of threatening and potentially self-destructive risks (p. 24), especially where this is undertaken in writing (p. 24, see also pp. 28, 82). The task requires 'innocence' (p. 28) – despite the overwhelming proof that 'murder is stronger than love' (p. 88) – as well as a willingness to abandon all previous strategies (pp. 28, 30, 36, 40).

Cixous suggests in *Vivre l'orange* that a keynote of Lispector's writing is its refusal to shy away from or exclude whatever is difficult, painful or potentially menacing to the self (pp. 58, 76, 92).[27] Again, the emphasis is on a way of *including*, expressed in the recognition: 'we do not know how to forget the dead without forgetting life' (p. 90, see also p. 100). As in *The Book of Promethea*, Cixous stresses the importance of this mode of writing which, despite its problems and dangers, can aid us to live more fully (pp. 106, 108) and hence initiate changes in the prevailing schema.

In *The Book of Promethea*, the relation to the other – figured in the love relation with Promethea – entails transformation of the self. This is described in the opening pages of the 'First notebook' (pp. 79–85), where the self must descend from the tower in which she has lived 'barefoot . . . to meet the other' (p. 82). Here the various changes the self undergoes – 'changes of economy. Hairstyle. Makeup. Changes of taste, stubbornness. Dreams' (p. 81, translation corrected) – are imaged in a sudden outpouring of the 'words she did not want to say' (p. 83). The outburst is 'immodest, immediate, inconsiderate' (p. 83), and thus contravenes all previous restrictions (p. 83), but is also a release since it is perhaps the closest the I has come to expressing her 'secrets' (p. 83). In a comic twist, the text represents this outpouring with a line of dots – '". . . . . ."' (p. 83) since to reproduce it would be to lessen both its truth (p. 83) and its impact (p. 84). The self's transformation involves 'learning dispossession' (p. 85): 'dispossessing herself of all her reserves' (p. 85) and abandoning former strategies (p. 85). The accompanying move into the present – the actual present of the love relation – is portrayed as the means of advancing (p. 85). This theme of dispossession – on page 136 the text is described as a 'book on relinquishment, dispossession' – with its return to innocence (p. 85, see also p. 102), evokes *Ou l'art de l'innocence*. As in *Ou l'art de l'innocence*, it is a love relation with others that enables 'our own possibility of growth' (p. 105).

The difficulties of writing *The Book of Promethea* are constantly highlighted.[28] Writing cannot convey the physical reality of Promethea, nor the effect her presence has on the author (see p. 53). This inability of language to render present reality is figured on page 101, where the author is reduced to employing a series of dots: 'to try to name the . . . to try to name this . . . without naming it, to try to surround this . . . so Immediate, this so real Real'.[29] Even on those occasions where she succeeds in finding a written expression, what she achieves will be no more than 'three or four of your footprints' (p. 108) since she can never communicate the full reality in words (see pp. 158, 183). This general difficulty connects to the specific problem that here it is *happiness* the author is attempting to convey (see p. 134).[30] The author sets out her aims in writing in a passage that parallels Cixous' description of *écriture féminine*:

> I would have liked (me too) so much to film Eternity! To stop one fine instant and take it close up. Filming the way we live; slow motion or speeded up, skimming over time, with all our memories brought together, with our memories of different yesteryears, with east and north, deserts and citadels, with its lightning memory of the future, with our fates foreshortened, every instant with its radiant procession of reminiscences, forebodings, impending transmutations, with all its sparkle, its shadow, its echoes, and always the heart's music . . .
>
> And what else? Everything unsayable: laughter. Our cosmic mental geography. (p. 111)

Language may transport the author away from her subject, embroiling her in metaphors that obscure the truth of what she wants to convey and which adversely affect her (pp. 86–7, 183–4). Words are imbued with their over-usage (p. 183), and contain a history and etymology that frequently belie the author's intention (p. 210).

This latter point is a theme of a number of other texts written at this time. In *Ou l'art de l'innocence*, there is insistence on a more immediate form of understanding and knowledge which transmission distorts:

> all this is deliciously simple to understand in the warmth of immediate comprehension, but I have difficulties in rendering the nature of this pleasure understandable by external intelligence. Take for instance the simple idea: 'the origin of confidence is the milk sucked at the breast', as long as it is expressed in the warm from me to you, between us, it keeps its brilliant consistency of a certitude. But as soon as I express it in external surroundings, before suspicious peo-

> ple, with rejectile ears, far from the unconscious, oriented towards capturing almost sound-proof waves produced by the forming of concepts – almost always men, beings who have a horror of milk, my idea loses its warmth, I no longer feel the taste of its truth in my mouth, it falls from my lips like an artificial phrase. (pp. 218–19)[31]

Although the author's declared intention in writing here is to 'celebrate living' (p. 257) and create 'the book of You', what she produces 'is only shadow and allusion, not even of my hand, but already spoken by French' (p. 257). *Limonade tout était si infini* also addresses this discrepancy between desire and language. Here the author's task is defined as 'saying without detours the essential things in all their simplicity' (p. 165, see also pp. 11, 17). In *La Bataille d'Arcachon*, the problematic nature of language is imaged in terms of 'evil phrases':

> the evil ones are thick, opaque and they work like crooks: they divert attention onto themselves. They mirror. . . . I have thrown out a whole scene which I had allowed heaps of bulky phrases covered in decorations to parasite. (p. 71)

This difficulty connects with a further problem outlined in *The Book of Promethea*. Even if the author were to succeed in her aim of rendering her subject 'pulsating into tender palms of paper' (p. 102), there is always the danger that her gift will not be so received (p. 207).

The author's project of writing *The Book of Promethea* involves a dilemma of perspective: the author cannot live the love relation and write about it simultaneously (p. 93)[32] since writing requires a certain distance:

> because on the inside there is only the immediate present thundering past, there is only the present and a present that goes by like lightning, flash by flash, goes by spearing and lancing fire, every instant cuts through and there is not even the tiniest instant of past or future in which to set one's pen or slightly sidelong thought. . . . One is in the center, there is only center, no edge, no end. (p. 94)

Promethea herself interrupts the writing, with suggestions and remonstrations (see pp. 206–7). In addition, the author must deal with the self-doubt that constantly pursues her, hampering her ability to write (p. 108, see also p. 110).

The possibilities of language and writing are also highlighted in the text. The incessant (re)creation involved in living the love relation (p. 87) parallels and can be enhanced by writing.[33] There is evocation of a language and writing that will transcend the current order, as in the imagined 'name composed of several different colored words . . . that spoke several languages at once' (p. 98, see also p. 99).[34]

There is an insistence in all the text of this period on a writing that will aid us with living. In *Ou l'art de l'innocence*, the possibilities of language – 'language is like life inventing itself' (p. 8) – link to the vision of a writing 'limitless like life' that 'only asks us to tell more' (p. 9). This other language and writing are contrasted with the discourse of the 'men-men' (p. 9), who refuse 'the language that is creating and magnificent . . . and lavish' (p. 9) to 'hunt it or capture it in order to crucify it or stone it or rack it as soon as it sends them a word' (p. 9). A possible delineation of a new, feminine language and writing is given in the reference to Aura: 'if she wrote as things came to her, it would be beyond books, constellatory, radiating from all sides, resonating with every language at once' (p. 75). Even though the author ultimately fails in her attempt to write in an/other way in *Ou l'art de l'innocence* (see pp. 264, 275), there is insistence on the positive benefits of the endeavour. Through writing, the author transgresses 'the law of silence' (p. 260), and may even find unlooked-for and unexpected gains (see pp. 265, 280). Writing can propel the I beyond the ego towards others (pp. 271, 280), and offers a means of bridling language 'so that it ceases speaking before my thoughts' (p. 280).

In *Limonade tout était si infini*, the problem centres on the writing of a single, true phrase. The task is presented in terms of the oblivion which afflicts modern life:

> she had succeeded in confiding the phrase [*'la phrase'*]. No matter what happened to her in the future, inadequate being, impure, little gifted for grace, a thing of truth, a fragment of life, was saved. (p. 172)

Writing ensures the expression of this truth (see p. 20). Recalling Cixous' criticism of the art that endeavours to seduce its audience (see the Introduction above), the emphasis in *Limonade tout était si infini* is on a mutually enabling mode of living and writing (see p. 187) that will create – not a 'work of prey' (p. 193) – but a 'work of being' (p. 189).

A further aspect of the writing of *The Book of Promethea* which reflects Cixous' description of *écriture féminine* is the author's desire that it should be the reader who will finally write the book. This is imaged in the passage on page 210 in which the 'necklace' of Promethea's dreams is offered to the reader: 'everyone can try on the necklace; and you can add all the things you would really like to receive'.[35]

There is reference throughout *The Book of Promethea* to a writing of the body (see below), an emphasis that is also present in other texts written at this time. In *Illa,* there is evocation of the possibility of transmission 'from hand to hand' (p. 21) as well as the revelation of the 'body's secret: the body continues. After the separation' (p. 99).[36] This view of the body's role implies a different relation to others and language. The writer must learn:

> to say: egg, like I say to you: love; with astonishment and love: from contemplation. . . . Egg! And now we remember the egg . . . let it oscillate, ripen, while respecting it, grow and shine, in such a way that it gives itself to us alive, warm, raw and written according to our need. (p. 132)

In *Ou l'art de l'innocence* there is the highlighting of a body knowledge (p. 84, see also p. 218) linked to the language of lovers: 'presenting one common grammatical feature: the existence of a singular plural pulsional personal pronoun . . . bearing neither prohibition nor restriction' (pp. 91–2). This is figured in the text in the references to thoughts which derive directly from feelings (see pp. 102, 114), and thus predate the law's intervention (pp. 114, 115, see also p. 130), and in H's communication of her 'secret':

> what I am telling you now through emission of the body at high temperature, has not undergone any interpretation or mechanical, chemical or symbolic treatment from me, nor detour via the brain, I emit it to you purely, as it rises warm from my lungs to my glottis, do you feel? (p. 216)

This links to the possibility of an 'art of innocence' (see p. 134: 'the supreme knowledge: the knowing-not-to-know') in which the relationship to the body and others is maintained: 'a divinely knowing grace: she does not know lack thus she knows all. . . . She stays, naturally . . . beyond the Law' (p. 232). The result of such grace is works of art 'whose author is no one other than the Being-Alive of our living' (p. 232). The 'innocence' of *Ou l'art de l'innocence* is a reawakened 'feeling' that will undo the repressive prohibitions of the law without regression into non-communication (pp. 116, 144).

In *The Book of Promethea,* this emphasis on the body is expressed in the numerous references to the physical sensations generated by the love relation (see pp. 129–30, 181) and in the use of body imagery to describe the writing (see, for example, p. 136). Words are portrayed – not as separate from the body – but as connected to the body's experience. This is exemplified in the passage on page 148 where the I feels her whole life is at stake as she calls out to Promethea: 'I put my heart into this word'. This refusal to see the split between the physical realm of the body and the symbolic realm of language as complete and final is also portrayed in the author's comparison between her relationship to language and Promethea's. Unlike Promethea, who has not 'cut the cord binding words to her body' (p. 154), the author confesses: 'sometimes, like most people I know, I speak . . . a thoughtless, fickle, superficial language, likely to flip over to its opposites, one that does not really care at all about what it says' (p. 154). The easy, preformed mechanisms of language slide the author away from the truth: 'slipping up on a few words that are too polite, too polished, I skid sometimes, I miss the point of what I meant to say, I miss the truth' (p. 155). The solution, in *The Book of Promethea*, lies in following Promethea and working to repair the 'cord between my belly and my words' (p. 155).[37]

The form of *The Book of Promethea*, despite a number of innovative stylistic features, such as the fragmentation and occasional disappearance (see pp. 70, 82) of the writing subject, the use of parentheses (see p. 130) and unusual modes of narration (see the presentation of Promethea's 'class' in the manner of Jane Fonda's *Workout* pp. 172–4), is on the whole more conventional than that of other texts written during this period.[38] 'The Book' is composed of a series of short 'scenes', written for the most part in conventionally structured sentences which are in striking contrast to the long, unpunctuated segments of *Ou l'art de l'innocence*. The tone is easy, almost conversational.[39] Unlike other texts produced during this period, there is little play on words.[40] The recounting of the relationship between I/H and Promethea involves the reader, offering a framework of interest and organization that is radically different to the self-preoccupation and disorder of *Inside* and *Angst*. The dramatization of I/H and Promethea's endeavours to live a love relation also marks a significant development from the mere evocation of this in earlier work. However, despite this dramatizing of an/other model of relations, the other remains a personal other in *The Book of Promethea*. Although there is insistence that the love relation must include others beyond the interpersonal sphere, this is not accomplished in the text. Thus, while there is a progression beyond the exploration of the self in the embodying of an alternative pattern of self/other relations, its potential to transform the political, social and cultural schema remains visionary. Despite the numerous ways outlined above in which the writing of *The Book of Promethea* realizes Cixous' depiction of *écriture féminine*, this lack of any tangible engagement with the wider world mitigates its achievement. In the next period of writing, Cixous turns from this personal dramatization to history itself, a transition which entails the adoption of a different literary genre.

4

Cixous and the Theatre

> Pour que la porte s'ouvre qui donne sur Toi . . . il faut que moi-qui-ne-suis-pas-toi ait réussi à s'oublier.
>
> 'Qui es-tu?', in *Indiade ou l'Inde de leurs rêves*, p. 267

> For the door to open that gives onto You . . . I-who-am-not-you must have succeeded in forgetting myself.
>
> 'Who Are You?'

Although it can be argued that *The Book of Promethea*, for the reasons outlined in Chapter 3, offers the most complete illustration from Cixous' work up to 1983 of an *écriture féminine*, there nevertheless remains the problem that Promethea is a personal other drawn directly from Cixous' own life experience. In the two plays Cixous wrote in conjunction with the Théâtre du Soleil, *L'Histoire terrible mais inachevée de Norodom Sihanouk roi du Cambodge* ('The Terrible but Unfinished Story of Norodom Sihanouk King of Cambodia') and *Indiade ou l'Inde de leurs rêves* ('Indiada or the India of their Dreams'),[1] this focus alters to include the other(s) of history.

Cixous' transition to writing for the theatre and engagement with the historical realites of war in Cambodia and Indian Independence raises a number of questions in terms of her literary project. The adoption of traditional dramatic form, where considerations of staging curtail the extent to which the writer may allow the components of writing their own generation, appears at odds with Cixous' delineation of *écriture féminine*. Similarly, theatre's dependence on characters and the nature of spoken exchanges seem incompatible with a view of writing in which the multifarious possibilities produced by the signifying operation are to be reinscribed. Writing is only one element of theatre, a fact that would appear to contradict

Cixous' insistence on *writing*. The impact of the body and the unconscious – key aspects of Cixous' vision of *écriture féminine* – equally seem hard to equate with the theatre. It will be the task of this chapter to explore these apparent contradictions.

In the second of the two plays written for the Théâtre du Soleil, *Indiade ou l'Inde de leurs rêves*, Cixous outlines her motivations and experience of writing for the theatre in a series of postscripts.[2] 'Le Lieu du Crime, le lieu du Pardon' ('The Place of Crime, The Place of Forgiveness')[3] opens with the following question:

> how can the poet open his/her universe to people's destinies? S/he who is first of all an explorer of the Self, how, in what language foreign to his/her ego, by what means could s/he write much more and altogether other than Me? (p. 253)

Cixous' answer in these postscripts involves a review of her œuvre up to her liaison with the Théâtre du Soleil, and an examination of how the requirements of theatre have affected and enabled her writing.

In 'L'Incarnation' ('Incarnation')[4] Cixous describes her previous method of writing fiction and contrasts this with her work for the theatre:

> in the infancy of the work, there is the ego, its terrors, its questions, its who-will-I-bes, its cries of thirst, its somber and demonized chambers.
>
> I had to write certain texts in order to tidy these chambers and appease my ego. Once peace is obtained, in work as in life, one can hope that the ego will fall silent, leaving the terrain to the world. Diminished, enlarged, may it fade away altogether into the distance, and the immense naked beach on which it did its noisy exercises be returned finally to its foreign guests, to the non-egos, to the passers-by, to humanity. Enter then the Others! I have the honor of being the stage for the other. (p. 260)[5]

Cixous' account of the evolution of her writing is reiterated in the 'Conversations' in *Writing Differences*, where she stresses:

> the inaugural gesture of writing is always in a necessary relation to narcissism. . . . It takes time for 'I' to get used to 'I'. Time for the 'I' to be sure 'I' exists. Only then is there room for the other. (p. 153)

Commenting on Clarice Lispector's strategy of changing her sex in order to approach the other of Macabea in *The Hour of the*

Star, Cixous describes her own very different solution to writing others:

> I have only been able to resolve the question in an equivalent movement to Clarice's strategy which consists in making the author I am fade to the point of disappearing. I, the author, have to disappear so that you, so other, can appear. My answer has come through writing for the theatre.
>
> On the stage, I, the author, am no longer there, but there is the other. And even the absolute other, the absolute stranger . . .
>
> My work now is child of the theatre, product of the theatre, but I have had to go through all the various stages to come to this point. I have had to change genres and I've only been able to do that through working on the 'I'. And the work has taken time. (p. 153)

In 'Le Lieu du Crime, le lieu du Pardon', Cixous reflects on the nature of the theatre and suggests how it has enabled her to move away from a writing of the self to a writing of others. She argues that in the theatre it is impossible for the writer to install him- or herself at the centre of the text, since the theatre is by definition 'the land of others':

> there was the stage, the earth, where the ego remains imperceptible, the land of others. There their words make themselves heard, and their silences, their cries, their song, each according to his/her own world and in his/her foreign tongue. (p. 253)

In 'A Realm of Characters' in *Delighting the Heart: A Notebook by Women Writers*,[6] Cixous outlines how the theatre imposes a time-scale on the writer (p. 126)[7] as well as the creation of characters whose hopes, passions, conflicts, struggles, form the basis of the play (p. 126). In 'Le Lieu du Crime, le lieu du Pardon' Cixous explores how this requirement of inventing characters furnished her with the solution to a problem:

> how can I, who am of the literate species, ever give speech to an illiterate peasant woman without taking it away from her, with one stroke of my language, without burying her with one of my fine sentences? In my texts would there never be but people who know how to read and write, to juggle with signs? . . . For a long time I thought my texts would only live in those rare and desert places where only poems grow. (p. 253)

In 'A Realm of Characters' Cixous stresses that 'until quite recently none of my texts had characters in them' (p. 126),[8] and she explains how her discovery of the theatre involved the parallel discovery of others (p. 126).

Cixous' account of writing for the theatre in 'A Realm of Characters' is significantly presented in a form that echoes her depictions of *écriture féminine*. She argues that when she writes for the theatre she is inhabited by others, and that her task is to give birth to these others by listening to what they say:[9]

> writing for the theatre, I am haunted by a universe of fictitious but real people. It's the strangest, most magical experience. I live, inhabited by my characters, who give me the same feelings real people give me, except that they live inside me, I am their home. There are those I detest, those I rejoice in, those who make me laugh; some who exasperate me, others I love and admire. They are characters full of colour who tell me their lives. I note down everything they say. I write as quickly as I can, trying to get everything down. I listen for their voices, through their conflicts, their encounters, their struggles. (p. 126)[10]

The imaging of the writer's role as scribe is reminiscent of the description of the author's task in *The Book of Promethea* (see Chapter 3 above).[11]

In 'Qui es-tu?' ('Who Are You?'),[12] Cixous delineates this process of giving voice to the others who will inhabit and create the play as a parable:

> a man comes knocking at his friend's door: 'Who are you?' the friend asks. – 'It is I,' the visitor replies.
>
> – Then go away, I do not know you since you do not admit me . . .
>
> The man returns all aflamed with love and need, after a year of meditation. 'Who are you?' the friend asks. 'I am you'.
>
> Then the door opens, and you and I are at last sitting in the garden, you and I, with two faces but a single soul.
>
> For the door to open that gives onto You, the desired person, I-who-am-not-you must have succeeded in forgetting myself. (p. 267)

Cixous compares this work of opening to the other with the actor's task of recreating the character on stage. She suggests that it is a process involving humility, sacrifice and risk (p. 268), the courage to relinquish the secure but restrictive concerns of the ego (pp. 268, 269, 270) and, above all, attentiveness to the human heart (p. 268). This return to the heart is important since, Cixous writes, it is here that the author and actor may discover the passions and motivations of others.[13]

Cixous explores in the postscripts to *Indiade* and in 'A Realm of Characters' how the creation of characters places her in the position of receptacle and amanuensis. Her account echoes her earlier insistence that the feminine writer, like a good mother, must enable and give others birth. She suggests that the invention of characters required by the theatre has led to her involvement with a variety of others, some of whom would previously have been inaccessible to her, either because in the course of writing she would have transformed them into Cixous equivalents or because their motivations and actions are beyond her sphere of experience. This engagement with a variety of others – and particularly those who appear most foreign – is clearly important in terms of Cixous' project.

In 'Qui es-tu?', Cixous reiterates her insistence that it is the characters who create the play:

> I open the door. They enter. And it happens. I mean: they create the scene, do the work. Or they refuse to do it. A freedom reigns on the stage that no longer depends on any author, but only on their destinies. (p. 276)

She suggests that each character has 'their life, their path' (p. 276), so that 'the stage is full of worlds, each [character] speaking loudly, humbly or grandly, each thinking the world in their own way' (p. 276). The author's task is to ensure that each character has an opportunity to express him- or herself. Her role is to: 'give them space. Give them their importance in the story. Their chance. A destiny' (p. 275); she must allow 'the heart's beating to sound exactly' (p. 275). This living of her characters (p. 275) is a process Cixous compares with the writing of fiction. In 'Qui es-tu?' she suggests that often, when a scene fails, it is precisely because she has *written* and not lived:

> this is when 'It is I', the author, who starts *writing*. Yes, this happens. How? Well, the author lets him or herself be seduced by a theme that runs through a scene. A magnificent theme, a temptation. One could write a book of poems, a philosophic treatise on the subject of this theme. And it is here one forgets the stage, the theatre and its law: 'be here', 'be present'. (p. 275)

The highlighting of the present in this passage is also noteworthy in terms of Cixous' depiction of feminine writing.

In *The Book of Promethea*, the author describes her difficulties writing those others she does not love. She compares herself to

Promethea who embraces 'everyone . . . with love that fits each of their sizes perfectly' (p. 186). The author's love, by contrast, is 'limited, dull, lazy' (p. 185, translation corrected). The difficulty is sidestepped in the writing of Promethea since Promethea is an other the author loves. It is a problem the writer of a play on the partition of India and the war in Cambodia necessarily confronts.[14] Cixous analyses the task of writing others who are remote or unacceptable to her in 'L'Incarnation'. Here she employs the image of motherlove to delineate the role the author – and actors – must adopt (p. 263). In 'Qui es-tu?' she argues that a certain distance between author and character can even be an advantage, since it is harder for the author if the character is too close to ensure that their words and actions are not her own:

> in truth it is much harder to create characters with whom one feels emotional affinities than those with whom one does not feel the least familiarity. Harder to make the beings I love speak, for I must distance them from Me, render them foreign to me in order to free them from me and to free myself from them. Thus Nehru, who for me is too obvious, will have caused me more fond anxieties than the dissolute head-minister of an Indian province. His language was not foreign enough to me. And if I were, through lack of vigilance, to make a mistake and make him speak like me? For one must treat the near and the far, the loved and the hated, equally as if they are unknown. (p. 274)

The parallels with Cixous's evocation of feminine writing are again striking.

Cixous explores this relationship further in 'L'Incarnation', where she repeats her belief that the author's role is to give all the characters an equal chance (p. 264), including those she personally finds odious (p. 264). She suggests that the way to communicate those others she finds alien is to heed her own feelings and reactions:

> there are odious characters in my play. Hatred exalts them. What do I know about hatred? That which uneasy and trusting love made me suffer and discover. Like everyone else.
>
> In reality, I couldn't have endured meeting these odious ones. But in truth I let them take pleasure in their rage, by filtering through me. (p. 264)

This account again recalls Cixous' description of *écriture féminine*. In a passage reminiscent of her depiction of the feminine writer's role, Cixous compares the dramaturge's task with the actor's, emphasizing the importance of abandoning the ego and providing the other with maternal space:

> acrobats, the actors jump over the emptiness left by the ego. Such a detachment from self in order to join the other to whom we yield ourselves entirely, this is a form of sainthood.
>
> The actor is always something of a saint, something of a woman: life must be given while withdrawing onself. (p. 265)[15]

In 'L'Incarnation' Cixous outlines how in writing for the theatre she is, for the first time, able to include men among her literary others. Her explanation offers further illumination into her description of the theatre as the space of the human heart. She argues that in her previous fictional writing, because of her approach, she was unable to create characters who are authentically male:

> I have never dared to create a real male character in fictional texts. Why? Because I write with my body, and I'm a woman and a man is a man and I know nothing of his pleasure. And a man without a body and without pleasure, I can't do that. (p. 265)

In writing for the theatre, drama's capacity to focus on the essential combines with the actors' physical embodiment of the roles to enable the creation of men:

> at the theater it's the heart that sings, the chest opens, we see the heart rend itself. The human heart has no sex. The heart feels in the same way in a man's chest as in a woman's chest. This doesn't mean that the characters are half-creatures who stop at the waist. No, our creatures are lacking nothing, neither penis, nor breasts, nor loins, nor womb. But I don't have to write this. The actor, the actress gives us the whole body which we don't have to invent. And everything is lived and everything is true. This is the gift the theater gives to the author: incarnation. (pp. 265–6)[16]

This highlighting of the body evokes Cixous' descriptions of *écriture féminine.*

Cixous' emphasis on the human heart is echoed in her conception of what theatre is. In 'Le Lieu du Crime, le lieu du Pardon' she argues that the theatre:

> allows us to live what no other 'genre' does: the hell we have in being human. The Evil. What occurs in the theater is Passion, but the

> Passion according to Oedipus, according to Hamlet, according to you, according to Woyzeck, according to me, according to Othello, according to Cleopatra, according to Marie, according to this enigmatic, tortured, criminal, innocent human being that I am, who is thou or you.
>
> I believe that today more than ever we need our own theater, the theater whose stage is our heart, on which our destiny and our mystery are acted out, and whose curtain we see so rarely rise. (pp. 253–4, see also 'L'Incarnation' p. 264)

Cixous suggests that this return to the heart is especially important at the present time, in which the all-pervasive influence of the media shapes our thoughts and reactions, preventing us from hearing the truth (p. 254).[17] The theatre remains one of the few places in which such a return is permitted:

> what a relief when, entering this place, the lies which are our daily politenesses stop, and we begin to hear the dialogue of hearts! We would cry from it. And we rejoice that it's not forbidden, in this marvellous country, to utter cries, to strike blows, to translate the suffering that comes from being a human inhabitant of our epoch into breath, sweat, song.
>
> We are the characters of an epic that we are forbidden, by the laws of mediocrity and prudence, to live. (pp. 254–5)[18]

This stress on theatre's capacity to overcome the corruption and destruction of the current schema recalls Cixous' delineation of the aims of feminine writing.

Corruption is a key theme of *Sihanouk*. It is expressed initially through the character of Sihanouk, who describes his country's corruption as an illness:

> our country still suffers from corruption. It's a tropical, stubborn and contagious sickness. I wonder how to cure it for, you see, the problem is that everyone wants to catch it. (p. 22, see also p. 20)

While the various factions that vie with each other for control of Cambodia are presented, initially at least, in terms which make them appear plausible, even desirable, each becomes a prey to corruption. The dreams of the Khmer Rouge for a reborn, innocent Cambodia (see p. 61), for example, are sabotaged as victory becomes more important than its cost in human life:

> Khieu Samphan: we must not count our dead. We must from now on count only our victories. We alone are masters of the meanings of

> events. It is up to us to interpret them as it suits us. The massacre has served our cause, thus it is a good thing. (pp. 85–6)[19]

It is Sihanouk's capacity to remain attuned to the essential – expressed, for example, in his grief at Ho Chi Minh's death and decision to render him homage by attending his funeral even though it is politically unwise for him to do so (see pp. 104–5) – that keeps him, in spite of his vanity and political opportunism, at the play's centre.[20]

In 'Le Lieu du Crime, le lieu du Pardon' Cixous develops her thesis that it is by listening to the human heart that the author – as well as the actors and audience – create the play. She stresses: 'what causes wars, peace, massacres, heroisms – looking closely, pulling back the curtain, are tiny and powerful humans' (p. 255). It is this that the theatre explores: 'Theater has kept the secret of the History sung by Homer: History is made up of the stories of husbands, lovers, fathers, daughters, mothers, sons, stories of jealousy, pride, desire' (p. 255). Cixous continues this argument in the Introduction to *Indiade*. Puzzling as to why the struggle for Indian Independence – a fight which 'united and carried 400 million Indians from every religion and caste towards the same end' (p. 12) – should have resulted in partition, she suggests that the answer lies in the conjunction of history – 'the second world war, political chance, the English only too pleased to weaken the Freedom Fighters of the Indian Congress by pressurising the Muslim League' (p. 13, see also p. 15) – and the aspirations and weaknesses of individuals:

> separations, regions cast out of India, alliances of parties, torments of populations, promises made, kept, broken, events appear with the poignant and familiar forms of our passions. The heart's tempests, recognitions, repudiations, rediscoveries, it is all there. (p. 14)[21]

History, within which we are located and which we necessarily contribute to (p. 255), begins and is reflected in our individual history. In 'Le Lieu du Crime, le lieu du Pardon' Cixous writes: 'the human being needs to become human. Human? I mean s/he is the scene of the war between good and evil' (p. 255).[22] This emphasis offers an interesting interpretation of the personal struggles delineated in Cixous' early fiction. In her Introduction to *Indiade*, Cixous suggests that it is this link between individuals and history that the play explores: 'it is a play about the human being, the hero and the dust, the fight between the angel and the beast in each one of us' (p.

16). This combat is figured through India's partition, and the inner conflicts of individuals: Sikander: 'the Muslim in me esteems the great Jinnah, but the Indian does not like your threats and does not recognize your claim' (p. 69).

This view of history is present in Cixous' earlier stage play *La Pupille*.[23] Here history is depicted as an open space (p. 7), figured by a large, iridescent globe (p. 7). The Theatre (itself one of the play's participants) symbolizes the body of history, providing a forum for, and in turn formed by, the actors and audience:

> The Fool: 'look, the Theatre has a glass body. Everything is moving there. Let us go in, softly, violently! who knows what monster our adventure will engender? What mutations our entering will produce? History is not closed. Its body is theatre's space. We are in this body as the child in the mother. But a mother who is open, visible, explorable, universal. (pp. 7–8)[24]

The description is endorsed in the play by the Theatre itself:

> I am the lawless space of displacements, the limitless body of History . . .
>
> Nations travel on my body. A spark in the pit of my stomach and it's another history! And he, yonder, crossing me, he is my becoming. He is the nucleus without which I am inconceivable: me the shell, he the hatching. (p. 47, see also p. 110)

Cixous' plea for a mode of living closer to the heart, linking individuals beyond our narcissism and fear, is also expressed here (see pp. 13, 23, 25, 94).

Theatre's role in staging history means it is a place where death is necessarily encountered. For Cixous, this inclusion of death is essential. She writes in 'Le Lieu du Crime, le lieu du Pardon': 'I go to the theater because I need to understand or at least contemplate the act of death, or at least admit it, meditate on it' (p. 256). Recognition of death and human mortality are vital in enabling us to live. Cixous stresses: 'it is this . . . that the theater gives back to us: the living part of death, or else the mortal part of life' (p. 256). This highlighting of theatre's potential to enhance life through the acknowledging of death echoes Cixous' definition of *écriture féminine* and corroborates her view of theatre's importance in producing such a writing. The point is symbolized in *Indiade* by the tomb of the Soufi saint. In 'L'Ourse, la Tombe, les Etoiles' ('The Bear, the Tomb, the Stars'),[25] Cixous outlines the tomb's significance in life:

> place your hand on your death, O human, distinguish between the essential and the insignificant, and from this point on, you will know in which direction life is . . .
>
> Who is afraid of dying, is already dying. Sometimes one has to pass through what resembles death, the terrifying stripping away of self, the circle of fire, to resume life. (p. 251)[26]

Theatre's provision of a space in which the human passions and death may be explored connects to Cixous' depiction of *écriture féminine* in its refusal to shy away from whatever is difficult, painful or ugly.[27] Theatre forces confrontation with the truth, including our tendency to refute or repress this (see p. 256): 'what does it give us to see? Primitive passions: adoration, assassination. All the excesses I place at the door of my apartment: suicide, murder, the share of mourning' (p. 257). Theatre also invites us to recognize our own contribution:

> we are all victims, but we are also executioners. The Beast and the Knife. What does the Theatre tell us? There is death. What does the Theatre give us? Death . . .
>
> The stage gives it to us, restores it to us, this death of which we are ashamed, which we fear, which we repulse. It gives us, in a moment or slowly this source of so much meaning, death to live, the part of death in all life, and up to the drunken desire to kill Marie, the young woman or the old woman, the mother, the father, the child, the people. (p. 257)

This acknowledgement reflects back on our lives, affecting the way we think and act and helping us to distinguish the fine line between 'good and evil' (p. 258).

Cixous' view of theatre's power to present us with what we normally avoid or repress is graphically imaged in *La Pupille*. Greed and human cruelty are among the play's themes (see p. 27, also p. 118) and *La Pupille* re-enacts scenes of hatred, torture and murder (see, for example, pp. 81–3) through a kaleidoscopic representation of historic events (see, for example, the atrocities committed in Auschwitz and Vietnam, p. 39, the portrayal of Brazil's history, p. 47). However, a question is raised by *La Pupille* as to whether the symbolic re-enactment of such atrocities involves the audience in the way Cixous intends. My own experience of reading the text was to feel alienated by the various descriptions, perhaps because the stage directions do not have the impact of played scenes, but also, I feel, because there are no characters with whom it is possible to identify. This absence of any point of identification makes it hard to internalize and experience the play's events in ways which engage our emotional response. This lack of characterization distinguishes *La Pupille* from *Sihanouk* and *Indiade*, and corroborates Cixous' highlighting of her discovery of characters in writing for the theatre as vital in the development of her art.

Through its representations, the theatre can also keep alive what might otherwise be forgotten (p. 259).[28] This includes not only emotions and forms of behaviour repressed by the current schema, but also those others whose lives have been obliterated by history. The hope that through this remembering the sufferings of others might not have been in vain is forcefully depicted in *La Pupille*. Although there is insistence here, expressed by the persona of History, that 'the past is not model for the future' (p. 133), there is also affirmation that the portrayal of the events of history and baser motivations of humankind will induce a desire for change. This emphasis on memory and assertion of the possibility of transformation through the evocation of others' experience was powerfully figured in the Théâtre du Soleil's production of *Sihanouk* where the auditorium and stage were encircled by large papier mâché dolls, imaging the murdered Cambodian people.

Two further aspects to Cixous' writing for the theatre which link to her delineation of an *écriture féminine* are expressed in 'L'Incarnation'. Cixous suggests here that unlike the writing of fiction, the creation of others the theatre requires means the author does not write alone but at the behest of and in conjunction with others (p. 261). This notion of writing with others is augmented by the ever-present sense of the actors who will perform the roles and the play's eventual audience. Cixous' intense involvement in the rehearsals for both *Sihanouk* and *Indiade* at the Théâtre du Soleil greatly affected the writing of the two plays,[29] as did her awareness of the audience.[30] This sense of collaboration extends to the extra-linguistic resources of theatre. In the Introduction to *Indiade*, Cixous lists some of the components she as author has not been able to include in the text of the play (see pp. 16–17), 'unspoken' elements she nevertheless hopes will be heard. The dramatic possibilites of representation through gesture and symbolic objects, music, costume, set, dance and mime all contribute to the play's expression. The Théâtre du Soleil's production of *Indiade*, for example, drew on music, lighting, costume, movement, gesture and even the physical environment of the theatre to communicate the experience of India.[31] This emphasis on the extra-linguistic resources of theatre throws Cixous' description of *écriture féminine* into interesting relief: on the one hand, it supports her view that a text is the product of its communication with an audience while, on the other, questioning her conviction in *writing* as revolutionary.

A second aspect linking Cixous' work for the theatre to her delineations of an *écriture féminine* concerns this issue of language. Throughout Cixous' œuvre there is insistence on a language that will convey the living present. In 'L'Incarnation', Cixous suggests that the nature of theatre engenders such a language:

> that which remains silent in reality and in literary writing resonates in the theater: the Spoken Word [*'La Parole'*]. Nothing more oral, nothing more naked than this language [*'cette langue'*]. Spoken words. I must write like the burning body speaks: the words delivered by the author to the character must be the same words moulded and given breath by living and thinking lips. (p. 261)

This has implications for the writing. Recalling the depictions of the author's role in *The Book of Promethea*, Cixous stresses that in writing for the theatre:

> I listen and I translate. My translation of the passions must be of an extreme fidelity.
>
> It's communicating the aliveness, the poignancy, the essential, the *secret* of each passion, from tormented depths without ego, by the image, the boat, the metaphor which will lead the eloquent blood out into the air of the theater, to the audience's ear. (p. 262)[32]

The author must overcome her egotistical desire to *write*, as well as the temptation to describe:

> I want to 'write'. To meditate. No! Spoken words are needed. *The* spoken word (*'La Parole'*) – not chatter, not written words [*'les mots'*]. To announce, designate, name. But *not describe*: that is what the actor will do with their body. (p. 262)[33]

The endeavour to communicate as accurately as possible the living truth of thoughts, emotions and actions necessitates a language that will neither analyse nor explain,[34] but will aid the actor in their task of embodying the truth (p. 262). In 'Qui es-tu?', Cixous elaborates on this point by stressing that truth can only ever be present, a 'truth' the ephemeral nature of theatre respects: 'the truth of the character is in the moment: immediate, precise, ephemeral and poignant. . . . Tomorrow, he will have changed his mind, his heart, his truth and he will say something else' (p. 275).[35]

Cixous' account of the freedoms and opportunities offered by the theatre presents an interesting commentary on her fictional texts and vision of an *écriture féminine*. Whereas in the fiction there is emphasis on a minimum of organization and control, order and revision are necessary components in writing for the theatre. In 'A Realm of Characters', Cixous highlights how the audience's needs affect the way she writes (see p. 126), making it impossible, for instance, to include lengthy passages of description during which there is no action. She also outlines how the written text is cut and altered during rehearsals (p. 128) to comply with the requirements of staging. While the fiction is offered to the reader in its entirety and it becomes the readers' prerogative to make their own 'order', staging imposes this task on the author and/or director.[36] A tension thus arises between Cixous' description of the feminine writer enabling her subject to create the writing and the theatre writer's obligation to furnish a text that is producible and comprehensible within a limited playing time. Therefore, although Cixous' view that it is the characters who engender the play appears to accord with her delineation of *écriture féminine*, the form of theatre nevertheless requires the controlling presence of an author to organize what they say.

The plays also develop those themes Cixous sees as crucial components of *écriture féminine*. In the Introduction to *Indiade*, Cixous argues that the story of India's partition is one of love (see pp. 13–14). This is figured in the play in the parable of the two brothers born from a single mother (p. 20, see also p. 37), and in Gandhi's speeches. For Gandhi, love is both the remedy and the cause of India's problems:

> Gandhi: love. That's the remedy. Let us love one another. That's the secret. The key to the lock in the door. Do we love one another?
>
> . . . .
>
> There's no love without fear. Nor even at times without a kind of disgust, yes, of repulsion. We human beings, Hindu or Muslim, male or female, we are all so different. We are very odd. There in front of me is another, nothing like me! (pp. 80–1)[37]

Gandhi's views are echoed in the speeches and actions of a number of the play's characters. Nehru ascribes the cause of India's difficulties – not to Jinnah and the Muslim League – but to an inability to love:[38]

> It is our fault. It is mysterious human weakness. We do not love one another enough. I myself divide so often, my soul is a battle field from which my thinking only emerges at the price of a massacre of desires. (p. 164)[39]

Rajkumar, whose anger leads him to avenge the theft of his home and family by murder, forfeits his humanity in the process (p. 186).[40] The play's insistence on relating to others as *other* – beyond our fear and desire to convert the other to our own religion, political party or way of living – expressed particularly through the character of Gandhi, links the themes of *Indiade* to those of Cixous' fiction. One of the strengths of *Indiade* is that this view is tested to its limit. The refusal of Mohamed Ali Jinnah, head of the Muslim League in favour of partition, to accept Gandhi's truce is voiced in a context it is not easy to refute:[41]

> Jinnah: what can love mean between two nations so ill-matched in strength. Tell me! No, don't! Not another word. It's the Muslims you're asking, you're asking *us* to perform the *labour* of love, to put up with your numbers, your weight, your crass indifference. (p. 83)[42]

Gandhi's idealism is contextualized within the play in terms of India's poor, expressed through the character of Inder: 'my aim? To fill my stomach' (p. 97, see also pp. 90, 104, the song of the Hindu soldier, p. 108). Gandhi's position, despite its problems, is nevertheless validated by the revelation of Jinnah's motives. In the last speech of Act I, Jinnah shows the loss of love to be the true spur to his actions:

> once before, Death, in your impatience, you tore out a heart that only beat for my wife, my lovely Rani, which so grieved and tormented me. Now you are slowly eating Jinnah away. Yet even if I'm left without liver or kidneys, if I must breathe without lungs, move without muscles or scan the horizon without eyes, I shall still cling to this world till I have snatched my country from Asia's tenacious grasp, my country, my offspring, my memorial.
>
> You prowl round the core of my being, Death. Yet your cruelty revives me, your stinking breath fills me with immortal courage. Without you, without your filthy fidelity, Jinnah might never have been able to withstand the countless enemies ranged against him.
>
> The British, the Hindus: haughty Nehru and false-hearted Gandhi. My own brainless and lawless co-religionists. Slaves of Empires and the Gods. All against me. On my side: my secret, my death and my strength. I am the League. Myself alone. (p. 73)[43]

This highlighting of death, loss and personal ambition as the key to Jinnah's politics is reiterated in a later speech in which Jinnah claims Pakistan as 'my creation, my work, my planet!' (p. 162). A further incident that confirms Jinnah in his course and emphasizes his separation from the heart of life is contained in his refusal to allow his daughter's love:

> Jinnah: To be in love. I remember. Who is it?
> Dina: Will you give us your blessing? It is Rustom Waddiah.
> ....
> Jinnah: Never! I tell you no! Never a Parsee for the daughter of Jinnah! No!
> Dina: Why never a Parsee? Aren't I a Parsee's daughter? Aren't I the fruit of your love for a girl of my age, a Parsee who taught you everything? Why never a Parsee? Can you deny my mother, the girl you loved, your tears and my own birth? Do you want to lock me out of Paradise, because you lost yours? (pp. 118–19)[44]

Jinnah's consequent decision to repudiate his daughter strengthens his resolve. He vows never again to question his aim (p. 121, see also Jinnah's reaction to what he perceives to be Nehru's betrayal, p. 109). His speech is commented by Haridasi, speaker of the Prologue and witness of the play's events. As a woman Haridasi finds the acquiescence of Jinnah's sister Fatima hard to understand: 'what good is it that you are a woman, nothing stirs in your breast' (p. 122). Jinnah's reactions are framed in the play by Gandhi's very different response to his wife's death (pp. 75–6).[45]

Fear is identified as a key factor in the motivation of the various characters and events that lead to partition. Fear – of the other, of counter-attack – is the cause of the massacres between Hindus and Muslims: Gandhi: 'they frighten each other. And there they are . . . slaughtering each other to infinity' (p. 129). The destructive nature of fear is imaged by the bear, Moona Baloo, whose aggression is the result of fear: Haridasi: 'poor Moona Baloo! She is so gentle! She is like a real person. It is fear that turns her into a beast' (p. 110).[46] Fear – of making a mistake – is also depicted as a reason for Nehru's decision finally to accept partition:

> Nehru: at times I think the courageous move is to accept it thankfully, for our country's sake, to end its anguish. But at others I think it's

> cowardice parading as courage to give my consent. I think Pandit Nehru's a hopeless case! He takes himself to be India's mentor. But while he's been blundering on blindfold he's been straying for weeks over the borderline into Partition. Do I know if I'm lying?
>
> With every fibre of my being I strain for the truth. I swear I'm more afraid of deceiving myself than of losing the battle. Oh God, I'm so afraid. (p. 151)[47]

The changing nature of truth is also a theme of the play. Each of the characters is portrayed as seeking – and acting from – their own perception and understanding of the truth. Jinnah's vision of Pakistan is presented as a valid and even beautiful one, while Nehru's incessant quest for the truth (see p. 151) is delineated as the mainspring of his politics.[48] This notion of the relative nature of truth depending on the perspective from which it is viewed is also a theme of *Sihanouk*. The various plans for Cambodia are depicted in such a way that each appears plausible, even necessary,[49] and it is only the subsequent attempt to implement the vision that reveals its inherent flaws. In Act I, scene 1, the Communist Khieu Samphan's criticisms of the network of privilege through which appointments are made is framed by a reminder of the conditions of Khieu Samphan's own education (pp. 21–3). Sihanouk, whose actions and speeches in the first part of this scene place him in a sympathetic light, is shown from a different viewpoint by Khieu Samphan following his exit (p. 25). This varying perspective extends to the numerous factions vying with one another for control of Cambodia. In the opening scene, for example, the beginnings of the Khmer Rouge movement are described in terms which make the movement seem attractive: Saloth Sâr: 'we must do all we can to merit our people's love. . . . We must not differentiate ourselves from the peasant' (p. 25, see also p. 26, Khieu Samphan's vision of a reborn 'innocent Cambodia', p. 61).[50] Saloth Sâr's altruistic advice to Khieu Samphan is in turn contextualized by a speech in which hatred and the desire for victory are portrayed as motivating influences alongside the concern for justice and equality (pp. 28–9). Even Lon Nol's alliance with America is at first presented in terms which make it appear the lesser of two evils (see his speech beginning 'soon Cambodia will be no more than a goldfish in China's bowl', p. 74). The endeavour to think and act truthfully without taking into account the shifting political situation is depicted as virtually impossible. The Queen Mother's agonized decision as to whether or not to recall her son is set within the framework of the ulterior motives that govern international advice (pp. 125–8). Despite Kossomak's efforts, her eventual choice proves to have been an error: 'I thought I was doing right, and the right turns back and strikes like hate' (p. 158). The vision of truth is further complicated in the play by the realization that to remain neutral is not only impossible but is in itself tantamount to taking sides. Sihanouk's attempt to play the card of political neutrality (see p. 45) makes him the prey of warring factions (see p. 89: Macclintock: 'we must force Sihanouk to choose between two neutralities, pro-Communist neutrality and pro-American neutrality' and the Vietnamese exploitation of Cambodian neutrality, pp. 113, 178). This view contrasts with the more idealistic notion presented in Cixous' fiction of the possibility of keeping all paths open (see Chapters 2 and 3 above). Here, history forces Sihanouk to decide (see p. 189, also Penn Nouth's insistence that it is only those who are not directly implicated in Cambodia's history who have the luxury to 'plead the cause of neutrality', p. 190). In Act IV, scene 4, this difficulty of discerning the truth from the necessarily limited perspective of participation is imaged in the view from the aeroplane window:

> Sihanouk: Look at that dull brown carpet which seems so lifeless. That's Mongolia. And it's when we're down below, with the banana trees no higher than our noses, that for carpets like this, more or less highly coloured, we keep our thousand-year-old hatreds on the boil and spend our whole lives dreaming we are slaughtering our neighbours . . .
>
> Princess: Oh, if only we could be quite detached from all this![51] (p. 164)[52]

The answer in *Sihanouk* – evoking Cixous' insistence on a return to the essential – is figured as a return to the 'inner paths' (p. 165). This is expressed in the 'Prologue' to the 'Second Epoch',[53] in which Cambodia is described as a 'desolation camp':

> Our hearts are lying so low, they've lost contact with our tongues,
> And it's hard to tell what our leading characters are thinking.
> It's a time of mistrust. A cold sun is rising in the North.
> No more kingdom, no memories left.
> On every side destiny reigns. (p. 194)[54]

Sihanouk, as the representative of Cambodia (see p. 195), is depicted as a puppet in the hands of more powerful forces:

> Now the Prince is in Peking
> And Cambodia is at a loss,

Not knowing where to look for itself,
In Phnom Penh or Peking,
Whether inside its frontiers or without,
Not knowing what sort of place it is,
What side it's on or how to describe itself,
As royalist or republican,
Or from what point in the compass blows the disordering wind,
From America or China.
Wondering in which foreign tongue,
To what gods, which masters to address itself,
Which popes or Papas now should be disobeyed.
A sharp-toothed era has torn this land to pieces. (p. 194)[55]

The difficulty affects even the author, who must negotiate her way through the various bids for truth: 'when infidelity rules, how hard it is to make a faithful chronicle'.[56] Communication of the truth depends as much on the reader/spectator as on the author/characters of the play (p. 194):

For, just like lies, truth
Lives because of those who listen.
No truth without ears. (p. 194)[57]

The emphasis on listening extends to a *collective* listening, recalling Cixous' belief in the multiple nature of truth and corresponding need for a plurality of perspectives from which to hear it:

I believe the truth lies concealed in all of us,[58]
Even if, short-sighted as most humans are,
I don't always manage to see it. (p. 195)[59]

Cixous' work for the theatre thus presents a number of points of divergence from her conception of an *écriture féminine*. Key among these is the form theatre imposes on writing, necessitating organization and control by the writer as well as accessibility and the immediate conveyance of meaning. These stand in stark contrast to the signifying play possible in fiction. The adoption of characters also distinguishes Cixous' work for the theatre from her fiction. However, there are senses in which the formal control and creation of recognizable characters contribute to a writing that engages its audience in the way Cixous' description of *écriture féminine* suggests. The increased degree of structural and linguistic arrangement, for example, prevents the bewildering confusion the reader may experience in the early fiction, making it possible to focus on the play's impact. The language employs metaphor, allusion, poetry and song, which work against the recuperation and closure Cixous condemns. The extra-linguistic elements of theatre contribute to this.[60] The inclusion of characters can similarly be seen as serving Cixous' project, providing points of identification for the audience through which to share in the play's passions and dilemmas. In this sense, it can be argued that Cixous' work for the theatre *gives* the text to the audience more completely than the fiction. Cixous' view of the actors' role in embodying language can equally be regarded as fulfilling her criteria for *écriture féminine*. In the plays, language is informed by the emotions and physical expressions of the actors. There are other ways too in which the plays attain Cixous' depiction of feminine writing. Her account of how writing for the theatre is dictated first by the characters then by the process of staging and rehearsal links to her description of the relationship between the feminine writer and her subject. The purpose of the writing, expressed through the plays' concerns with love, death and the nature of truth, also compasses Cixous' vision. Unlike the early fiction, these issues are tackled from the vantage point of history, although the interconnections between the political and personal are carefully maintained. India's partition, for instance, is shown first and foremost to derive from the failure of individuals to relate. However, as with the fiction, the question remains as to whether an alternative is presented. Gandhi's endeavour to create a world in which differences are respected is prevented in *Indiade* by the prevailing order of fear and repression, and the women's hopes at the end of *Sihanouk* are framed by the events of Cambodia's history. It can be argued that the engagement with history in the plays obstructs the imaging of an alternative, since to do so would be to contradict the facts. In the next period of Cixous' work, the concern with historical reality combines with a return to fiction.

5
Recent Writings

> Et le message? Ah le message. On ne l'aurait connu qu'à l'arrivée. C'est sûrement la vérité.
>
> *Jours de l'an*, p. 58
>
> And the message? Ah the message. We would only have known it on arrival. It is certainly the truth.
>
> 'Firstdays of the Year'

In her most recent writing, Cixous has again returned to fiction. The three texts published since *Indiade*[1] – *Manne aux Mandelstams aux Mandelas* ('Manna to the Mandelstams to the Mandelas'), *Jours de l'an* ('Firstdays of the Year') and *L'Ange au secret* ('The Secret Angel')[2] – draw on Cixous' work for the theatre and, in significant ways, move beyond the stage plays to produce a writing that powerfully evokes Cixous' depiction of *écriture féminine*. The question addressed in this chapter will be the extent to which Cixous' latest fiction employs her experience of writing for the theatre to embody an alternative to the current order.

I have chosen in this chapter to focus on *Manne* since it resumes Cixous' engagement with the writing of historical others – here Osip and Nadezhda Mandelstam and Nelson and Winnie Mandela – and, evoking *The Book of Promethea*, combines this with the delineation of an/other mode of living and relating. In *Manne* the capacity of love to transform the present pattern of self/other relations is envisioned within history.

A key component of Cixous' work for the theatre is her adoption of characters (see Chapter 4 above). This is continued in *Manne*, where the central viewpoint is that of Winnie (sometimes Zami) Mandela. The author outlines her relationship to Winnie Mandela in the opening pages of the text, in a formulation that recalls Cixous' account of how, in writing for the theatre, she was inhabited by the characters that engendered the play:

> if it comes to publication, this book will be the fruit of a haunting. I have such a desire to tell Zami Mandela's story. Because for some weeks, on her account, Africa dwells in me. . . . How this has happened I do not know. It takes place in the depths of my body behind thinking, there where ego stops governing and gives way to the world. (p. 18, see also p. 20)

In 'L'Incarnation' (see Chapter 4 above), Cixous argues that one of the gains working for the theatre brought her is the possibility of writing male others (p. 265). In her fiction prior to *Sihanouk*, the only male presences are the shadowy figures of father, male lovers, mythic heroes. In *Manne*, the central viewpoint includes the perspectives of Nelson Mandela and Osip Mandelstam, thereby extending the scope of the writing.[3]

In *Manne*, the relationship between the author and the others of the writing is elucidated. The author declares her feelings towards Winnie Mandela (see p. 19), and reveals her doubts as to her ability to accomplish her task: 'how will I dare speak of all these events that did not happen to me on the surface?' (p. 22). Exploration of this relation between the I writing and the others who are the subject of the text distinguishes the novel from Cixous' work for the theatre, where this connection is necessarily hidden.[4] The author of *Manne* suggests that while she cannot write from the position of her characters (see pp. 25, 29), her endeavour to portray their experiences is sincere: 'I try each morning to progress along the pathway that climbs in the direction of those I do not ever hope to reach; but I do not lose the hope of climbing and imagining in their direction' (p. 24). This links to Cixous' delineation of the feminine writer's task (see the Introduction pp. 11–14), and corroborates her belief in the importance of writing in enabling us to learn from others. In *Manne*, this combines with the need for testimony,[5] an emphasis recalling Cixous' view of the vital role of memory.

The danger of oblivion is figured in *Manne* in the context of South African apartheid through the persona of Alfios Sibisi, who is murdered and then 'disappeared' by the white authorities: 'Sibisi could just as well have dispensed with being born. Being born not to be, that is what happens in this country' (p. 31).[6] The relationship between author and character is complicated here by the author's realization that not only is she unable to imagine what Sibisi went through in prison, but that such a remembering is personally disabling:

> stories like Sibisi's I do not know how to recount. I stay at the bottom of the ladder leading to the heavens of echoless sand. I can only feel them while they are slipping away, weep for them while losing my tears, and then, so as to live, forget them.[7]
>
> So it goes; not only do we have to kill in order to live, kill the echo, we also have to silence ourselves and die, all this to stay, across earth, across blood, alive. (p. 32, see also pp. 105–6)[8]

It is nevertheless this 'fear' (see p. 37, also p. 40) that motivates the author to write.[9]

This exploration of the relationship between author and other, omitted from the theatre, is reflected in the positions adopted by the writing subject. These fluctuate, with the author occupying the place of I and the corresponding designation of others to the second or third person, or a collapsing of the differences between I, you and s/he as the author and another merge in the first person. This is illustrated in the account of Zami's childhood, where the positions shift back and forth between author and character:

> and now, with empty hands, what to do? Now this is hell: the child's fault. The world is her fault. The world's sickness is my fault. And I do not know how to avoid the crime. I do not know how to endure the other's lack without offence. It would be necessary to stop the current. But the air in the street turns into an ill music. And the child's breast fills with weighty feelings. (p. 68, see also p. 217)

It can be argued that this vacillation, which leaves the reader to decide who is speaking and which involves the reader in its address ('the world's sickness is my fault'), accomplishes Cixous' delineation for a feminine writing more completely than her work for the theatre, in its inscription of an alternative relation between subject and other and transmission of others' experiences.

There is also reference in *Manne* to the author's participation in the process of writing. On page 248, for example, the author describes her attempt to experience a character's situation by trying to imagine herself in prison:

> I look at the walls of the small room in which at this moment I am moving only my hand. And I call forth the prison's truth. I invoke the impossibility of leaving this room. I invoke the possibility of leaving

> this room. I invoke the impossibility of the wish. (p. 248, see also pp. 259, 293)

Despite the fact that in a number of important ways the exposition of the relationship between the author and others in *Manne* marks a development beyond Cixous' work for the theatre in terms of her description of *écriture féminine*, the villains of *Manne*, unlike those of the plays, are portrayed almost exclusively from the outside. This is exemplified in the portraits of the murdering Drs Lang, Tucker and Hersch (pp. 46–7). All three remain caricatures, without the detailed, inner examination given to the villains of the plays. In this sense, *Manne* appears less successful in the context of Cixous' project than her writing for the theatre.

The author suggests in *Manne* that one of the ways in which she is able to write what she has no personal experience of is through dreams (see p. 116). This emphasis on the power of dreams – so central a component to Cixous' vision of feminine writing – is developed in *Jours de l'an*. Here writing is both the author and the subject of the text. Dreams are presented as the source of writing (see p. 43), and are portrayed as essential since they are free from socially constructed taboos such as our fear and projections surrounding death (see pp. 259, 272).[10]

Other themes of *Manne* connect to Cixous' account of feminine writing. Love is a central concern, expressed particularly in the relationship between Winnie and Nelson Mandela. The portrayal of their love echoes Cixous' delineation of a mode of relating in which the differences of each are respected: 'they looked at one another in silence, as it is forbidden to look at someone, with a slow and delicate wonder' (p. 96). This depiction is reflected in the story of the antelope and hippopotamus (see p. 110), and in the description of Zami's imagined day with Nelson on his release from prison (pp. 222–6). The insistence on the present (p. 223) and a togetherness in which both lovers can exist (pp. 224, 225) is especially noteworthy in this episode. Love is also highlighted as central to the relationship between Osip and Nadezhda Mandelstam. It is portrayed as a love that enhances both, and as vital in overcoming the oppressive climate of their time:

> their song was so necessary that they feared neither the looks of the police, nor the blindness of heaven, nor the deafness of the time, nor absence, nor shadow, but they took all that there was of good in the world, they gave it themselves, they kept it between their bodies, they revealed themselves without fear since they saw nothing that

was not the other, they felt nothing that was not desire and illumination, each being entirely made of passion for the other. Each told the other. (p. 341)

Manne also involves a debate on the nature of truth. As in the plays, this hinges on the importance of recognizing and remembering what we normally repress (see p. 232, also p. 283).[11] This is depicted as Nelson Mandela's dream: 'in the world created by Nelson there will be no more obliteration, no more oblivion, only an immense ever-beginning future, an immense ever-continuing present from today into today' (p. 97). The emphasis on the present is again striking.

Fear, and particularly our fear of death, is similarly a key theme of the text (see, for example, p. 111). This is most emphatically portrayed in the story of Osip Mandelstam, whose fear of death prevents him from writing (see p. 164). It is Mandelstam's subsequent acceptance of death that enables him to write and, conversely, to live in the present (see p. 202, see also p. 228).

One of the threads that links Nelson Mandela and Osip Mandelstam is their political exile (see p. 290).[12] As in Cixous' plays, this historical reality is explored in personal terms. In an interview entitled 'A propos de *Manne*' ('On the Subject of *Manne*'),[13] Cixous suggests that what interested her in writing *Manne* was not so much the political facts of dictatorship and apartheid, but 'the way in which people rich in humanity live a fate that steals their lives, their joys, their years from them: how they live this in their flesh, in their imaginary, in their unconscious, in their real' (p. 217). This is exemplified in the account of the prison meeting between Nelson and Winnie Mandela. The barrier of the glass screen that prevents any real contact between them and which can be read as a metaphor for the repressive conditions of apartheid paradoxically becomes a means of reinventing the connection:

> all the strange ruses our species tirelessly invents for surmounting infernal separation and reclaiming the mother, the air, the water, the blueness, the milk, the honey, the marrowy, and all the goods privation kills in us, all the secrets of survival below zero. (p. 319)[14]

The emphasis on the possibility of transcending the current order through love and new invention is noteworthy here, and marks a significant development from the stage plays. As in the theatre, women's role is depicted as crucial in this transcendence. In *Manne*, it is Winnie Mandela who maintains the love relation through her letters to Nelson, while Nadezhda Mandelstam's determination to collect her husband's poems is portrayed as a means of keeping him alive.[15]

The role of writing in safeguarding the truth is a key theme of *Manne*, figured particularly in the story of Osip and Nadezhda Mandelstam. As Nelson Mandela is depicted as sacrificing his life in order that future generations may be free from the obliteration of differences sanctioned by apartheid, so Osip Mandelstam is portrayed as dedicating his life to preserving language:

> by dint of writing and wanting to write poems on the frozen ground, Osip was completely worn out, worn-out soles, worn-out leather, worn-out heart, holes in his courage, worn-out eyes trying to see if one day . . . there would exist a world where forests of symbols would spring up again, where, from the ashes, wonderful languages would be reborn, where the airways would no longer be forbidden to magical musics, to metaphors, to ageless travellers. (p. 141)

In 'Difficult Joys', a text based on a lecture given by Cixous in English at Liverpool University in 1989,[16] Cixous elaborates on the correlation between writing, death and the truth. She suggests that writing offers a means of vanquishing death (p. 20), allowing us to think: 'about the mystery of death, about our mortality, about the fact that we are strange things, we are completely alive and we know that there is some border there, the real limit' (p. 20). Confrontation with this 'real limit' – made possible in writing – contrasts with the socially constructed limits we adhere to in daily life:

> when we come to writing, we come to that point when we have to be completely and violently true, about everything that we don't take time or don't have the courage to deal with in ordinary life. Should we call it transgression? I don't know. It's really forbidden in our usual life to speak about what can hurt; we're organized not to hurt people. We're organized in order to live socially, not to be excessive. (p. 20)

This emphasis on writing's capacity to confront our socially constructed self with an/other order is reminiscent of Julia Kristeva's work on the transforming potential of language. In *La Révolution du langage poétique* (*Revolution in Poetic Language*),[17] Kristeva argues that writing has the potential to transport us beyond our established position through transgression and reinvention. In particular, her work on the role of pleasure in motivating the subject to recreate their relation to the social code throws an interesting light on Cixous' vision of feminine writing.[18]

This function of writing is explored in *Manne*. Karel, a white South African police officer, sickened by the ridiculously light fine imposed on himself and his colleagues for raping and inadvertently killing a young Boschiman girl (pp. 273–6),[19] has a sudden vision of the brute harshness of the world in which he lives: 'reality suddenly appeared to him such as it must aways have been behind his dream: coarse, with no taste, no heart' (p. 275). What is missing, he reflects, is poetry (p. 275). Karel's view is framed in the text by the account of Nelson Mandela's prison life, a world kept alive by writing:

> I would never have believed that a letter could be my mother and my boat! Look walls, look bars, I know how to pass through your teeth and your irons. And you, hysterical century, in vain you shout that I am dead forgotten and erased. (p. 310)[20]

Significantly, this creation depends not only on Winnie's letters, but also on Nelson's reading of them: 'everything depends on you who read it. The Universe in each letter, if you are child enough to receive it' (p. 310).[21]

Writing's ability to put us in another's place, extending our experience and enabling us to see from another's point of view, is also highlighted in *Manne*. It is imaged, for example, in the author's reading of a poem by Mandelstam, written in a language that is foreign to her:

> I look at it, I do not hear it, I see it, I borrow its stride, I follow it letter by letter, foreigner in a foreign street, without fearing to make a mistake, I do not read it, I let it run before me and without leaving it by a syllable, I go where it takes me. To Leningrad, to Veronej, where I have never been, I go to a foreign poem, without fearing for a single moment not to arrive.
>
> What we do not know in our language, we know it again in the other language. (p. 286)

There is also reference in *Manne* to the problems language poses. This is expressed in the author's admission that what she needs to communicate a sense of the Mandelstams' life is not words but a 'violoncello' whose notes weigh in the breast (p. 256) and, for the depiction of their exile, 'the famous rude hoarse raspy tongue of rock, tongue of tusks, of rack and rock, tongue dirtied with dung and daub, of flaking rhymes' (p. 315).[22]

In *Jours de l'an* writing is itself a theme of the text. There is evocation of a writing that is both feminine and female:[23] a writing of the other, derived from and received by the body, drawing on extra-linguistic channels of communication and dedicated to expressing the truth. This mode of writing is imaged at the beginning of *Jours de l'an* in a passage recalling Cixous' delineation of *écriture féminine*:

> writing had come back, the course, the slender mute current with singing arms, the blood's flow in the veins between bodies, the wordless dialogue from blood to blood, with no sense of distances, the magical flow full of mute words running from one commune to another, from one life to another, the strange legend inaudible if it is not from one heart to another, the tale that weaves itself above, the weave quivering with secrecy,
>
> Writing, this bond, this growth, this orientation had come back,
>
> Again the void is filled with voices, the heart is the entire body. It was the missing land, the harbour, the other shore, and over there the unknown house, the sister who would receive the letter and take it in. (p. 5)

The reference to the sister who will receive the letter is evocative of women's role in *Manne*. Significantly in terms of Cixous' project, the return to writing described in the opening passage of *Jours de l'an* involves a return to the present time: 'and suddenly, today, the present opens, the spirit of time enters, passing through its own breast' (p. 7).[24] The subject of *Jours de l'an* is described as that which has hitherto been excluded by the author from her writing (see pp. 8, 9). This revelation offers an interesting commentary on Cixous' work for the theatre, which is here envisaged as incomplete. The new endeavour to incorporate what has previously been omitted takes the writing closer to the truth:

> the book I wanted to write, the one I dread writing is the one that would begin thus: I am at last going to tell you, and for the first time everything I now know about the most hidden truth [*'la vérité'*]. (p. 16)

This 'most hidden truth' is imaged in 'the living heart' (p. 18). The endeavour to write this 'truth' has implications for the writer who, like Rembrandt, must disinvest herself of her own emotional preconceptions: '"the world is a breast whose living heart I want to paint", he said, "And to paint the world's heart, one has to paint with the heart equally bare"' (p. 18, see also pp. 24, 157, 253). Importantly in terms of the development of Cixous' œuvre, this position of 'heart equally bare' is depicted as deriving from knowledge of the self:[25]

> for it is necessary, I believe, I do believe it, and I would like not to believe it, to have an idea or a suspicion of oneself in order to be able to begin to write, at least a point, an axe, a root of a flower, a beating in the temple, a centre of gravity or a sex. (pp. 27–8)

The author's answer to the question – recalling the question of the early fiction – 'in what am I me?' (p. 30) here involves the assertion of a position:[26]

> in what am I me? In beginning. In dreaming. In desiring to write. It is a woman who desires to write this book. Not without men. But a woman. The person who already perhaps, perhaps doesn't write, this book, the author of all the difficulties, the author of the desire, is, I can vouch for it (more or less), a woman. (p. 30)[27]

The 'most hidden truth' in *Jours de l'an* is revealed as death (see p. 49).[28] In order to write this 'truth' the author must open herself to the unknown and be prepared to risk (see p. 139). The author's account of the impact of such writing recalls Cixous' description of *écriture féminine* and, interestingly, her comments on her work for the theatre:

> living is advancing toward the unknown to the point of losing oneself.
>
> At the risk of losing oneself. The risk is necessary.
>
> (At least for an author. An author is a person to whom life arrives by unknown chapters. Life of which the author is not the author. My story has for authors the characters I love and who call to me.) (p. 53)

The author's declaration that death is 'the principle character' (p. 35) and 'true' author (see pp. 78–9) of the book extends the range of others in Cixous' œuvre and echoes her assertion that death must be acknowledged to bring the writing closer to a feminine mode. In *Jours de l'an*, acceptance of human mortality as a prerequisite for living and writing is portrayed in terms of the author's own experience:

> I took a step. I was in the cemetery, below. For the first time. Intimidated. I climb among the tombs. Here no one to lie to. . . . I climb, shaken by the idea of again seeing, of seeing, of seeing again, of

meeting my father and the stranger. Young, rejuvenated, I greet, I am greeted. We are among the unknown here. Fountains, doves, freshness in the midst of the fire, come. In my womb a birth is gently born.

Cemetery: my native foreign country. Above, to the right *the first unmeeting* happens, face to face with the granite end page: stone speaks. (p. 79)[29]

This encounter is contrasted in the text with our symbolic reconstructions of death, which prevent life:

'Death', what a story! And to say that we invented it, invented it so well that we no longer even know we are the authors of its stories. . . . Then we arm it with the words that diminish us. (p. 255, see also p. 257)[30]

L'Ange au secret similarly includes exploration of the relationship between writing and truth. As in *Jours de l'an*, the others who initiate the writing are not characters as such, but the voices, fears and pulsions that inhabit the author:

we close our eyelids, and with all our blood, all our fire, with humility, condensed into an intensity, we call of it to our own, you who have been walking in my flesh for tens of years, you whose mystery has overtaken my nerves, will you climb on board, can you be part of this journey, you my orangy blacknesses, you the secret colour of my colours, you who are for more than half in the light of my depths, you who are the force of my substance, you my wild animals, my alarms, you my disarmed weapons for the use of writing, military arrows daggers sabres plumes with sometimes red sometimes violet inks, you to whom I drink, you the salt and piquancy on my thoughts, come and be my character. (pp. 17–18, see also pp. 66, 112)[31]

This openness, incurring the danger that the author will be overwhelmed and thus unable to write (see pp. 18–19), turns writing into a battle-ground (p. 18). The invasion and ensuing battle is none the less necessary, since it brings the author to other experiences and prevents her writing solely from her own viewpoint (see, for example, p. 20). The terrain is an inner one:

they are my mines, my reserve difficult to access, but teeming if I reach there, with thoughts, passions, kinships, before me my personal foreign land: everything in this near yonder is mine, everything is strange to me. . . . The world, before me, so great, is internal, it is the immense hidden life behind the restricted life, it is the first forest

> that spreads itself out under the bed, the marshland of women and poets. (p. 25)

Although this emphasis in *L'Ange au secret* on a return to an internal landscape removes the writing from the historical engagement of *Manne* and the two plays, it supports Cixous' view, expressed in the postscripts to *Indiade*, that history is the culmination of the passions, fears and projections of individuals (see Chapter 4 above). In *L'Ange au secret*, the individual's adoption of the social constructions that organize our response to death and each other is contrasted with a way of living – enabled by writing – that would question and reframe these (see, for example, the author's insistence: 'the subject of my story is my fear' p. 28, also p. 35).[32] This return to the terrain of the early fiction throws an interesting light on Cixous' account of the development of her œuvre in 'From the Scene of the Unconscious'.

As in *Manne*, a central concern of *Jours de l'an* is the relation between the author and her subject. Evoking Cixous' description of the feminine writer's role, the author stresses: 'thoughts come released, and impassioned, from all sides . . . they fall upon us . . . transport us, turn us' (p. 54).[33] Truth, depicted here as collective (see p. 170),[34] is seen to reside *between* the author and others that generate the writing (p. 163). Exploration of this relationship includes analysis of that between the author Hélène Cixous and the author of the text. On page 100, for example, the author Hélène Cixous reveals that, unlike the author of the book, she has children – a fact which prevents her from saying certain things (see also pp. 126–7). This difference is figured in the text in a movement between the first and third subject positions (see, for example, p. 10: 'certain of Celan's poems, thought the author. To which I clung', also p. 8)[35] and in the occasional use of 'we' (p. 9).[36]

The equation between truth and death in *Jours de l'an* means that any acquisition of truth in life is impossible. This is expressed in the imagined promise of writing: 'each moment of your journey will be a fight to see more clearly what you will never see. I promise you blindness and the fight against blindness' (p. 134). It is also imaged in the 'Histoire idéale' ('Ideal Story') the author is preparing to write and which closes the text (pp. 207–76). 'Une Histoire idéale' is a love-story: 'the study of love, without death's help' (p. 210). The 'ideal' nature of the relationship between the two protagonists is portrayed as inhuman, since it exists beyond separation and death. The couple are: 'as if punished with good fortune. Forgive me, I describe clumsily, because, I must confess this here, I experience a great repulsion in loving them. If I am an "author", and prone to a little asceticism, I don't go to the point of "understanding" an inhuman state' (p. 212, see also pp. 215, 216).[37] This 'ideal' life is contrasted with the author's approach:

> I took in my parenthesis arms the entire human being including women, girls, female lovers, desires, demons, there is no one I have not included in my parenthesis arms . . .
>
> fearlessly and shamelessly. . . . In ten thousand dreams I understood everything and loved everything carnally. (p. 243, see also pp. 244–6)

This description, in its highlighting of the need to be open and all-embracing, its depiction of the relationship between author and others and emphasis on the freedom of dreams, recalls Cixous' delineation of feminine writing.

There is also discussion in *Jours de l'an* of the difficulties of writing (see p. 139). In 'Une Histoire idéale', there is insistence that our negative symbolic reconstructions require that we constantly overhaul language so as not to be caught in its trap (see p. 256). Words are 'our antique and enemy inventions' (p. 256) which the writer must guard against and work to reinvest (p. 256). This potential reformulation opens a new space for the writer: 'before me the field of time: everything to cultivate. . . . The universe to rewrite' (p. 258). Writing plays a crucial role in this reformulation, since it can reinvent our symbolic relation to the world (see pp. 177–8).[38] The importance of our endeavour to symbolize is underscored: 'we need images, we cannot live without our images, we need to be portrayed or described or represented' (p. 113). Interestingly, the author highlights here the need for constant correction and rewriting in this symbolization process: 'I write my avowals with severity. As I rework I cross out, I correct, ceaselessly redressing the mistakes' (p. 147).[39] This emphasis on the need for the author to order and control writing recalls Cixous' descriptions of her work for the theatre.[40] In 'Une Histoire idéale', this view is extended to envision an/other language based on love (see p. 213). Echoing the insistence on the collective nature of truth, this language is imaged as one where the differences between I and you would be simultaneously respected and surmounted in a plural 'we':

> how strange you are to me, foreign woman, foreign man, my love,
> As I am to myself, and I let myself go to you as far as almost,
> as far as almost approaching the never attained, never desired state of appropriation

> How without attributing you to me, will this 'we' yet be formed? 'We' this high high vital creation secret. (pp. 216–17, see also p. 222)[41]

The section of 'Une Histoire idéale' attributed to Clarice (p. 250) also contains description of a language which, in its evocation of love, parallels Cixous' delineations of feminine writing:

> another word than the word 'love', my love: it concerns this labour at the extreme and ultimate limit of thought. It means piercing old opaqued thinking. And for this rid ourselves of the words that cling to our feet, to our knees, to our eyelids by their thousand tiny frightened fingers, begging us not to advance. Not any further. And which hold us back and tell us the worst, the lifeless and soiled and chilly terrestrial version of the human condition. Get rid of the words that separate us from the world, and that cry out their fear, and that are made to dissuade us from reaching and leaving, and from touching and going beyond and tasting. (pp. 250–1)

This is contrasted with the pre-Oedipal relation to the world in which: 'we went without counting, we knew how to take pleasure in the heavy as in the light, losing was a find, each feeling a benediction' (p. 252, see also p. 253). The text ends with a reaffirmation of the possibility of (re)creating this paradise, in which 'between language and ourselves there was neither obedience nor disobedience, only exact conjugation of feeling and music' (p. 251).[42]

Cixous' most recent fiction thus draws on her work for the theatre to produce a writing which, while it involves a return to the terrain of the early texts, moves beyond the personal towards the embodying of an/other mode of living and relating. In *Manne*, this endeavour is portrayed through the dramatized experiences of individuals within history. These others – Nelson and Winnie Mandela, Osip and Nadezhda Mandelstam – derive from their real-life counterparts and, more significantly than in the theatre, from the author's attempt to parallel and convey their struggles. Unlike the plays, the relation between the author and her subject is a principal focus of the text. Exploration of the process and purpose of writing – omitted from the theatre – also contributes to the concerns Cixous lists as the components of *écriture féminine*. *Manne* combines a greater degree of formal order than the early fiction with a number of innovative elements. These include the composition of the text as a series of fragments, often set out as poetry with each new thought or idea beginning a new line and with an unconventional use of punctuation (see, for example, p. 25). The thread linking the two stories – that of Osip and Nadezhda Mandelstam and Nelson and Winnie Mandela – revolves around their 'gift' to the world – expressed as 'manna' – and the figuring of this 'manna' in their respective names. In *Jours de l'an*, parentheses are used to distinguish the author's thoughts (see p. 37). Some pages end in mid-sentence, as the author breaks off one train of thought to begin another (see, for example, pp. 48–9). In *L'Ange au secret*, this stylistic experimentation includes abrupt changes of page (see pp. 92–3) and unconventional punctuation. As is the case with the later fiction generally, the word-play of the early texts is almost non-existent (though see for example 'Nimporte' – literally 'no matter' – p. 17). The author suggests in *L'Ange au secret* that the thread which weaves the writing is 'red' (see the references to the geranium, p. 112, the section entitled 'let us follow the geranium', pp. 113–30, the author's insistence p. 116: 'let us be guided by the scarlet seed'), and the constant evocation of red becomes a key organizing influence in the text (see also the play on 'le jeu' – game – and 'le feu' – fire – in this respect, for example p. 223). There is nevertheless a sense in the later fiction that, despite the source of the writing in *Manne* and implicit view that history is the result of individual decisions, the return to a more personal terrain removes the writing from any significant influence in the political and social spheres. Perhaps, as has been suggested here, the question should be rephrased in terms of the transforming effect the writing has on the reader. In this case, in spite of the representation of repression and endeavour to inscribe an alternative in *Manne*, it is possibly Cixous' work for the theatre that is most successful, combining, as it does, confrontation with the forces of the law and the undeniable pleasures of the plays to prompt reformulation of our relation to ourselves, others and the world.

Conclusion

As Cixous' article 'From the Scene of the Unconscious to the Scene of History' outlines, there is a progression in Cixous' œuvre from the exploration of our subjective relation to the world of the early fiction, to an increasing engagement, in the later writing, with the ways this relation might be reformed.

In *Inside*, the question 'Who am I?' is cast in terms of primary loss and entrance 'inside' the symbolic order that shapes our responses to ourselves, others and the world. The highlighting of language as the arena where death and the law are constructed, and the corresponding insistence on language's potential to refigure these structures, is echoed in the formal and linguistic experimentation of this phase of Cixous' work.

In the next period of writing, the paradoxical role of language is imaged in the themes of *Angst*: to remain 'inside' the symbiosis of presymbolic union is to forgo subjectivity and hence the possibility of intervention, whereas the self's emergence entails acceptance of a schema 'inside' which *she* has no place. In *Angst*, the focus on the dead father alters to the living mother whose role in inducing subjectivity is portrayed as exemplary in the creation of an/other order.

The Book of Promethea, as illustrative of the next group of texts, moves beyond the preoccupations with self-formation, engaging with the others of Promethea and writing to envision alternative modes of perception, relation and representation. Evoking Cixous' descriptions of feminine writing, the foregrounding of the mother's role in giving birth to the self and others conjoins with the author's own analyses of the processes and purpose of writing. Here, an/

other writing involves the abandoning of past narratives, strategies and perspectives to centre on the present truth of lived experience.

In 'From the Scene of the Unconscious to the Scene of History' Cixous suggests that the self-exploration undertaken in the early fiction was the necessary prerequisite to a writing of others. In her two stage plays written in conjunction with the Théâtre du Soleil, 'The Terrible but Unfinished Story of Norodom Sihanouk King of Cambodia' and 'Indiada or the India of their Dreams', the focus changes from the endeavour to love another figured in the author's relation with Promethea to an encounter with the others of history. In the postscripts to *Indiade*, Cixous argues that theatre can re-enact the scene of our primary struggles, thereby returning us to those experiences and confrontations which cumulatively comprise history. The correlation between the enabling mother and the feminine writer is continued in Cixous' writing on the theatre as she describes how, in the theatre, the author writes in co-operation with others – the director, actors, audience and characters who create the play.

In Cixous' most recent writing, the engagement with the others of history combines with a return to the inner terrain of the early fiction. 'Manna for the Mandelstams for the Mandelas' presents the revolutionary potential of an/other mode of living, through characters who derive partly from their historical counterparts and partly from the author's endeavour to write. Language is depicted as the forum for change, since it carries the existing political, social and cultural codes and offers a means to transgress and recast these. Through the scenarios of apartheid and totalitarianism, acceptance of the established formulations is contrasted with a response – enabled by writing – that strives to challenge and reinvent.

Cixous' delineation of an *écriture féminine* provides a fruitful frame from which to consider her œuvre. While the first group of texts, centring here on *Inside*, contain a number of elements Cixous describes as exemplary of feminine writing, I have suggested that their self-preoccupation and formal disorder limit their sphere of interest and influence on the reader. Despite the portrayal of the self's relation to others and the forces of social order in *Angst*, it has been my contention that this next phase of Cixous' writing is essentially descriptive. *The Book of Promethea*, while it embodies the endeavour to live and love differently, none the less remains within the arena of interpersonal relations. Although Cixous' stage plays fulfil her criteria for an *écriture féminine* in terms of the way they are written and their subject matter, their formal construction and failure to realize an alternative raise a number of questions. The theatre's requirements for action, immediate communication and the maintenance of audience interest contradict Cixous' insistence that writing should be allowed its own gestation, and the women's hope, in *Sihanouk*, for a Cambodia in which differences and national identity are respected is impeded by the reality of Cambodia's history. Cixous' most recent fiction, in its conjugation of the author's and others' attempts to formulate an alternative, might therefore be seen to extend Cixous' work in the theatre, though it can also be argued that the fragmentary nature of its composition *gives* the experience to the reader less effectively than the more accessible *The Book of Promethea* or the plays. Perhaps, in the final analysis, a link might be drawn between Cixous' correlation of the enabling mother and the feminine writer and *écriture féminine*. If the ultimate aim of *écriture féminine* is to induce us to re-examine our connection to the world, then perhaps – like the mother who gives birth in a simultaneous movement of separation and support – the securities and pleasures of the text are important in aiding the reader to transgress the established structures, and reinvent the framework through which our understanding, identities and relations with others are built.

Notes

Preface

1 This aspect of Cixous' work as well as her relationship to other French feminists, philosophers and critics is the subject of my *Language and Sexual Difference: Feminist Writing in France* (Macmillan, Basingstoke, and St Martin's Press, New York, 1991).
2 This study was written in 1992 and revised for publication in 1993/4.
3 'De la scène de l'Inconscient à la scène de l'Histoire: Chemin d'une écriture', in Françoise Van Rossum-Guyon and Myriam Díaz-Diocaretz (eds), *Hélène Cixous: Chemins d'une écriture* (Rodopi, Amsterdam, and Presses Universitaires de Vincennes, Saint Denis, 1990), pp. 15–34. The translations from this article are by Deborah Jenson with occasional modifications by myself. Page references are to the French text.
4 Cixous was born in Algeria. Her father was French and her mother is German. Here she lists the languages she heard as a child as 'Spanish, Arabic, German, French' (p. 16).
5 Cixous cites her first, full-length work of fiction, *Inside* (*Dedans*), as an example: '*Inside* was necessarily written inside the father, in seeking him even unto death and in *returning*' (p. 19). *Inside* is discussed in this context in ch. 1 below.
6 'Domingo, antes de dormir', in *Para nao esquecer* (Atica, São Paulo, 1978). The key passages are reproduced on pp. 17–18 of Cixous' article in both a French translation and the original Brazilian.
7 'And the mother? [Et la mère?] She is music, she is there, behind, the force that breathes, the mother who for all French writing is obviously the sea [la mer]' (p. 19). This relation to the mother is also explored in Cixous' early fiction, in texts like *Souffles* ('Breaths'), and will be discussed in ch. 2 below.

8 Jacques Lacan's description of the role of language in compensating the emerging self for the loss of the m/other in relation to the father is instructive here. See, for a detailed account of Lacan's view of self-development, *Language and Sexual Difference: Feminist Writing in France*, pp. 44–8, 72, 92, 97–8.

9 Macabea is the central character in Clarice Lispector's *A hora da estrela*, 5th edn (Livraria José Olimpio Editora, Rio de Janeiro, 1979). The English edition is translated as *The Hour of the Star* by Giovanni Pontiero (Carcanet, Manchester, 1986).

10 The reference is to *L'Histoire terrible mais inachevée de Norodom Sihanouk roi du Cambodge* ('The Terrible but Unfinished Story of Norodom Sihanouk King of Cambodia'), Théâtre du Soleil, Paris, 1985.

11 Though Cixous began writing for the theatre much earlier, it is her liason with the Théâtre du Soleil she is describing here. See ch. 4 below for further discussion of this point and a detailed outline of Cixous' work for the theatre.

12 The writer's obligation to history is explored in some detail in 'From the Scene of the Unconscious'. See pp. 25–8, also pp. 33–4.

13 'Conversations', in Susan Sellers (ed.), *Writing Differences: Readings from the Seminar of Hélène Cixous* (Open University Press, Milton Keynes, and St Martin's Press, New York, 1988), pp. 141–9. Cixous' essays 'Extreme Fidelity' and 'Tancredi Continues' in this collection also provide good illustrations of this approach in practice.

Introduction: *Cixous and* écriture féminine

1 *La Jeune Née*, with Catherine Clément (Union Générale d'Editions, Paris, 1975). The English translation is by Betsy Wing (University of Minnesota Press, Minneapolis, and Manchester University Press, Manchester, 1986).

2 See *The Newly Born Woman*, pp. 63–5, 68–72. Nicole Ward Jouve, in her article 'Many Rills, Will They Ever Run into One River, a River with Two Banks?', in Susan Sellers (ed.), *Delighting the Heart: A Notebook by Women Writers* (The Women's Press, London, 1989, reissued 1994), pp. 211–30, offers an interesting commentary on this difficulty of theorizing women's/feminine writing:

> you can say, 'Yes, this is a feminine, or a female, or a woman's practice, yes, a certain inwardness, stream-of-consciousness, refusal of fetishism, fluidity of style, punning, subversion of logic, of phallogocentrism, re-vision, the re-writing of myths, and fairy-tales, deconstruction of gender roles, silences, secrets, being-in-darkness, regressing, all that, one way or another, as well as certain subject matters, certain experiences, that, for biological, social or economic reasons, only a woman could have, can all be

called "feminine"'? You can say that truthfully. But the proposition cannot be reversed. (p. 211)

3 See, for a detailed account of Freud's theories of human development and Cixous' reaction to these, my discussion in *Language and Sexual Difference*, pp. 40–4, 56–9, 72, 80–3.
4 See *The Newly Born Woman*, pp. 81–6.
5 See 'Conversations' in *Writing Differences*, pp. 144–5, for an example of Cixous' defence of Freud. Here she pays tribute to his work on the unconscious, and argues that it would be absurd not to make use of his research because of his inherently male approach.
6 See *The Newly Born Woman*, pp. 84–5.
7 See, for example, Freud's papers on 'Libidinal Types' and 'Female Sexuality', in James Strachey (ed.), *The Standard Edition of the Complete Psychological Works of Sigmund Freud*, 24 vols (Hogarth Press, London, 1953–74).
8 See Cixous' account of libidinal economies in 'Extreme Fidelity', in *Writing Differences*, pp. 14–18:

> what can we assign as descriptive traits to these economies? Let us consider our behaviour in life with others, in all the major experiences we encounter, which are the experiences of separation; the experiences, in love, of possession, of dispossession, of incorporation, and non-incorporation, the experiences of mourning, of real mourning, all the experiences which are governed by variable behaviours, economies, structures. How do we lose? How do we keep? Do we remember? Do we forget? (p. 18)

9 *Writing Differences*, pp. 9–36. A revised French version of this text, which was originally written for translation into English and publication in *Writing Differences*, appears in *L'Heure de Clarice Lispector* (Des femmes, Paris, 1989), as 'L'Auteur en vérité', pp. 123–68.
10 It is noteworthy that what Perceval sees – a lance dripping with blood – *suggests* castration.
11 See her recent preface to Susan Sellers (ed.), *The Hélène Cixous Reader* (Routledge, London and New York, 1994), pp. xv–xxiii.
12 'The relationship to pleasure and the law, the individual's response to this strange, antagonistic relationship indicates, whether we are men or women, different paths through life. It is not anatomical sex that determines anything here. It is, on the contrary, history from which one never escapes, individual and collective history, the cultural schema and the way the individual negotiates with these schema, with these data, adapts to them and reproduces them, or else gets round them, overcomes them, goes beyond them, gets through them – there are a thousand formulae – and joins up with a universe which I would

call "without fear or reproach". It happens that culturally, women have more of a chance of gaining access to pleasure, because of the cultural and political division of the sexes, which is based on sexual difference, on the way society uses the body' ('Extreme Fidelity', p. 18).

13 See also Cixous' comment in 'Conversations' concerning women's sex-specific experience of childbirth, p. 151.

14 See Cixous' comments on this point in 'Conversations', pp. 151–2.

15 *La Venue à l'écriture*, with Madeleine Gagnon and Annie Leclerc (10/18, Paris, 1977). The title essay is reprinted in *Entre l'écriture* (Des femmes, Paris, 1986), pp. 9–69. The English translation of the title essay is 'Coming to Writing' by Deborah Jenson, in *'Coming to Writing' and Other Essays* (Harvard University Press, Mass., Cambridge, and London, 1991), pp. 1–58.

16 The links with Julia Kristeva's work on the power of the pre-symbolic 'chora' to influence and disrupt the subject in language are interesting here. For a full discussion of this point see my account in *Language and Sexual Difference*, pp. 48–52, 93, 98–113, also pp. 73–5.

17 Cixous reiterates this point in 'From the Scene of the Unconscious', stressing that German was the language she learned to sing in (p. 16).

18 See *The Newly Born Woman*, pp. 85–98.

19 She writes in *The Newly Born Woman*:

> what *he* wants, whether on the level of cultural or of personal exchanges, whether it is a question of capital or of affectivity (or of love, of *jouissance*) – is that he gain more masculinity: plus-value of virility, authority, power, money, or pleasure, all of which reenforce his phallocentric narcissism at the same time. Moreover, that is what society is made for – how it is made; and men can hardly get out of it. An unenviable fate they've made for themselves. A man is always proving something; he has to 'show off', show up the others. Masculine profit is almost always mixed up with a success that is socially defined. (p. 87)

20 See also Verena Andermatt Conley's compilation and translation of material from Cixous' research seminar, *Readings: The Poetics of Blanchot, Joyce, Kafka, Kleist, Lispector, Tsvetayeva* (Harvester Wheatsheaf, Hemel Hempstead, 1992), for further exploration of the parallels between the enabling mother and feminine writer. Reading Clarice Lispector's *Felicidade clandestina* ('Clandestine Felicity') (Nova Fronteira, Rio de Janeiro, 1971), in which Lispector describes an attempt to enable a young girl to take pleasure in a baby chick, Cixous writes:

> the good mother is the one who does not take herself for a mother and succeeds in absenting herself. She does not precede,

> she follows. She has to let the child *make* her into a mother. She has to be the locus and not the master of birth. She has to let happen the ultimate scene of encounter between the little girl and the chick – in other words, the scene between the little girl and herself. . . . It is another analysis of the child's coming upon herself, of the process of individuation and of difference. It is not analyzed theoretically but told, written. To resolve birth, the mother has to accept dissolution. (pp. 80–1)

21 'She doesn't watch herself, she doesn't measure herself, she doesn't examine herself, not the image, not the copy' ('Coming to Writing', p. 51).

22 See note 20 above.

23 Cixous suggests that this male discourse is 'homogeneous with phallocentric tradition, to the point of being phallocentrism-looking-at-itself, taking pleasure in repeating itself' (p. 97). See also her comment on the 'naming trick' that has resulted in men's appropriation of the origin: 'men's cleverness was in passing themselves off as fathers and "repatriating" women's fruits as their own' (p. 101).

24 'Le Dernier Tableau ou le portrait de Dieu', in *Entre l'écriture* (Des femmes, Paris, 1986), pp. 171–201. The English translation is by Sarah Cornell and Susan Sellers in *'Coming to Writing' and Other Essays*, pp. 104–31.

25 'It's all there: where separation doesn't separate; where absence is animated, taken back from silence and stillness. . . . My voice repels death; my death; your death; my voice is my other. I write and you are not dead. The other is safe if I write' ('Coming to Writing', p. 4).

26 Karen Blixen (Isak Dinesen), *Out of Africa* (1937) (Penguin, Harmondsworth, 1982). The example is taken from Hélène Cixous' seminar.

27 *A Paixão segundo G.H.* (Editora Nova Fronteira, Rio de Janeiro, 1979). The passage is one quoted and worked on in Cixous' seminar. The translation is by Hélène Cixous, Sarah Cornell and Regina Helena de Oliveira Machado.

28 'L'Approche de Clarice Lispector', in *Entre l'écriture*, pp. 115–38. The English translation is by Sarah Cornell and Susan Sellers in *'Coming to Writing' and Other Essays*, pp. 59–77.

29 There is a strong echo of the feminine article (*la*) on the first word.

30 See, for example, pp. 91–8.

31 For readers of French, Cixous' 'La Missexualité ou jouis-je?', in *Entre l'écriture*, pp. 75–95, provides a further detailed exposition of her work on the possibilities generated by the signifying process. Readers of English might consult *Vivre l'orange/To Live the Orange* (see note 32 below), the English translation of which was revised by Cixous, or the more recent *Three Steps on the Ladder of Writing* (Columbia, New York, 1993). Although *Three Steps* is not a work of fiction it is based on

lectures originally written in English, and the final published version has been extensively reworked by Cixous.

32 'These pearls, these diamonds, these signifiers that flash with a thousand meanings, I admit it, I have often filched them from my unconscious' ('Coming to Writing', p. 46). See also Cixous' comments in 'The "Double World"of Writing, in *Delighting the Heart*, p. 18, on how the inspiration for her writing comes from her dreams. Cixous similarly stresses in 'Coming to Writing': 'the more you let yourself dream, the more you let yourself be worked through, the more you let yourself be disturbed, pursued, threatened, loved, the more you write, the more you escape the censor' (p. 55).

33 See also Cixous' comment in *The Newly Born Woman*: 'this cannot be accomplished, of course, without political transformations that are equally radical' (p. 83).

34 See *The Newly Born Woman*, pp. 147–60.

35 In 'The Last Painting or the Portrait of God' Cixous writes: 'the ego is the last root preventing flight. Or the last anchor. One has to unfasten oneself the best one can. . . . At that moment, when the ego no longer weighs him down, the [artist] becomes permeable, becomes immense and virgin, and becomes woman. He allows himself to be worked in' (p. 113, translation corrected).

36 *Vivre l'orange/To Live the Orange*, English text translated by Hélène Cixous, Sarah Cornell and Ann Liddle (Des femmes, Paris, 1979). *Vivre l'orange/To Live the Orange* is reprinted in *L'Heure de Clarice Lispector*, pp. 8–111.

37 The feminine writer must 'write to the living in life,' Cixous suggests ('The Last Painting or the Portrait of God', p. 105).

38 See also for a revised version of this material 'Freincipe de plaisir ou paradoxe perdu' (1983), reprinted in *Entre l'écriture*, pp. 99–112.

39 In 'The Last Painting or the Portrait of God' Cixous suggests that her difference as a writer from those painters she most admires is precisely this desire for the inside. Describing the painter's relation to still life, she argues that her difference as a writer lies in her 'way of loving an interior apple as much as an exterior apple. . . . Myself, I would have eaten it. In this way, I am different from those I would like to resemble. In my need to touch the apple without seeing it. To know it in the dark' (p. 130).

40 The reference, as Cixous herself emphasizes, is to Lacan's account of individuation.

41 Cixous writes: 'Joyce . . . has elaborated a rapport with castration, something inevitable for a boy. Generally, men are caught in this space; some women too, but only through identification. As Freud described it, the boy begins to symbolize from the threat of castration, from resistance to castration' (p. 8). Cixous stresses here that despite Joyce's transgressive position he is nevertheless dependent on the law.

42 See also Cixous' introduction to the French edition of Carroll's text *De l'autre côté du miroir* (Flammarion, Paris, 1971), pp. 13–34.

Chapter 1 *The Early Texts*

1 *Dedans* (Grasset, Paris, 1969). The English translation is by Carol Barko (Schocken Books, New York, 1986).
2 *Le Prénom de Dieu* (Grasset, Paris, 1967).
3 *L'Exil de James Joyce ou l'art du remplacement* (Grasset, Paris, 1969). The English translation is by Sally Purcell (David Lewis, New York and John Calder, London, 1976; reprinted Riverrun, New York, 1980).
4 See 'De la scène de l'Inconscient à la scène de l'Histoire: Chemin d'une écriture', in Françoise Van Rossum-Guyon and Myriam Díaz-Diocaretz (eds), *Hélène Cixous: Chemins d'une écriture* (Rodopi, Amsterdam, and Presses Universitaires de Vincennes, Saint Denis, 1990), pp. 18–19, and the Preface above.
5 See the Introduction above.
6 See pp. xii–xiii, above.
7 A figure of enclosure as a place of death is contained in the title of *Tombe* ('Tomb') (Editions de Seuil, Paris, 1973), imaged in the text as 'inside' the (father's) mouth/language:

> His death like a bad joke still I have said nothing . . .
> I still have not opened the now useless mouth (coffer of the
> second time born). If one were to open it
> One would see his dead tongue of a darkish colour
> Expired swollen motionless decayed
> Useless
> I sucked and suckled and chewed it when
> My name was his name.
>
> (pp. 6–7)

8 The mother's role in the acquisition of language is figured in *Inside* partly through the voice of the grand/mother (see pp. 105–6).
9 The acquisition of language is a theme of a number of texts of this period. *Tombe*, for example, explores the birth of the self through language from the 'tomb' of non-separation and the father's death.
10 The division between words and things is also imaged in the text in the section on p. 66–72. Here the mellifluous sound of the grand/mother's voice, which generates sensations of security and love, is contrasted with the meaning of what she says (p. 68). The I endeavours to comply with the grand/mother's request to 'say some thing' (*'dis quelque*

chose') (p. 69) despite its impossibility: one can only say words, not things (p. 69).

11 In *Les Commencements* ('The Beginnings') (Grasset, Paris, 1970) it is the *choice* between mother and father that initiates separation into the adult wor(l)d: 'the first question was: Who do you love best? daddy or mummy? Death entered with the *or*' (p. 39).

12 The figure three is a recurrent motif in the fiction of this period. Its correlation with the Oedipal triangle is present in *Les Commencements*, where three is acknowledged as the number necessary for existence (see p. 35). 'The third loss', that which follows the loss of the father and mother, is also a key theme (see p. 105), recalling the I's preoccupation with death in *Inside*. This loss, which brings knowledge (p. 162), is depicted as splitting the I into three, figured by the terms 'where', 'I' and 'time' (p. 162). The figure is later characterized as past, present and future time (see the 'triple times triptych', p. 176). In *Tombe*, the number three is imaged as death (see p. 26), while in *Le Troisième Corps* ('The Third Body') (Grasset, Paris, 1970) the figure three has numerous connotations, including that of the third body referenced in the title. The insistence on a third term is noteworthy in conjunction with Cixous' endeavour to move beyond symbiosis and the restrictive binary structure that underpins our thinking.

13 In *Le Troisième Corps* only writing is viewed as able to overcome these constraints (see p. 66, also p. 207). In *Les Commencements* the formulation of a new 'discourse of love' is imaged as a means of not dying (p. 229, see also p. 250).

14 The birth of the self is itself figured as a death in *Les Commencements* in the image of a stillborn child (see pp. 165–6).

15 The eighth subsection of Part One opens with the mother's negative word: 'NOTHING' (p. 49).

16 This role is fused in *Les Commencements*, where both father and mother inculcate the law (see, for example, p. 152).

17 This invention is also figured in *Le Troisième Corps* (see p. 27). Here, it is the conjunction of the two lovers' languages that creates a body outside the law: 'at the crossing of our tongues a third body came to us, there where there is no law' (p. 107). Writing, in particular, is seen as enabling such a break (see pp. 55, 70).

18 'The only incontestable difference is not that of sex or age or strength, but that of the living and the dead: the former have all the power, which they don't always know how to use, the others have only knowledge without power' (p. 79).

19 This dream of union with the father is also present in *Les Commencements* (see pp. 34, 105).

20 On p. 97 symbiosis with the father is depicted as:

> Him.
> Me around and inside us.

Us.
Death around and inside us.

The consequences of the self's failure to emerge from 'inside' are figured in *Neutre* ('Neutral') (Grasset, Paris, 1972) in 'a bloody scene in which the mirror [breaks] over' William Wilson, preventing him 'access to the symbolic . . . it is thus impossible for William Wilson to come to language' (p. 92).

21 This self-inflicted castration is echoed in *Les Commencements* in an episode in which the I distinguishes a cat as you. As a result of this distinction: 'I had to begin everything again from the age of ten as if I still knew nothing, and I did what the captured animals do in the legends who sacrifice their tails in order to escape from the trap, I too cut this first tail of my existence' (p. 203).

22 In *Tombe*, the creation of a relationship between self and other in which both can exist is depicted in terms of the paradox of having (see, for example, p. 74). The destructive effects of another's desire is also a theme of the text (see pp. 112, 117).

23 In *Le Troisième Corps*, gender is also seen to depend on the other's viewpoint: 'the subject, according to whether I look with an even eye or an odd eye, is masculine or feminine: that does not depend on the being but on the eye' (p. 112). In *Les Commencements*, this notion of perspective in the attribution of gender (see, for example, p. 101) is broadened to include the role of language (see p. 20). The I of the text shifts between a masculine, feminine and bisexual-plural gender (see, for example, pp. 143, 230). In *Neutre*, the 'blood' of the text is depicted as neutral, while its subject is the 'unfortunate victim of genetic coding' (p. 68). The power of the look in determining gender is also a theme of *Tombe* (see, for example, p. 5). Interestingly, it is death that is seen to give the necessary perspective here (p. 23). The plurality and mobility of gender is similarly an issue in *Tombe* (see p. 38), where the divisive law of gender is described in the following terms:

> I fear the sheathed knife which slices love by the middle, the law of genders which separates one from the other from its self ('*son même*') and which assigns you here and assigns me there, I fear the split and the order of bodies. (p. 41)

24 See p. 11 above.

25 See also *Les Commencements*: 'but if I am, who then?' (p. 118). In *Neutre*, the question 'Who am I?' is answered with the realization that I exists only in relation to others (see pp. 79, 183). *Tombe* similarly stresses self-identity in relation to others – 'The One will not be without the Other' (p. 104) – rather than through the impositions of the law (see p. 88).

26 In *Les Commencements*, the self's birth includes a dream of origins

predating their organization by image, language, thought and religion (pp. 158–60).

27 See 'the old head of my race is full of stories about our dead' (p. 67).

28 The role of lovers in the self's construction is explored in *Le Troisième Corps* (see pp. 19, 20–1, 46, 66). In *Les Commencements* (p. 75, and see also p. 87), the relation between self and lover is figured in terms of the conventional master/slave model:

> – Say: 'I am your slave, amen.'
> – No
> – Say: 'you are my master, amen.'

The obliteration of the self to conform to others' views is also imaged in *Les Commencements* (p. 106) in terms of a lobster displayed ready to eat:

> I feel keenly the resemblance between this lobster displayed on the pewter dish, and what most people try to make of me (. . .)
>
> I am a tongue one must silence, though whose virtue must be kept. One cuts it out, slices it up, eats it.

29 In *Les Commencements*, the necessity of beginning is imaged as death *within* the enclosure if beginning is denied (see p. 163, also pp. 152, 157). Here beginning is explicitly linked to beginning to write: the 'third body' ('*troisième corps*') *is* writing (p. 13), and the *fort–da* is explicitly textual (p. 14, see also p. 141).

30 The dangers of a fantasized reunion with the dead father are graphically depicted here, as the I imagines herself prevented from re-entering this 'inside' by the terrifying spectre of an other, older self wearing the faded 'dress . . . for my death' (pp. 134–5).

31 Words are seen to contain the memory of what is no more, a function contrasted with the role of objects (see, for example, the episode in which the father's imprint is removed from the bed, p. 40).

32 The town, which is the town of the I's birth (p. 91), is described as having 'no beginning nor end' (p. 95): 'you could drive night and day without coming to an exit or entrance' (p. 95).

33 This can be compared with the description of the role of the writer in *Le Troisième Corps*: 'even if it's me who's writing, I touch nothing, I don't steal, on the contrary I lend. The rest is Nature' (p. 220).

34 See, for example, the comment: 'nor did I care to learn if death had any sense of time, of youth, of age; I've never been afraid of my death; I've nothing more, nor anyone, to lose' (p. 8).

35 The formal innovations of *Le Troisième Corps* include the incorporation of blank spaces (see, for example, p. 144 which is entirely blank except

for a question printed at the bottom of the page), the use of other languages (see for example the employment of mathematics p. 149), and the play with signifiers to challenge the conventional form and meaning of words (see for example the game played with the letter 'z' on pp. 164, 166). In *Les Commencements*, the notion of narrative order is exploded by the opening question – 'And where to begin? Which beginning, more than others, begins?' (p. 12) – as well as by the insistence that the text has numerous '*commencements*' and thus can begin anywhere (see p. 32). *Tombe* opens with a sequence of propositions listed in numerical order (pp. 6–14), contains an irregular use of punctuation (see for example the use of commas at the *beginning* of an indented line p. 5, a feature already employed in *Neutre* [see pp. 139–40]), and includes the insertion of italicized type or type in block capitals between lines, insertions in the margins, and in parentheses. *Tombe* also has extended word-play, as in the various derivations of the word '*menthe*' (mint): '*lamente*' (lament), '*l'amante*' (the lover), '*mente*' (lie) (see p. 19).

36 See pp. 117, 104–5.

Chapter 2 *Creating a Feminine Subject*

1 Although, as is the case when subdividing any œuvre, the break is in many ways an arbitrary one, there is, as I endeavour to show, an argument for suggesting that while Cixous' early texts concentrate on the relation to the father this second group focuses on the mother.

2 *Angst* (Editions Des femmes, Paris, 1977). The English translation is by Jo Levy (John Calder, London, and Riverrun Press, New York, 1985).

3 See, for a discussion of Freudian and Lacanian theories of the self's formation in relation to Cixous' work, my account in *Language and Sexual Difference: Feminist Writing in France* (Macmillan, Basingstoke, and St Martin's Press, New York, 1991), pp. 40–8.

4 See also p. 8: 'here: no more inside'.

5 This concern recalls the 'who am I?' of the early texts. It is a theme of other texts written in the same period as *Angst*. In *Souffles* ('Breaths') (Editions Des femmes, Paris, 1975), the form the self will take is humorously figured in a series of questions: 'must I decide on a form for myself. . . . Slip on a woman's skin and wig?' (p. 27, see also p. 11). The opening section of *La* (Gallimard, Paris, 1976) evokes *Angst* in its depiction of an I that is formless and outside (see p. 7). In *Préparatifs de noces au delà de l'abîme* ('Preparations for Marriage beyond the Abyss') (Editions Des femmes, Paris, 1978), the appellation I covers the self's indecision: 'you no longer know who to appear . . . for behind the voice that says I, no one comes, no one dreams, and you feel you are

waking no one. . . . I does not catch hold of any me' (p. 49). The question also arises in *Le Portrait du soleil* ('The Portrait of the Sun') (Denoël, Paris, 1974) (see pp. 7, 16, 84).

6 *Révolutions pour plus d'un Faust* (Editions de Seuil, Paris, 1975).

7 The 'you' is foregrounded in *Préparatifs de noces au delà de l'abîme* as the text shifts from I to you to she (see, for example, p. 8: 'without I scarcely if you have enough of she', also p. 7).

8 'There [*Là* – the evocation of the feminine article is striking] . . . they transform themselves into blood and words [*en sangs et en sons*], they push words to my surface, love letters for Absence, letters of caress for the time of Estrangement' (p. 31).

9 This conjunction of the father, mother and God is humorously figured in the 'TwiceGod' ('*Dieubis*') of *Le Portrait du soleil* (see, for example, p. 15). It is also present in the fantasized 'unique being, of three mixed genders male and female and partially divine' of *Préparatifs de noces au delà de l'abîme* (p. 29).

10 In *La* it is the mother's continuing presence – *là* ('there') – that enables the self's (re)birth (see p. 44, also pp. 54–5). In *Souffles* the mother's role is similarly presented as one the self must take on for herself (see pp. 73–4). In *Préparatifs de noces au delà de l'abîme*, the mother's role is divided between the mother 'who lays down the law' (p. 126, see also p. 125) and the mother the I must become (see pp. 129, 131, 134).

11 The scene is entitled 'the Horriginary Scene' ('*la Scène Horriginaire*') (p. 66).

12 See also *Le Portrait du soleil* (pp. 39, 85).

13 In *Souffles* this order is described as 'rules of unity, of non-contradiction, and other police formalities' (p. 28). It is an order the I fears: 'I am scared of being stopped by an officer of all the police forces that are looking for me for hesitation, excess of birth, sexual indecision and other attempts' (p. 29).

14 This is also a theme of *Révolutions pour plus d'un Faust*. Here the issue of origin is linked to sight: 'it happens that the Eye engenders men and it happens that men engender the Eye that engenders them' (p. 77). This is humorously figured in the tale of the 'royal god' (p. 79) whose perceived lack of the phallus (p. 80) entails its invention. In *Souffles*, the question of origin is explored in a horrific episode in which the mother is tortured for her secret (pp. 62–5, 69). A similar episode occurs in *La* (p. 198). The role of language in the appropriation of the origin is also a theme of *Préparatifs de noces au delà de l'abîme* (see, for example, p. 28).

15 In *Le Portrait du soleil*, the force of the existing order is such that the I knows without apparently having learned what is required: 'I had never done it before, at least I cannot remember any precedent, however my movements were sure, I invented nothing, I did not hesitate, there was born each second in my body the whole of a familiar order' (p. 15). In *Préparatifs de noces au delà de l'abîme* the I's accession to the

social order is described as 'a profound struggle . . . between your law body and your pleasure body' (p. 71).

16 This image of a crossroads also occurs in *Le Portrait du soleil* in terms of past, present and future time (p. 12). In *Préparatifs de noces au delà de l'abîme* the image is figured in the description of two paths: '*if, once outside, instead of letting yourself be taken by the first path that comes, you take the risk on the left* . . . the risk can transport you' (p. 103).

17 In *La*, language is also depicted as the mother's gift (see pp. 90, 125). It is attributed with the potential to carry the I beyond the interdictions of the law (see pp. 90, 113, 116).

18 This episode is echoed in *Le Portrait du soleil* in a comic reworking of Lacan's account of the mirror stage. Not only does the I have difficulty recognizing herself, she has similar difficulties pronouncing herself: 'each time I saw myself I absolutely did not recognize *Myself*: yet I was completely alone, and the image could not define anyone other than she who could only be me. It would have been necessary to begin a sentence with I, but the sentence came out headless, the subject did not appear' (p. 16). In *Préparatifs de noces au delà de l'abîme* language is deemed responsible for the self's castration: 'nothing more than a name . . . had slit my throat' (p. 15, see also p. 11).

19 See also p. 47: 'the pack of words . . . are doing their dirty work and making their filthy prophesies, blaspheming and lying right inside my own mouth.'

20 See also the description of the impact of his words:

> recaptured. Stopped. Condemned to listen to them. They were strange, passing strange; terrible, more than terrible; they had absolute power over blood and mind. Terribly appealing and threatening. Who could have escaped them? No woman. Nothing could resist them. They would have captured me even if I had shut my eyes. As if it had been written that I would obey them. And each letter repeated that necessity. They read themselves to me without pity. . . . As soon as a letter referred to me a mist formed in front of my eyes. I felt myself summoned by the sentence that rejected me. . . . They fell on me, or I fell into their bottomless space, with no safety net. . . . I fell under their charm which I loathed. (pp. 135–6)

21 See also: 'I would have liked to hear a sentence with room for me in it' (p. 200).

22 The difference between a poetic and philosophical approach is a major concern of *Révolutions pour plus d'un Faust* (see, for example, p. 46, also p. 58). Socrates' answer to the young man's: 'I want to know everything! explain everything to me!', for example, is to insist that 'the only means of making ourselves masters of multiplicity is to create categories' (p. 59). Plato and Aristotle are depicted erecting 'a dome that

hides the gaping sky with the help of mathematical concepts distributed and connected by rigid . . . threads. They then contemplate their sky of concepts with a smile' (p. 66, see also p. 64). These positions are contrasted with the insistence of the Fool: 'it is not in knowledge, it is in creation that we find our joy. You, if you want to create, beware the passive eye. Don't content yourself with what has already been seen. Invent new possibilities for seeing. Dare to invent the eyes that see what *will be* visible' (p. 67). The futility of the philosophical approach is figured in Socrates' narcissism and the dissolution of the conceptual dome: '*Socrates*: "Look at me looking? Admire me seeing!" Socrates' eyes take in fragments of earth, diverge, dilate, become monstrous mouths. The world shudders; the conceptual dome vibrates and splits on all sides' (p. 67). The power of poetry to overcome the machinations of the law is also a theme of *Un K incompréhensible: Pierre Goldman* ('An Incomprehensible K[ase]: Pierre Goldman') (Christian Bourgois, Paris, 1975) (see p. 17). In *Préparatifs de noces au delà de l'abîme*, writing similarly presents itself as a means of circumventing the law's dictates (p. 145, see also pp. 38–9).

23 This description, reminiscent of Cixous' depictions of *écriture féminine*, is echoed in *La*: 'a rain of flying verbal images . . . contaminates the genders and the numbers, passes from one edge to the other edge of its most gaping abyss by enchantment, enbirthment, enjambement, throws a verbal bridge between its desires and its realities' (p. 248, see also the description of the 'Effelle tower', p. 278).

24 On p. 116 this is imaged as 'writing against the law of no-return'. This is also a theme of *La*, where writing is pitted against the 'enemies of life' (p. 207, see also p. 208 and the insistence, p. 270, on the necessity of writing 'against death').

25 The necessity of this recognition in *Révolutions pour plus d'un Faust* is also figured in the collision between the imaginary and the real. Within '*the imaginary*' (p. 114), there is no separation and this has a negative effect on the two 'similars' ('*semblables*'):

> the two beings face each other, in the blinded way of lovers of a same sex, each one looking for his same in the other and looking for the other in the same. However each one being still no more than a same and only wanting the other, but without leaving the other the place to be and confusing one with the other in looking with hatred for themselves in an eternal and illusory alikeness. (p. 114, see also pp. 91, 138)

26 In *Préparatifs de noces au delà de l'abîme* madness is figured in terms of what it would mean to be 'delivered from the self' with no language or law (p. 15): 'all is silence and madness' (p. 16, see also pp. 17, 136).

27 See also the episode on p. 172 in which the woman's refusal to flee from the fire is labelled madness.

28 The law is the theme of *Un K incompréhensible: Pierre Goldman*. Here Cixous expresses her outrage at Goldman's trial and reflects on the nature of the law. Of particular interest in terms of Cixous' work on femininity is her insistence that allegiance to the law depends on the self: 'it is our docility, our individual and collective consent that creates its power' (p. 86, see also pp. 7, 78). For Cixous it is Goldman's refusal to adhere to the law that condemns him. He is described as outside 'the general schooling ('*manège*') of the law' (p. 18) – defined here as 'the law of repression of the not-same, of the other' (p. 73) – and thus 'from the point of view of the social establishment the uncontrollable element' (p. 18, see also p. 21). 'It is necessary to eliminate him one way or the other' (p. 18).

29 Madness is also a theme of *Révolutions pour plus d'un Faust*. Here the language of the Fool – pitted against the law's machinations (the law is portrayed as the 'father of all phantasms' [p. 80]) – borders on nonsense: 'without sentences and without points and without direction' (p. 82). The solution is shown to reside in a third ear, eye and mode of thinking – imaged as 'a third language' – that will bring into being an/other schema (pp. 83–4, see also p. 192) and the concomitant freeing of the self (p. 193).

30 The feminine I that comes into being in *Souffles* is the product of labour, figured in the feminine '*Voix-Là!* ('Voice-Present') (p. 11): the French plays on the feminine gender of voice (*la voix*), on the echo with *la voie* (the way) and on the expression *voilà*: there is. It is this 'present' of the voice – deriving from 'the time when the soul still spoke flesh' (p. 10) – that brings the I to life. In *Souffles* it is women (see p. 184) who recognize the valorized object for what it is (see pp. 170–1, 182–6) and risk the prohibitions of the law (p. 186).

31 The plural possibilities of the self are also imaged in *Révolutions pour plus d'un Faust*, in the I's perception of the Fool (for example p. 24: 'I see springing from where you speak several bodies . . . O you more than one and never one'), in the Fool's admonition: 'do the infinite round of your multiplicity' (p. 31), and in the Homuncule's answer to the I's question: 'this is why I am so beautiful: because I have the great desire to be all the individuals I can give birth to' (p. 34). There is insistence here that the differences of others must be recognized and valued, rather than denied, made use of or condemned (see, for example, p. 76). This theme of plurality is also figured in '*A Workshop of the Other*', (see p. 90). In *La* the plural self is indicated in the repeated use of a plural form (see, for example, p. 28).

32 This choice is portrayed in *Le Portrait du soleil* – 'I hesitated over the subject of my own constitution, sometimes turning to the masculine sometimes moving to the feminine' (p. 132) – in relation to the law of gender (see p. 37). In *Révolutions pour plus d'un Faust* there is a 'sexual

celebration' (p. 68) advocating interaction rather than exclusion (p. 69). In *Souffles* the differences between a masculine and feminine gender are imaged in terms of defence or openness to the other. *His* mode – 'to shield his flame, he invented hard forms for himself, volumes closed tight as fists' (p. 30, see also p. 31) – is contrasted with the comportment of the feminine I: 'I in my need to always leave from me to you, streaming, risking the assault of an evil blast, I'm off, inventing extensions for myself, supplenesses' (p. 30). In *Portrait de Dora* ('Portrait of Dora') (Des femmes, Paris, 1976), Madame K. tells Dora that sex roles must be learned (p. 40). In *La* there is a blurring of gender roles as in the 'beautiful young masculine mother' (p. 87, the movement between masculine and feminine subject pronouns is also noteworthy here). This plurality is contrasted with the traditional masculine position figured in the 'retiring-God' who is 'Master of his possessions' (p. 131). The absurdity of using the masculine to legislate for difference is also expressed here: 'only an idiot can announce: "A masculine symbol serves to designate a part of the female genital equipment"' (p. 239).

33 The page reference is to the French edition since the postscript is missing from the English translation.

34 The woman evoked is reminiscent of Sakundeva in *La Prise de l'école de Madhubaï* (1984) ('The Taking of Madhubaï School') (Des femmes, Paris, 1986).

35 In *Un K incompréhensible: Pierre Goldman* Cixous describes how her realization of the role of others (p. 38) and the need to remember (p. 34) required time:

> I know how limited I am, how I am shut inside the narrowness of my cultural and social figure, my skin, I want to talk about my interior keenness, how partial it is, selective, blocked here by ignorance, here by egotism, here by lassitudes. I have surprised myself at blindnesses that it has taken me time to disclose, to name, to pursue: I have been slow, terribly slow to approach certain people. . . . One never feels, one never touches, one never sees the other enough. (p. 38, see also p. 49)

The description is interesting in terms of Cixous' account of her writing biography. Cixous compares her position to Goldman's:

> a sensitivity, above all an imagination, a possibility of being affected, touched, altered, changed, by an encounter with the other; because there is in him what there is not in the keepers of the Château, of the Law, of paradise always already lost for the human being, the living space of becoming, the infinite fabric of possibility, the place – for the other. (pp. 51–2)

36 The form of *Révolutions pour plus d'un Faust* is almost theatrical in its attribution of voices to such personae as 'The Fool', 'The Poet' and 'The Philosopher' and in its assigning parts of the text to different locations (see, for example, *'A Non Dialectic Workshop'*, *'The Heliopolitical Workshop'*, *'A Matrix Workshop'*). There are also numerous theatrical images, as in the description of the text as a 'ballet of the world's ancient and new images' (p. 10) and the depiction of the players as puppets (see p. 12). *Souffles* includes sections of text in italics and different sized type to differentiate between the I's statements. The insistence on an/other language and writing is also figured in a play on syntax and meaning:

> labour! Re-compose de com re com pose. . . .
> In the womb where the tongue at work comes and goes where mash matter march masticate the hatchet tongue which has not finished ruminating and recommencing, retouching, moistening, moulding,
> The new dough! (p. 114, see also the various configurations of *'voler'* [to fly/steal] p. 179)

La is a collage of short passages, some of which are divided by asterisks and some of which have headings. A number of the texts are printed only on the right hand side of the page, while others are printed in the form of poetry with each new phrase on a separate line. There is word-play in such phrases as 'nuitamment je se fuit' ('nightably I flees itself') (p. 13), in the distinction between 'jedus' ('Ishould') and 'jedit' ('Isaid') (see p. 23) – distinguishing the self that is obedient to the law from the speaking self who may thus alter its impact – and in the 'Noun Nounet Non Non' ('Noun Nounand No No') associated with 'vieux-le-dieu-qui-pénètre-victorieux, le prime maire de Mêmeplus' ('god-the-old-who-penetrates-victorious, the prime mayor of Sameplus') (p. 132). *Partie* ('Part') (Des femmes, Paris, 1976) can be opened and read from either end, while the text itself works on the meanings and possibilities generated by the writing process. These include the constant evocation of the sexual body: 'outrecuisse danse et l'impatience de *Si, Je* ne serait jamais venu à sexpression' ('ultrathigh dances and the impatience of *If, I* would never come to sexpression') ('Si-je', p. 14); 'tout ceci serait la seinscription mictique d'un albalphabet de lait-trait dans le moir, l'écriture étant donc d'origine mammispermique et phonolactique' ('all this would be the micturitic breastscription of an albalphabet of [literate] milk-trace in the [ego-black] moire, writing thus being mammispermic and phonolactic in origin') ('Si-je', p. 15). There is also an innovative use of textual layout and typography. *Préparatifs de noces au delà de l'abîme* comprises short passages prefaced with a heading in bold. The texts also contain sections in italic. Word-play is featured in such transpositions as that between 'elle-même' (she-herself) and 'elle m'aime' (she loves me) (p. 27), in the play on 'mère'/'mer' (mother/sea) (see, for example, 'la mermoire' [the (mother)memory/seamoire], p. 30), and in the various configurations of 'si' (if): 'ciel' (sky), 'sielle' (if she), 'silence' (silence), 'silenciel' (silentsky).

37 See also the play on 'seinceste' (breastincest) (French text, p. 99).

38 The English translation gives 'the 20th comes, he doesn't come. Who will vanquish these vain days for me'/'leaving – 20 – day of plenty – day of vanity – or the 23rd' (p. 40). Examples of word-play in other texts written during this period include the naming of the town in *Le Portrait du soleil* as Masterdam and the play on the letter 'K': 'j'aimais le dos de Mme K. Parce K'il était d'une blancheur ravissante Kand Dora l'embrassait elle projetait une ombre noire Komme une enKre' ('I loved Mme K's back beKause it was of a bewitching whiteness when Dora kissed her she projected a shadow black as inK') (p. 127). The letter 'K', deriving from Freud's case study (see *Portrait de Dora*), links to the K in *Angst* and the 'K' (Kafka, case) of *Un K incompréhensible: Pierre Goldman*.

39 In *Révolutions pour plus d'un Faust* the reader is addressed directly (see, for example, p. 12). The reader's role is depicted in terms of giving birth to the writing (p. 88, see also p. 52: 'to you if you wish to bring these things to an integral form, and to you to invent') and as in continual flux (see p. 45).

Chapter 3 *Writing with the Voice of the Other*

1 *Le Livre de Promethea* (Gallimard, Paris, 1983). The English translation is by Betsy Wing (University of Nebraska Press, Lincoln and London, 1991).

2 See also p. 208: 'the author of what I describe is not myself, it is the Other'. There is a similar insistence in *Illa* (Editions Des femmes, Paris, 1980): 'I had not written this child by myself, I wrote it with them, the women, and it shone by itself, it radiated with us' (p. 206). See also the comments in *Ou l'art de l'innocence* ('Or the Art of Innocence') (Editions Des femmes, Paris, 1981) that 'I am not the one who found at least half the words which sprout from each page' (p. 16) and 'I am always on the trail of phrases which run ahead with all their might' (p. 53).

3 See p. 53: 'consequently: everything that follows has moved through my hand and onto the paper when there was real contact with Promethea. I have often put my left hand between her breasts and with the rapid motions of my docile right hand it was written. I am only that cardiograph' and p. 91: 'all I am doing here, anyhow, is putting down traces of Promethea. Only the paper is mine. The rest: light, movement, and breath, the fate of our book and of our

adventure, is hers. The style is principally hers as well' (see also p. 121).

This view of the author as recorder or teller is also a theme of *La Bataille d'Arcachon* ('The Battle of Arcachon') (Editions Trois, Québec, 1986), written in the same year as *Le Livre de Promethea* appeared. There are numerous references in *La Bataille d'Arcachon* to the author waiting for her characters' next move, as on p. 10 where she explains: 'I am telling you of the departure. I could not do it before because I was waiting for H to succeed in recovering an anchoring point in life' (see also p. 146). The author's respect and concern for her 'characters' figured here in her decision to wait for H before proceeding is also a consistent theme of both texts, echoing the insistence that the other must be accorded their space.

4 Cixous' opera, *Le Nom d'Oedipe* ('The Name of Oedipus') (Editions Des femmes, Paris, 1978), figures this split in its subdivision of the voices of the various personae. The opening sequence, for example, interweaves the different voice-divisions to create a simultaneous affirmation, echo and negation (p. 13, see also the play on the various configurations of 'sans/sens/sang' [without/meaning/blood] here). *Anankè* (Editions Des femmes, Paris, 1979) opens with the question: 'which (feminine) I can really say I?' (*quelle je peux bien dire je?*) (p. 10). As in *The Book of Promethea*, the question is echoed in a division between I and she (see, for example, p. 29) and the difference between the I writing and the text's subject, whose various configurations influence and alter the writing I (see pp. 28–9, also the epigraph to the 'Orange chapter' pp. 33, 35, 36, 37, and the epigraph to the 'Green chapter', p. 187). In *Limonade tout était si infini* ('Lemonade Everything Was So Infinite') (Editions Des femmes, Paris, 1982), the subject includes I and she. There is also the frequent disappearance of the subject from the writing (see pp. 14, 52, 92). In *La Bataille d'Arcachon* the distinction between I as teller of the tale and H and Promethea (sometimes grouped together as they [*elles*]) as its participants and creators is clearly drawn (see, for example, p. 9).

5 This division is figured slightly differently in *Illa* where the I is both '(myself and the other: she who writes)' (p. 191).

6 In *Anankè* this doubt is explicitly linked to the conflicting motivations of the body which prevent the self from adopting a definitive subject position (see p. 37).

7 This is also figured in the occasional disappearance of the I from the text (see, for example, pp. 70, 80).

8 *Illa* similarly explores women's role in the (re)birth of the feminine subject (see, for example, pp. 109–11, 113, 118, 171, 173, 178, 179, 197, 198), in contradistinction to the way the I was previously dictated to (pp. 112, 120, 127, 205). In *Ou l'art de l'innocence* there is insistence that the writing derives through a relation with female/feminine others (see, for example, pp. 129, 290). The text's 'other' title, printed inside

the cover, includes the English word 'with' – *With ou l'art de l'innocence* – and this 'with' is highlighted as the writing's beginning (p. 173). In *Limonade tout était si infini* living requires others: 'to live life truly essentially is too great a joy for whosoever would confront it alone' (p. 68) and the inscription – the safeguarding – of this mode of living is writing's aim (see p. 214, and particularly the reference to 'a place where creating is synonymous with giving'). As in *The Book of Promethea,* this capacity to *live* life (see p. 258) derives from the recognition of mortality (see p. 220). In *La Bataille d'Arcachon,* the regressive desire for merger with another is prevented as Promethea mother's H towards self-birth (see p. 11).

9 In *Limonade tout était si infini* women's annihilation is delineated in terms of a war waged by men against women's possession of the truth (p. 74). The answer to the mystery of origin necessitates its concealment: 'because it was so terribly simple . . . [the Ancients] diluted it, encased it in metal, poured life into the molds, rolled the apples in gold. The juice stopped flowing. And from this point on we no longer understood anything. Because the apples died of it. Little by little the world has been covered in gold, it has been cold, slow, heavy, and odourless . . .' (p. 299).

10 This echoes the depiction of woman in *Illa* as mother *and* daughter: 'always at the work of the other. In labour. . . . Supple, welcoming, infinitely comprehensive . . . naturally faithful to the nature of life which is differences, chance, antitheses. . . . Not choosing a path in order to reject the other, does not elect, does not abase, lets herself be inspired by the risk' (p. 39). This insistence on the possibility of both paths extends the image of the crossroads in the texts preceding *Vivre l'orange/To Live the Orange* where the I was immobilized by her incapacity to choose. Here, the I realizes: 'each path up until the revelation: we learn, as we journey, that there is no arriving. There are only paths' (p. 131). In *Illa* it is the relationship *between* women that gives birth to writing (p. 90, see also pp. 91, 124). In *Limonade tout était si infini* being a woman and being with women are deemed vital:

> and immediately without any holding back, she, her whole being transformed in an outpouring of joy, flung herself towards her. And the mystery of this calm was that it had the power of making her feel her own mystery. She was a woman . . . being-a-woman only realized itself in the depths of the body, there was a vital sense to being-a-woman, and it could only be accomplished through encountering the body of another woman. (p. 55)

11 In *Ou l'art de l'innocence* this earlier phase of the author's life and work is portrayed through Cordelia (see pp. 30, 38). Cordelia is described as

'caught in the cold plaster of language' (p. 28), and links to a decade of the author's life (p. 44) in which 'the good light, the one which moves, pours, sheds visibility on everything that is really alive, already shone far ahead of me' (p. 45, see also the reference to this decade as a period of 'mourning' for the father, pp. 59–60). The end of the decade comes with the author's realization of her mistaken endeavour to create a god (p. 46), and substitute past and future narratives (see pp. 49, 50) for life in the present.

There is a similar description in *Limonade tout était si infini* (see pp. 123, 194), contrasted with the author's discovery (p. 213) of a means of living *beyond* separation and the law:

> there was a place – perhaps it was a time – in which no name any longer had this malefic power to recapture and separate. And then things called, and one responded, one was free and young with no after-thought. One was an Other-person; being the happy, free, non-servile person of the other. Living near-to-the-wild-heart-of-life. Living in the middle of life's current. (p. 214)

12 See p. 54: 'Promethea's book is a rough draft. . . . I will not touch this draft'. Also p. 61: 'I would like Promethea's book to stay where it belongs, on its true page: therefore I feel obliged to leave it in its authentic, immediate state, disorganized and even dated (not taking into account my ex-taste for discretion in writing).'

13 The insistence on a return to a position preceding the manuals of the law is also present in *Illa* (see p. 12). In *Ou l'art de l'innocence* this is figured in terms of 'the three morals' taught in school: 'moral geography (including the study of frontiers, enclosure and initiation in racisms); moral calculation (inhibition; greed; prudence and the different ancient and modern methods of life economics); and flying-low, which is a believing-living, following the rules of death' (p. 69). In *Limonade tout était si infini* the author's aim of thinking within the present (see p. 33) necessitates a departure 'with no watch, with no date limit, with no reserve' (p. 51).

14 Promethea is described as 'the great magical mare' (p. 11, see also p. 93) who transports the author at a gallop (p. 78).

15 There is also insistence that this position must not be abused by the author: 'I do have a sense of responsibility. I certainly do not want to wrongly benefit from a work that I am only part of' (p. 13, see also p. 38).

16 There are meditations on the process and purpose of writing in a number of the texts written during this period which echo Cixous' delineations of *écriture féminine*. *Anankè* outlines its aim to 'realize the unrealizable: a birth from the heart' (p. 187) and stresses the role of

others in this process (p. 187). *Illa* contains numerous references to a writing that will enable us to 'live totally alive' (p. 173) derived through our relations with others and involving our advancement 'in the light of questions' (p. 208). In *Ou l'art de l'innocence* writing is compared to loving (p. 138), an approach contrasted with the comportment of the 'men-men' who 'do not want to receive, but to take by wounding' (p. 211).

17 See also pp. 131–2: 'sometimes I desire you the way a queen desires a slave: I would like to belong to you and have you order me and humble me and provide me with the realm of obedience. Sometimes I want to rule over you with all the fierceness of the slave bent over the queen' (see also pp. 143–4, 177–8). In *La Bataille d'Arcachon* this side to love is figured in the narcissistic pleasures derived from hurting and torturing the other (see pp. 46, 51), H's 'bad character' (p. 43) and the ridiculous behaviour of the lovers (see p. 146).

18 The potentially destructive effects to the self of merging with another are figured in *Le Nom d'Oedipe*. Here Oedipus' desire – 'I no longer want to have a name. No other name than you' (p. 70) – precipitates the tragedy (see also pp. 80–1). In *Ou l'art de l'innocence* the question of an appropriate distance involves the splitting of the I between I, you (see p. 171) and the text's various personae. The I's desire to become Aura is seen as dangerous since it would necessarily efface these other personae (p. 78).

19 This notion of the right distance to the other in relation to (re)birth is also a theme of *Illa* (see pp. 16–17, 20, 36–7, 38).

20 See also *Illa* (pp. 151, 154, 155, 160).

21 In *The Book of Promethea* this is connected to the more general problem: 'what does one do to succeed in having (anew) something one already has?' (p. 165). In *Illa* there is comparison between a mode of living, loving and writing which appropriates (see, for example, pp. 136–7) and an approach which: 'gives. . . . What we have lost. What we never had. What we no longer knew how to have' (p. 147). This is echoed in *Ou l'art de l'innocence* where 'knowing how to have what one has' is described as 'an inexhaustible richness' (p. 290). In *La Bataille d'Arcachon*, H's inability to live her happiness (p. 48) is presented as her greatest obstacle. It is her narcissism that prevents her from receiving Promethea's gift: 'never had one made her such a huge gift of herself. Her cup was overflowing. Bashful and delighted, she felt like the fisherman's wife who was so insatiable that in the end she had nothing since she had never known how to have anything of what she received' (p. 56).

22 This is a theme explored in *La Bataille d'Arcachon*. Here a day of perfect happiness between the lovers is achieved by excluding all external news (pp. 39–40). The final 'victory' of *La Bataille d'Arcachon* is the recognition that love cannot ignore what is happening in the wider world but must, on the contrary, work to include this (see, for exam-

ple, H's attempt to keep the newspapers out of the bedroom pp. 155–6). Love *is* the incessant battle to maintain a relationship between the self, the other and the world.

23 In *Illa* the author defines her task as 'living along the thread of nows' (p. 170), a process requiring constant readjustment (p. 173; see also *Ou l'art de l'innocence*, p. 239, and *Limonade tout était si infini*, p. 262).

24 In *Limonade tout était si infini* the question of history is figured by the 'question-of-war' (p. 70). Here the state of 'being in paradise' (p. 72), in which we finally become 'capable of discovering the treasures of life' (p. 72) is threatened by war: 'war stuns it, deafens it, war makes its stupidity reign over the world'. The nature of this war is described as: 'a war of the nullification of women and similar beings . . . a war aimed at weakening and reducing half of the world, and at enslaving nine-tenths of the other half of the world' (p. 74). Its methods include 'the development of unbelievably perfected, in other words perverse, psychological weapons' (p. 74) and 'the utilization of means of aggression which are strictly insidious, invisible, inaudible, and have a radical force of destruction hitherto never attained' (p. 74). Its purpose is the obliteration of differences (p. 75) and re-education (p. 75) according to 'the Great Logic of Destructions' (p. 77). Impetus for the war comes from the 'men-men' (p. 76) and their need: 'to wall themselves in, to shelter themselves in order to keep well away from each other; need to have borders; need to have wars to keep at a distance for are afraid of touching' (p. 76, see also p. 98). Their 'masculine-interest' is depicted as a desire to 'preserve oneself, protect oneself . . . defining oneself . . . in selfsatisfaction' (p. 120). It is this fear and repression that comprise History, presented here as 'the notebook of the world's repetitions/rehearsals' (p. 85) used to prohibit change (p. 86). It is in this sense that living/loving and writing are potentially revolutionary (p. 86). Writing, with its capacity to inscribe an 'enjoying living' (p. 87, see also pp. 73, 86, 117, 123), is contrasted with a mode of living and writing 'having no other aim than to preserve, survive, reproduce . . . develop the means of defence, commodity exchange' (p. 82). The challenge in *Limonade tout était si infini* is that of living – in contradistinction to our habitual mode of existing 'far from life' (p. 173) – with others, in the knowledge of war, without repeating its model of destruction nor underestimating the difficulty of more peaceful solutions (see p. 176).

25 See also *Limonade tout était si infini* where the conditions for living and writing are described as: 'first going to live. To encounter the other. Going to the other. Encounter the world. Benedictions happened at the points of encounter' (p. 153).

26 See also the references to the work of Clarice Lispector in *Illa* (for example, p. 131). The insistence in *Illa* on a new approach and inscription of the other echoes Cixous' description of Lispector's writing in *Vivre l'orange* (see *Illa*, pp. 136, 137, 147, 178–9). Pages 198–9 of *Illa* offer

a comparison of men's and women's writing which can be read in the context of Cixous' delineations of *écriture féminine* and her work on Lispector (see, for example: 'she writes without foresight, towards the encounter with what comes' (p. 199), 'there are silences and she hears these, and there are words which shine . . . and she listens to them giving her entire body' (p. 199)) There are similar references to Lispector's work in *Limonade tout était si infini* (see, for example, pp. 202, 214, the emphasis on the 'absolute respect for the other', p. 215).

27 In *La Bataille d'Arcachon* there are numerous meditations on the process and purpose of writing which parallel Cixous' reading of Lispector (see, for example, p. 71, and the homage to Lispector's *Agua Viva*, p. 19).

28 This can be compared with similar reflections in *Ou l'art de l'innocence*, (see, for example, p. 276; see also *Limonade tout était si infini*, p. 135). In *La Bataille d'Arcachon* there are numerous references to the way language reduces and distorts life (see, for example, p. 65), as well as meditations by the author on the difficulties of her art (pp. 65, 70).

29 The lacunae within language are also referred to in *Illa* in relation to women's birth:

> (and what I have glimpsed, I am not able to say, what happens in between two stories, the thing that accomplishes, and inaugurates, does not have a name either in one language nor in the other, the instant in which is born what is not yet, a woman . . .) (p. 36)

In *La Bataille d'Arcachon* H is similarly reduced to silence 'since she found that words did not manage to approach the vision delicately enough' (p. 116).

30 This is also the problem of *Limonade tout était si infini*. Here, the author is personally unprepared for happiness (p. 52) and so has 'everything to invent' (p. 52, see also p. 53: 'the good fortune of being happy, she would work on this, she would learn it. It is much easier to work with the aid of misfortune on unhappiness').

31 This can be compared with a similar passage in *Illa*:

> we have been taught the language which speaks from on high, from afar, which listens to itself, which has ears only for itself, the deaf language, deafening, speaking to us in advance. We have been taught the language that translates everything in itself – only understanding through translation; only speaking its language, only listening to its grammar: and we are separated from things by its order. (p. 136, see also p. 137)

32 See also p. 108: 'just stop loving me, Promethea, long enough for me to finish writing this page' (also pp. 137, 187). This difficulty of living *and* writing is also expressed in *Illa*: '"I cannot write, my passionate hands want to touch your neck . . ." and then not one word more' (p. 122).

33 This is also evoked in *Limonade tout était si infini* where the endeavour to write a letter is justified in terms of communicating joy (p. 70). In *La Bataille d'Arcachon* language is portrayed as an aid to transmitting love (see pp. 54–5).

34 This depiction of an/other language and writing is also a theme of *Illa* (see pp. 103, 178–9). In *La Bataille d'Arcachon* there is a link between an alternative language and music, figured in the delicate, infinitely varied yet harmonious pealings of the five bells (p. 55).

35 This insistence on the role of the reader is also present in *Limonade tout était si infini*. Here, the author compares her reaction to those works of art which appear as trophies (p. 194, see also p. 193) of the artist's struggle – 'someone had wanted to win. And this desire revealed itself' (p. 195) – with her reaction to works of art which embody 'a moment of life, found, saved' (p. 194). In the first case there is no place for the spectator/reader beyond that of admirer (p. 190), whereas in the second case art gives rise to further creation (p. 196).

36 See also the 'lessons in touching, enjoying, listening that women have given me, with their hands . . . to know skin, to speak nakedly before languages' (p. 101); 'to her I owe the first body that grows outside laws. The first knowing-woman. . . . she told me everything, without a word: "I will be a woman, you the same", and we understood everything in the intimacy of the mystery' (p. 107); 'below in the room of pulsions in which their milky a, i, o, u made their tongues beat to the same strong, slow and maternal cadence, we must desire to invent the thinking that does not separate' (p. 119).

37 See also the reference in *Illa* to the 'paper phrases' (p. 188) that derive from 'thoughts cut off from the body that supplies them' (p. 188).

38 *Illa*, for example, is composed of a series of fragments, many of which begin in mid-sentence (see p. 17), some of which are in parentheses or set between quotation marks (pp. 16–17), while others include text in italics or block capitals (p. 18). *Ou l'art de l'innocence* is subdivided between a number of voices, and comprises sections of text that do not employ the conventional format of paragraphs, sentences and punctuation (see p. 305).

39 The style of *Limonade tout était si infini* parallels *The Book of Promethea* in this respect, although it is without *The Book of Promethea's* conversational ease (see, for example, the extended sentence on pp. 140–1). In the final pages of *Limonade tout était si infini* the author discusses the question of style, acknowledging the temptation to ornament her

writing – a temptation she must guard against: 'so hard to disembellish. Habit. Must unlearn' (p. 263). She gives her aim as the writing of 'human-phrases' (p. 260) which 'have no need of seduction or explanation' (p. 261). This necessarily involves a move away from conventional literary practice, altering both its content and its form:

> without drama? Without intrigue. The essential drama: living.
> Action consists of the essential: living, loving. Knowing that one will die: remain living. (p. 261)

40 This can be contrasted with the word-play of *Anankè*, exemplified in the days of the week (*'l'undit'* [the French plays with the idea of the unsaid, creating a homophone for the French word for 'Monday' – *'lundi'*], p. 122, *'je-dit'* [literally 'I-said', the homophone is with *'jeudi'* – 'Thursday'], p. 127), and the description of hair-cutting as *'Cutting treatment'* (p. 126) a *'quoi-faire'* for women (p. 126 – literally 'what to do', the expression is a homophone for *coiffure* – hairstyle) trimming 'the last manbilical [*hombilical*] link' (p. 126). In *Illa* there is play on the persona of Angela – *'ange est là'* (literally 'angel is there', p. 129) – as well as on the 'relation' of the other *'en soi(e)'* (p. 81 – the French juxtaposes the expressions 'in oneself' and 'in silk' while the added 'e' in parentheses evokes the feminine). In *Ou l'art de l'innocence* there is word-play on the *'hommes de taire'* (literally 'men who suppress', there is also the echo of *pommes de terre* – potatoes, p. 11, see also p. 14), who silence and reduce the inventive possibilities of language. This attitude to language is contrasted with an approach that merges attentive listening/understanding and feeling: *'je sentends'* – 'I hearfeel' (p. 18). Some of the word-play in *Ou l'art de l'innocence* involves the feminizing of words, as in 'seintillements' – a play on feelings, containing the French word for breast (*sein*) (p. 66) – and 'la soleille' (the sun) (p. 245), or the creation of neologisms (see pp. 155, 189, 200, 302).

Chapter 4 *Cixous and the Theatre*

1 *L'Histoire terrible mais inachevée de Norodom Sihanouk roi du Cambodge* (Théâtre du Soleil, Paris, 1985) and *Indiade ou l'Inde de leurs rêves* (Théâtre du Soleil, Paris, 1987). The Théâtre du Soleil publication of *Indiade* includes the essays 'Le Lieu du Crime, le lieu du Pardon', 'L'Ourse, la Tombe, les Etoiles', 'Qui es-tu' and L'Incarnation'. Full details are given below.
2 See pp. 247–78 of *Indiade ou l'Inde de leurs rêves*.
3 'Le Lieu du Crime, le lieu du Pardon', *Indiade ou l'Inde de leurs rêves*, pp. 253–9. I am indebted to Catherine MacGillivray for allowing me to use her translation of this text and that of 'L'Incarnation'. Both translations

appear in Susan Sellers (ed.), *The Hélène Cixous Reader* (Routledge, London and New York, 1994).

4 'L'Incarnation', *Indiade ou l'Inde de leurs rêves*, pp. 260–6.

5 In 'Le Chemin de Légende' ('The Pathway of Legend'), the 1984 preface to *La Prise de l'ecole de Madhubaï* in the Des femmes edition of the play, Cixous notes:

> to write for the theatre: it is necessary to go away from the self, leave, journey in obscurity for a long time . . . until one feels the space become a country that is extremely foreign . . . until one awakes, metamorphosed into someone I has never met . . .
>
> It is not me, and yet I am it. What remains of myself when I become an old woman or a minister? Almost nothing, the beating of wonder in my breast. (p. 7)

She compares this mode of writing with that of conventional narrative in which 'the author, in general, holds very tightly to his ego' (p. 8).

6 'A Realm of Characters', in Susan Sellers (ed.), *Delighting the Heart: A Notebook by Women Writers* (The Women's Press, London, 1989, reissued 1994), pp. 126–8.

7 'When I write fiction, I let my meaning gather slowly, I give my reader as long as she needs to understand. In the theatre, my writing must be efficient, there must be an immediate explosion of meaning. The spectator has three hours, whereas a reader has the whole of eternity if she wishes. Theatre is the art of urgency. Everything happens in the present. In the ten seconds after the actors are on stage the audience must have understood. In this sense I find writing for the theatre a perpetual apprenticeship. I have a tendency to hang about *en route*, pausing here, stopping to reflect there, and the theatre doesn't allow me to do this' (A Realm of Characters', p. 126).

8 It is nevertheless interesting to note that many of Cixous' fictional texts involve a subdivision of the writing between different voices or personae. This is true even of her first fictional collection *Le Prénom de Dieu* (see, for example, p. 15). The fact that Cixous wrote a number of plays before *Sihanouk* should similarly be emphasized.

9 The parallel with Cixous' highlighting of the mother's role as a model for the feminine writer is noteworthy here.

10 See also 'Qui es-tu?', in *Indiade ou l'Inde de leurs rêves*, where Cixous describes writing for the theatre as 'the art of listening to others. For fifty characters, multiply your small ears and hold your breath' (p. 276).

11 See also 'Qui es-tu?', p. 277.

12 'Qui es-tu?', pp. 267–8. The 'you' of this question is significant in terms of its progression from the 'who am I?' of the early texts.

13 See, for example, 'L'Incarnation', p. 266.

14 It is also a problem confronted in *La Bataille d'Arcachon* (Editions Trois, Québec, 1986), albeit humorously, as the author struggles with her dislike of H (see pp. 20, 43, 93).

15 In 'A Realm of Characters', Cixous comments on the fact that the others she is engaged in writing in *Sihanouk* and *Indiade* are historical others. She explains how this fact necessitates a period of research into the lives of these others, a period of research she must then struggle to undo:

> for both *Sihanouk* and *Indiade* I began with long months of historic research. I have always envied Shakespeare who was able to draw on the chronicles of Plutarch and Holinshed for the subject-matter of his historic tragedies, but as far as contemporary history is concerned, these chronicles don't exist. I was first of all obliged to become the chronicler of my story. And this task turned out to be a handicap. I emerged from months of painstaking historic research weighed down with documents and facts, and I then found I had to fight against this great mass of accumulated knowledge in order to be able to write.' (p. 127)

16 See also 'From the Scene of the Unconscious', in Françoise Van Rossum-Guyon and Myriam Diaz-Diocaretz (eds), *Hélène Cixous: Chemins d'une écriture* (Rodopi, Amsterdam, and Presses Universitaires de Vincennes, Saint Denis, 1990), p. 31. A number of the ideas and even, as here, some of the passages from the postscripts are repeated in this article.

17 See p. 254:

> to tell the truth, we go to the theater as rarely as to our heart, and it's going to the heart, ours and that of things, that we feel the lack of. We live on the outside of things, in a world whose walls have been replaced by television screens, a world which has lost its thickness, its depths, its treasures, and we take newspaper columns for our thoughts.

Cixous similarly comments on this point in 'Le Chemin de Légende'. She suggests that in contrast to the world in which we live, which has been 'flattened, chopped up by walls and partitions, and barred at the two extremities' (p. 8), the world of the theatre is 'open on all sides, and continues to infinity' (p. 8); as a result, 'what can no longer happen in the machine-world still happens in the theatre' (p. 10). In the theatre, Cixous writes: 'we recover what, being so submissively yoked in our miserly daily banality, we have lost . . . the hope that things that have been our History and existence, and which are so relentlessly programmed by the great social machines, will escape all prevision; present themselves to chance, to the human' (p. 9). The theme is reiterated in *La Pupille* (Cahiers Renaud Barrault, Gallimard, Paris, 1972), where in the horrific world frequented by The Pupil and The Fool love and art are outlawed (p. 20). The solution is seen to lie in a return to the heart, a return heralded by The Theatre who warns: 'a permanent puppet army, made up of a half-billion civil servants and five hundred million soldiers will cover society's body with a mottled membrane, blocking its pores and will suffocate it and substitute Repression and Capital interest for the real needs and desires of the masses!' (p. 119). This insistence on the stultifying effects of the mass media is evoked in *Sihanouk*, where reports of Khmer Rouge atrocities fail to mobilize international outrage (p. 282, see also the American purchase of Lon Nol's government: 'we'll give him the title of national hero for outstanding contribution to the nation's aid' p. 285).

18 See also 'L'Incarnation':

> here we are in a sanctuary of recollection. The actors do before us what we no longer do: they cry, they laugh, they shout, they dance in anger, they explode with joy, and see how we who were living dry and weaned on the floor of forgetfulness above childhood, we rush down to the ground floor, there where the heart gives onto earth, earth made of earth, of water, of roots, of blood, the earth that keeps imprints, and suddenly we recover the cake of life. (p. 261)

'A Realm of Characters' similarly stresses theatre's capacity to return to the essential, highlighting this as a key motivation for writing:

> one can give these characters enormous richness, all the richness and potential all of us have but which becomes crushed and thwarted in the onslaught of everyday life. In the theatre, we are no longer in the realm of the banal. I don't believe we can mobilise people in order to recount platitudes. I'm looking to write the essential, and this is what the characters who inhabit me, talk to me, sing to me, help me to achieve. (p. 127)

19 The Khmer Rouge vision for a new and more just society is expressed by Khieu Samphan: 'I have always wanted the birth of a new society, of an incomparable purity, with no towns, no commerce, no compromising germs' (p. 298, see also his description of the old Cambodia, p. 337). The Khmer Rouge's abandoning of what is essential is imaged in the leaders' decision to 'disappear' in a fabricated radio broadcast announcing their execution without informing their families of the truth. Their decision not to tell the truth to their wives and mothers reinforces women's role in the play as keepers of the truth (see below). This is evoked in Act II, scene 5, where Khieu Samphan and Hou Yon reflect on the progress of the revolution:

Hou Yon:	We are driving the world so strenuously that sometimes it seems to me we will cut the roots of human reality in a single stroke! Why aren't you married?
Khieu Samphan:	I swore not to take a wife before our victory.
Hou Yon:	As for me, it is children I would not want to have. (p. 278, see also the lessons of the Khmer camp, p. 368: 'we have succeeded in abolishing all feeling towards the family')

20 Sihanouk's vanity is most forcefully revealed in his demand in Act V, scene 1, that the Ambassador receive him 'on his knees' (p. 184). It is contained in this scene in his refusal to allow himself to be represented at Ho Chi Minh's funeral: 'no one represents Sihanouk! I am irreplaceable' (p. 105). Sihanouk's capacity to remain attuned to the essential despite the shifting positions he adopts politically is emphasized throughout the play. See, for example, p. 335: 'I do not want to force a smile! I want to shout! I want to cry! I want to be a man again!'. Unlike the Khmer Rouge leaders, whose desire for revolution leads them to falsify the past and blinds them to the sufferings of the people (see p. 337), Sihanouk is depicted even at the end of the play, despite his protestations, as able to distinguish the truth:

> for a year, I lie like I breathe. No, I don't breathe: I lie, I lie, I lie . . .
>
> But the worst is not the shame. It is that by dint of lying I construct the Tower of Lies, I myself create the hell of false truths. And by dint of calling darkness 'radiant', and prison 'sweet liberty', I end up forgetting what real light, real truth is. (p. 358)

21 In the Prologue to *Indiade* this struggle is imaged as a parable of a mother and two sons:

Haridasi:	A mother and two sons. Two brothers, a single mother. The story begins. (p. 20, see also p. 37)

It is the jealousies and collisions of the two brothers that lead to combat. There are numerous references in the play to India as a mother being divided by her sons, and the parable is evoked in an exchange between Haridasi, Sarojini and Ima, herself the mother of two sons:

Sarojini: It is our sons who are always dreaming so violently of departure. As if that was growing up: going away.
Ima: Yes, it's true, they leave us without realising.
Haridasi: And once they've arrived there, then they remember. But it is too late. While they were travelling, the mother died.' (pp. 154–5)

22 This can be compared with a similar insistence in *La Pupille*, where The Fool invites The Pupil to consider 'the four movements of man in History: Birth, Construction, Destruction, Death' (p. 28) and suggests 'there is no absolute ending. What is absolute, is the struggle: where there is war, there is life' (p. 28, this combat is also figured through the characters of Faust [see pp. 101, 102–3] and the tempest [p. 105]).
23 *La Pupille* (Cahiers Renaud Barrault, Gallimard, Paris, 1972).
24 See also The Fool's assertion: 'it is real, open, vulnerable. . . . Following the intensity of the vision that pierces it, it becomes the scene of moral, political and biological vicissitudes' (p. 8).
25 'L'Ourse, la Tombe, les Etoiles', in *Indiade ou l'Inde de leurs rêves*, pp. 247–52.
26 The insistence is paralleled in Sihanouk's realisation: 'all I have endured in order not to die and in order not to let die is worse than dying' (*Sihanouk*, p. 358).
27 In *La Pupille* death is figured in a number of horrific guises (see, for example, 'Brute Death', p. 15).
28 This is an explicit aim of *Indiade*, expressed through the character of Gandhi (see p. 40, also Cixous' Introduction to the play, p. 13).
29 See Cixous' description in 'A Realm of Characters' of how the plays changed during rehearsals (pp. 127–8).
30 See 'A Realm of Characters', p. 126.
31 The large entrance hall to the Théâtre du Soleil's base at Vincennes was decorated in an Indian manner. The décor was enhanced by photographs, the burning of incense, and even the serving of Indian food and drinks at the bar.
32 See also p. 264: 'I write by ear: my ear strained towards the musics of the heart. . . . These are the passions, the pulsions' (p. 262).
33 In the text of *Sihanouk* this point is highlighted through the occasional representation of a character's reaction by a series of dots and exclamation marks (see pp. 31, 58, 288).
34 See p. 262: 'no commentary, no analysis. Sensation, the stage, metaphor'.
35 It is noteworthy that in *Ou l'art de l'innocence* the author rejects the notion of writing for the theatre because of theatre's tendency to end with the representation of a truth: 'what worries me about our tragedies, is that at the end a truth triumphs and calls itself the truth. And what is it. Isn't it simply the strongest?' (p. 58).

36 In the published text of *Indiade* there are various alternatives to the text performed by the Théâtre du Soleil (see pp. 201–40). See also the variant to Act V in *Sihanouk* (pp. 413–23).
37 I am indebted to Donald Watson for allowing me to use his translation here.
38 See also Cixous' comment in 'L'Ourse, la Tombe, les Etoiles': 'that the human is defined by love of the other, we average Westerners, we scarcely imagine. For this does violence to our habitual violence' (p. 249).
39 Donald Watson's translation.
40 See also Ghaffar Khan's speech, Act IV, scene 2 (p. 166).
41 This realism is also present in *La Pupille* where the idealistic insistence on freedom of speech for all during the early days of the French Revolution is depicted as impossible and a freedom the revolutionaries cannot afford. While each revolutionary 'presents his vision and tells his story' (p. 121), the enemy prepares to counter-attack.
42 Donald Watson's translation.
43 Donald Watson's translation.
44 Donald Watson's translation.
45 The difference between the two characters is also figured in Gandhi's association with 'yes' and Jinnah's declaration: 'no is my sword, the secret of my strength, my battle horse. I will not swerve from it' (p. 118).
46 See also p. 191 and Cixous' commentary on the bear's role in the play in 'L'Ourse, la Tombe, les Etoiles', p. 249.
47 Donald Watson's translation.
48 See also p. 107: 'the shadow changes position depending on the hour, man too' and Sarojini's speech, p. 152: 'may God give you the strength to endure our . . . contradictions'.
49 Only the American position is exempt from this at least initially sympathetic portrayal. Despite the protestations and resignations of Watts and Dean (pp. 230, 279), the strategy of Kissinger and the White House is depicted in grotesquely simple terms (see pp. 228–31), without any more principled motivation than the lust for conquest.
50 Saloth Sâr's speech to Khieu Samphan is in turn commented by Khieu Samphan's mother, Khieu Samnol. Khieu Samphan's wish to follow Saloth Sâr leads him to reject the food his mother has prepared for him:

Khieu Samnol: Well, son, are you coming? The fish will be cold.
Khieu Samphan: I don't want to eat your fish, mother.
Khieu Samnol: But why not, my boy? This morning you told me to buy some.
Khieu Samphan: This week, mother, I shall eat no fish.
Khieu Samnol: Why, is it pig-week?

Khieu Samphan: For a few days I intend to fast.
Khieu Samnol: Are you ill? I bet it's that Saloth Sâr who's taken away your appetite.
Khieu Samphan: I'm not ill, mother, I'm very happy. I beg you, venerable mother, not to question me.
Khieu Samnol: Venerable mother! I'd rather see you ill than all peculiar. (p. 27, Donald Watson's translation)

As in *Indiade*, the role of the women in *Sihanouk* is to bring the male characters back to a sense of the essential, imaged here in the food Khieu Samnol has prepared (see also pp. 53–5 and especially Khieu Samnol's condemnation of the Communists: 'they no longer know how to live, how to laugh, how to enjoy', p. 55). The opening exchange is echoed later in the play after Khieu Samnol's removal to the Khmer camps: Khieu Samnol: 'I am going to ask the big chief organizer Khieu Samphan: "Comrade, how does one live without eating?"' (p. 323). Women's role in safeguarding the essential is also figured in the scene between Sihanouk and his wife (p. 164, see also p. 365), and in Madame Lamné's attempts to teach Khieu Samnol the lessons of the camp: 'because I'm against death and for life' (p. 367, see also p. 369). The final invocation to keep alive the language and national dance of Cambodia, with which the play ends, is also given to two of the female characters, the Queen Mother, Kossomak, and Mom Savay (p. 407).

51 Donald Watson's translation.

52 The impossibility of such a perspective is revealed as the plane's viewpoint is obscured by clouds: Sihanouk: 'these clouds are so dense, they look like a belt of ice-bound land that cuts us off from the living earth' (p. 166, Donald Watson's translation).

53 The considerable length of *Sihanouk* necessitated its division into two parts.

54 Donald Watson's translation.

55 Donald Watson's translation.

56 The text even goes so far as to suggest:

One piece of advice: if a character you respect
Swears before witnesses that the darkest of night
Is the brightest of days, don't trust him.
(p. 194, Donald Watson's translation)

The insistence on the reader/spectator's participation in the creation of truth is noteworthy here. The author's limited and changing perspective is also evoked in this speech (see, for example: 'I beg your pardon. What I have just announced is to be the second scene of our play: once more the author has had second thoughts' p. 195, Donald Watson's translation).

57 Donald Watson's translation.
58 It is to this 'truth' (*'la vérité'*) that the play is dedicated (p. 195, see also p. 308). The implication is that without attention to the truth the patterns of hatred and destruction will merely repeat themselves (see, for example, Yukanthor's reaction to his killing of Kamaphibal: 'I have killed a Khmer Rouge. . . . O tender-hearted Buddha! And to think that there was a time when I prayed to kill an American' (p. 375, see also Hou Yon's speech p. 313).
59 Donald Watson's translation.
60 The Théâtre du Soleil's productions of both *Sihanouk* and *Indiade* used live music to accompany the speeches to great effect.

Chapter 5 *Recent Writings*

1 Since the research for this study was completed, Cixous has published a play script and two novels. These are *On ne part pas, on ne revient pas* ('One Does Not Leave, One Does Not Return') (Des femmes Antoinette Fouque, Paris, 1991), *Déluge* ('Deluge') (Des femmes Antoinette Fouque, Paris, 1992) and *Beethoven à jamais* ('Forever Beethoven') (Des femmes Antoinette Fouque, Paris, 1993).
2 *Manne aux Mandelstams aux Mandelas* (Des femmes, Paris, 1988), *Jours de l'an* (Des femmes, Paris, 1990), *L'Ange au secret* (Des femmes, Paris, 1991).
3 See also Cixous' comments on this point in the interview with Françoise Van Rossum-Guyon 'A propos de *Manne*' ('On the Subject of *Manne*'), in *Hélène Cixous: Chemins d'une écriture*, p. 231.
4 The Prologue to the 'Second Epoch' of *Sihanouk* is an exception (see p. 195). Interestingly, this Prologue was omitted from the Théâtre du Soleil's production of the play.
5 See p. 26: 'without a witness to die our death how to suffer our suffering? I need you to give me my suffering and my death. I need you to give me my pleasure. May my sufferings be mine, and my pleasures also!' (see also p. 293). I am indebted to Catherine MacGillivray for allowing me to use her translation here.
6 Catherine MacGillivray's translation.
7 See also the author's confession reading about Steven Biko: 'I have too great a desire to live and too little compassion, how could I look the country of Abandonment in the face, without failing and without falling into a faint like a corpse' (p. 37).
8 Catherine MacGillivray's translation.
9 See also p. 50 where the author argues that, in order to write, she deliberately chose others whose stories are finally ones of hope.
10 See also 'Difficult Joys':

> we should write as we dream; we should even try and write, we should all do it for ourselves, it's very healthy, because it's the

> only place where we never lie. At night we don't lie. Now if we think that our whole lives are built on lying – they are strange buildings – we should try and write as our dreams teach us; shamelessly, fearlessly, and by facing what is inside every human being – sheer violence, disgust, terror, shit, invention, poetry. Our dreams are the greater poets. In our dreams we are criminals; we kill, and we kill with a lot of enjoyment. But we are also the happiest people on earth; we all make love as we never make love in life. So at least let's not forget that we have secret authors hidden in our unconscious – and try to go to school at night. (p. 22)

In *L'Ange au secret* dreams enable the author to encounter those others she lacks (p. 17), and to experience the emotions and actions she is prevented from in real life. Dreams provide a return to 'life before the law' (p. 226). Like writing, they take us back to 'the cradles of humanity' (p. 226), where 'we are cannibals. We are candid. We are disgusting. We are disgusted. Without disapproval. We are free to vomit and to adore. . . . There is no: no. God the police only comes at daybreak' (p. 226, see also the insistence on the crimes the author has committed 'in dreams', p. 105). It is this return to our true selves – 'without the shadow of a lie' (p. 227) – that the author seeks in writing (p. 227).

11 See also the reasons for the retelling of the ostrich's story (p. 9).

12 In the interview with Françoise Van Rossum-Guyon on the composition of *Manne*, Cixous explains how what interested her in Mandela and Mandelstam was that both men were 'the subjects, the heroes of a fate which is for me the tragic modern fate: banishment, exclusion, rejection, and at the same time resistance to this rejection' (p. 219). She also comments here on the linguistic link between their names (p. 220).

13 'A Propos de *Manne*', in Françoise Van Rossum-Guyon and Myriam Diaz-Diocaretz (eds), *Hélène Cixous: Chemins d'une écriture* (Presses Universitaires de Vincennes, Saint-Denis, and Rodopi, Amsterdam, 1990), pp. 213–34.

14 Catherine MacGillivray's translation.

15 See also the description of Winnie Mandela as poet:

> never has Zami been never more will be in such pure surrender to the Mandela destiny. Day without I and without you. She opened her hands. No more mine. No more his. She forgot herself as the poet forgets themself under the impact of a poem. Only the poem is. Only the Mandela destiny is. (pp. 277–8)

16 'Difficult Joys', in Helen Wilcox, Keith McWatters, Ann Thompson and Linda R. Williams (eds), *The Body and the Text: Hélène Cixous, Reading and Teaching* (Harvester Wheatsheaf, Hemel Hempstead, 1990), pp. 5–30.

17 Julia Kristeva, *La Révolution du langage poétique* (Seuil, Paris, 1974). The English translation is *Revolution in Poetic Language*, by Margaret Waller (Columbia University Press, New York, 1984).
18 See *Revolution in Poetic Language*, pp. 97, 153, 180.
19 The scene is echoed in *L'Ange au secret* in the author's reflection on the rape of a white woman by thirty black men in Central Park (see pp. 77–9). Here it is the men's fear that is depicted as leading to the rape.
20 Catherine MacGillivray's translation.
21 Catherine MacGillivray's translation. See also p. 312: 'reading is a limitless journey, in the letter is all the air in the world and almost all the earth'. This emphasis is also figured in the prisoners' sighting of the whale (p. 323). The whale becomes a crucial symbol in the prisoners' struggle to maintain morale.
22 'La fameuse rude rauque râpeuse langue de roc, langue à crocs, de ric et de roc, langue crottée de crottes et croûtes, aux rimes écailleuses'; Catherine MacGillivray's translation. This concern with language is also a theme of *L'Ange au secret* (see, for example, p. 190).
23 In *Manne* this correlation is figured in the link between those writers who have preserved life in the face of death and '[the] women, mothers sisters, without whom there would be neither soaring nor ascension nor erection nor resurrection' (p. 13).
24 See also p. 205: 'I am swimming in reality. I see! I am the chosen one of a miracle. I go in, I go out, the doors remain open. Quick. The Present has begun. Yes! I'm coming quickly'.
25 There are various references in *Jours de l'an* to the evolution of Cixous' writing from the initial focus on the father's death (see, for example, pp. 69, 74, also pp. 66–7).
26 See pp. 45–6:

> time our painter is slow. It takes him twenty years to assemble a portrait that will be our result. After which we remain like ourselves for ten, twenty years, meanwhile time continues its work, noting and retaining our elements that are in transformation, up to the moment when we make the aquaintance of the person we have ended up by being, and everything has changed. And it will all change again. The person we have been, is not an 'I was', the character of our past. It follows us, but at a distance. And sometimes it can even become the character of one of our books.
>
> This is how it is that I have behind me one, two, three, four deceased (and perhaps others of whom there remains only the bones and dust), one of whom is a mummy, and one who could be my friend. I detest the other two. (See also p. 165)

27 This emphasis on womanhood is echoed in a later passage where the author describes how, aided by her sisters, she gives birth to writing:

> would a man ever have been able to know this proud state that slightly swells the author's body, this state of the pregnant heart? I brood, I am heavy with, I am rather more than me. . . . I take women by the waist, my future and former sisters. The earth turns, and it's done. Now night is falling. The moment of giving birth arrives. The ritual hour. All is dark. In the strange chamber, O the moment of strange joy. I wait. I surrender myself with no preconception to the innocence of the event. Never have I been so strange. Life gives me the gift of one moment after the other and each moment is a surprise. (pp. 30–1, see also p. 32)

In *L'Ange au secret* this emphasis is figured in the author's declaration that her writing derives 'from my mother's aliveness. Everything I write, I write from my mother's aliveness' (p. 167). The mother's questions and comments punctuate the text (see pp. 133–4). Her presence in *L'Ange au secret* contrasts with the focus on the father in the early fiction, endorsing Cixous' view of the link between the feminine writer and enabling mother.

28 'My death. Which is your death. Your death which is my death. This is the character of what will be this book if it lives' (p. 49).

29 See also p. 83: 'without my father to give me death, without death to give me the keys to the gate, the entry to all entries, without my father to break my walls and my bones, what would have happened to me?' The correlation between our symbolic reconstruction of death and the law which prevents us from living is highlighted later in the text (see p. 203).

L'Ange au secret similarly marks a return to the themes and imagery of *Inside*. The text opens 'inside' the 'old house' (p. 9). The 'railings' – described as bars of death (p. 10) – that encircle the house are here acknowledged as necessary in constituting difference: 'without railings, no outside, no inside of them, no difference' (p. 9). This 'inside' is depicted as the starting point for subjectivity and writing (p. 11). The father's death is also portrayed in *L'Ange au secret* through the exploration of 'my father's legacy . . . T.B.' (p. 61). The legacy is figured in the various images of tuberculosis and death, as well as in the references to T.B. (Thomas Bernhard) who, like the author's father, died of tuberculosis.

30 In *L'Ange au secret*, the return to the childhood home – linked as it is to the scene of (the father's) death – initiates both subjectivity and writing (see p. 13). Here the mother is located with the author/daughter 'inside' the house (p. 14), where death is comprehended as 'the whole breadth of life' (p. 14). Childhood acceptance of death is a key theme of *L'Ange au secret*, and is contrasted with the adult constructions and taboos that later surround it. These reconstructions are figured in the image of the wind that prevents departure: 'we had invented the

winds, the great winds of fear' (p. 23). Adult repression and fear of death is depicted as depriving us of our humanity (p. 115), and the author argues for a return to the scene of genesis – with a different outcome: 'before the desired forbidden tree, and tempted by "the Voice": *Bite!*' (p. 115).

31 See also p. 95: 'for this journey I have promised myself to let myself be guided by the voices I am scared of'.

32 It is noteworthy that in so far as there are 'characters' in *L'Ange au secret*, these are the writers the author has read. Their role, the author stresses, is that of guide: they are there 'to help us to abandon ourselves' (p. 42).

33 See also writing's promise to the author: 'I will give you children, countless children of every size and colour' (p. 136).

34 In *L'Ange au secret* this insistence on the collective nature of truth is expressed in a call to the text's readers: 'everything depends on the reader: truth is there. It escapes me. I beg you, catch hold of it! While it's alive! There! There! There! It is yours!' (p. 257).

35 See also p. 153: 'why did I speak of the author as if she were not me? Because she is not me. She leaves me and goes where I do not wish to go. Often I feel she is my enemy. Not a hostile one, but one who goes beyond me, disconcerting me. . . . Sometimes we are almost one. . . . Often it is as if she were dead while I live. And the other way round'; p. 154: 'one difference between the author and I: the author is the daughter of dead-fathers. As for me I am on the living mother's side', pp. 270, 276.

36 This 'we' also embraces the reader (see 'Une Histoire idéale' ['An Ideal Story'] p. 209). There is a similar use of 'we' in *L'Ange au secret* (see, for example, p. 11: '(listen to me, you, readers, lost with me, for I also speak to you about you, about your journey into caves, and why we have loved so much').

37 This 'ideal' relation is contrasted with the reality of love, which is here seen as destructive, involving the very worst of human desire (see pp. 164–5).

38 In *L'Ange au secret* the importance of writing is portrayed as its capacity to propel us beyond ourselves: 'we write above ourselves, beyond ourselves' (p. 93).

39 This passage can be compared to that on p. 202: 'writing books. This marvellous and terrible act that is no more than hope and can hope for no more than to hope. Cannot hope either to win, or to succeed, or to achieve, or to arrive'.

40 Writing is none the less acknowledged as the source here. See p. 196: 'I still do not know up to what point the author must go to obey this book'; p. 274: 'for ten days I have been trying to write a last page for this book. I have written dozens of them. All rejected. The book doesn't want any of them. One cannot force a book'. There is a similar insistence in *L'Ange au secret* (see, for example, p. 11: 'when we "begin"

to write, there are days, weeks even, and often months when it has begun – to write itself yes – to write itself, it happens by itself, it makes itself').

41 See also p. 260: 'in the future of the future we will invent an ever more ideal story. With another word than the word "us". With other "words" than our words, unknown ones in musical colours'.

42 This portrayal of a return to a childhood relation to the world and others is also present in *L'Ange au secret* (see p. 117).

Bibliography

BY HÉLÈNE CIXOUS

(The place of publication for all Cixous' books and articles in French is Paris, unless otherwise indicated.)

Books

1967 *Le Prénom de Dieu*, Grasset.
1969 *Dedans*, Grasset.
L'Exil de James Joyce ou l'art du remplacement, Grasset.
1970 *Les Commencements*, Grasset.
Le Troisième Corps, Grasset.
1971 *Un Vrai Jardin*, L'Herne.
1972 *Neutre*, Grasset.
La Pupille, Cahiers Renaud-Barrault, Gallimard.
1973 *Tombe*, Seuil.
1974 *Portrait du soleil*, Denoël.
Prénoms de personne, Seuil.
1975 *La Jeune Née*, in collaboration with Catherine Clément, 10/18.
Un K. incompréhensible: Pierre Goldman, Bourgois.
Révolutions pour plus d'un Faust, Seuil.
Souffles, Des femmes.
1976 *La*, Gallimard; Des femmes, 1979.
Partie, Des femmes.
Portrait de Dora, Des femmes.
1977 *Angst*, Des femmes.
La Venue à l'écriture, with Madeleine Gagnon and Annie Leclerc, Union Générale d'Editions. The title essay of this collection, by

Hélène Cixous, is reprinted in *Entre l'écriture* (Des femmes, 1986), pp. 9–69.
1978 *Chant du corps interdit/Le Nom d'Oedipe*, Des femmes.
Préparatifs de noces au delà de l'abîme, Des femmes.
1979 *Anankè*, Des femmes.
Vivre l'orange/To Live the Orange, Des femmes.
1980 *Illa*, Des femmes.
1981 *(With) Ou l'art de l'innocence*, Des femmes.
1982 *Limonade tout était si infini*, Des femmes.
1983 *Le Livre de Promethea*, Gallimard.
1984 *La Prise de l'école de Madhubaï*, Avant-scène.
1985 *L'Histoire terrible mais inachevée de Norodom Sihanouk roi du Cambodge*, Théâtre du Soleil.
1986 *La Bataille d'Arcachon*, Collection Topaze, Trois, Québec.
Entre l'écriture, Des femmes.
Hélène Cixous: Théâtre, Des femmes.
1987 *L'Indiade ou l'Inde de leurs rêves*, Théâtre du Soleil.
1988 *Manne aux Mandelstams aux Mandelas*, Des femmes Antoinette Fouque.
1989 *L'Heure de Clarice Lispector*, Des femmes Antoinette Fouque.
1990 *Jours de l'an*, Des femmes Antoinette Fouque.
1991 *L'Ange au secret*, Des femmes Antoinette Fouque.
On ne part pas, on ne revient pas, Des femmes Antoinette Fouque.
1992 *Déluge*, Des femmes Antoinette Fouque.
Les Euménides (translation), Théâtre du Soleil.
1993 *Beethoven à jamais ou l'existence de Dieu*, Des femmes Antoinette Fouque.
1994 *Hélène Cixous: Photos de Racines*, with Mireille Calle-Gruber, Des femmes Antoinette Fouque.
L'Histoire (qu'on ne connaîtra jamais), Des femmes Antoinette Fouque.
La Ville parjure ou le réveil des Erinyes, Théâtre du Soleil.

Screenplay

1989 *'La Nuit miraculeuse'*, with Ariane Mnouchkine, broadcast on La Sept and FR3.

Articles

1964
'Conrad Aiken', *Les Langues Modernes* (May–June), pp. 271–3.
'Nathaniel West', *Les Langues Modernes* (May–June), pp. 72–3.
'Stephen, Hamlet, Will: Joyce par-delà Shakespeare', *Etudes Anglaises* (October–December), pp. 571–85.

'Time and Reality in Contemporary Fiction', *Etudes Anglaises* (July–September), pp. 301–2.

'Une Farce Tragique', *Les Langues Modernes* (May–June), p. 303.

1965

'L'Avant-portrait ou la bifurcation d'une vocation', *Tel Quel* 22 (summer), pp. 69–76.

'Une Chronique vériste', *Les Langues Modernes* (May–June), pp. 376–7.

'Un Paritéméraire', *Etudes Anglaises* (April–June), pp. 396–7.

'Un Voyage inachevé de la conscience', *Les Langues Modernes* (May–June), p. 513.

1966

'L'Allégorie du mal dans l'œuvre de William Golding', *Critique* 2339 (April), pp. 309–20.

'Portrait de sa femme par l'artiste', *Les Lettres Nouvelles* 15 (March–April), pp. 41–67.

'Vers une lecture détachée du *Prometheus Unbound*', *Les Langues Modernes* (September–October), pp. 582–94.

'William Golding: Mode allégorique et symbolisme ironique d'une esthétique des ténèbres', *Les Langues Modernes* (September–October), pp. 528–41.

1967

'A Jérusalem par Paul Bailey: Jeunes romanciers et vieilles folles', *Le Monde* (12 July).

'Camp retranché de J.C. Powys: Un Univers fantastique', *Le Monde* (29 March).

'La Correspondance de Joyce: Publiée à Londres', *Le Monde* (1 February).

'Les Deux voies du Catholicisme anglais', *Le Monde* (10 May).

'Iris Murdoch et *La Gouvernante italienne*: "L'Art dans le filet" des idées', *Le Monde* (20 December).

'James Joyce et la mort de Parnell', *Les Langues Modernes* (March–April), pp. 142–7.

'James Joyce's *Letters* Vol. II–III', *Les Lettres Nouvelles 58* (March–April), pp. 173–83.

'*Le Journal de Dublin* par Stanislas Joyce: Le Frère de l'artiste', *Le Monde* (22 November).

'Jules César: Un Repas sacré: Discours autour d'un meurtre rituel', *Les Langues Modernes* (January–February), pp. 53–5.

'Langage et regard dans le roman expérimental: Grande Bretagne', *Le Monde* (18 May).

'La Langue de Kipling et la Renaissance hindoue', *Le Monde* (3 May).

'La Leçon d'Ezra Pound: Un Art de lire', *Le Monde* (27 January).

'Nigel Dennis: Une solitude bien ordonnée: L'Héritage de Swift', *Le Monde* (7 October).

'Le Nouveau fantastique dans le roman d'aujourd'hui: Grande Bretagne', *Le Monde* (28 June).

'La Présence permanente du tragique', *Les Langues Modernes* (January–February), pp. 109–10.

'*La Pyramide* par William Golding: Fables internales', *Le Monde* (26 July).
'Une Science de la littérature', *Le Monde* (25 October).
'Situation de Saul Bellow', *Les Lettres Nouvelles* 58 (March–April), pp. 130–45.
'Survivances d'un mythe: Le gentleman', *Le Monde* (5 April).
1968
'Les Conversations cruelles d'Ivy Compton Burnett', *Les Lettres Nouvelles* (May–June), pp. 157–67.
'La Farce macabre de Muriel Spark: Un Catholicisme grinçant', *Le Monde* (17 January).
'Le Génie excentrique d'Ivy Compton Burnett', *Le Monde* (9 March).
'Hors chat', *Nouveaux Cahiers* 18, pp. 17–20.
'Iris Murdoch: L'Art poétique d'aimer bien', *Le Monde* (22 June).
'Nicholas Mosley et ses accidents: Un Dissident du roman anglais', *Le Monde* (22 June).
'L'Œuvre mystificatrice d'Anthony Burgess: Tendre le miroir à la culture', *Le Monde* (23 November).
'Relecture d'Alice *Aux Pays des merveilles*: A l'occasion d'une nouvelle traduction', *Le Monde* (3 August).
'Le Retour de Beardsley ou les dentelles du péché', *Le Monde* (28 February).
1969
Les Etats-Unis d'aujourd'hui par les textes, introduction and co-editor with Marianne Debouzy and Pierre Dommergues (Colin).
'Le Prix Nobel est attribué à Samuel Beckett: Le Maître du texte pour rien', *Le Monde* (24 October).
1970
'Henry James: L'Ecriture comme placement ou de l'ambiguité de l'intérêt', *Poétique* 1, pp. 35–50.
'Joyce et la ruse de l'écriture', *Poétique* 4, pp. 419–32.
'Présentation', with Gérard Genette and Tzvetan Todorov, *Poétique* 1, pp. 1–2.
'La Réponse de Hélène Cixous', *Les Letters Françaises* 4 (25 November–1 December).
1971
'Au sujet de Humpty toujours déjà tombé', *Lewis Carroll*, ed. Henri Parisot (Herne).
'D'Une Lecture qui joue à travailler', introduction to *De l'autre côté du miroir* by Lewis Carroll (Aubier-Flammarion).
'La Déroute du sujet ou le voyage imaginaire de Dora', *Littérature et Psychanalyse* 3 (October), pp. 79–86.
'Une Lecture imprudente', *Le Monde* (5 November).
1972
'La Fiction et ses fantômes: Une Lecture de l'*Unheimliche* de Freud', *Poétique* 10, pp. 199–216.
'Un Modèle de modernité: La Puissante machine d'écriture', *Le Monde* (23 June).
'Poe relu: Une Poétique du revenir', *Critique* 28/2 (April), pp. 299–328.

1973
'L'Affiche décolle', *Cahiers Renaud-Barrault* 83 (Gallimard).
'Electre. L'Après Médée', *Festival d'automne de Paris* (Gallimard).
'L'Essor de Plusje', *Arc* 54, pp. 46–52.
'Littérasophe et Philosofiture', with Gilles Deleuze, Emission Dialogues with Roger Pillaudin, France-Culture (transmitted 13 November), text available.
'Le Non-nom: Elles volent', *Gramma* (April), pp. 18–26.
'Le Prix Nobel de littérature est décerné à l'écrivain australien Patrick White: L'Epopée d'un continent', *Le Monde* (20 October).
'La Textrémité', *Nouvelle Revue de Psychanalyse* VII (spring), pp. 335–50.
1974
'Le Bon Pied, le bon oeil', *Cahiers Renaud-Barrault* 87 (Gallimard).
'D'Un Oeil en coin', '*Ulysses* cinquante ans après: Témoignages Franco-Anglaises sur le chef-d'œuvre de James Joyce', *Etudes Anglaises* 53, pp. 161–7.
'Le Livre des morts', *Cahiers Renaud-Barrault* 89 (Gallimard).
'Les Morts-contreparties', introduction to *Dubliners* by James Joyce (Aubier-Flammarion).
1975
'A Propos de Marguerite Duras', with Michel Foucault, *Cahiers Renaud-Barrault* 89 (Gallimard).
'Les Femmes écrivains et leur colloque', *Le Monde* (3 May).
'La Noire vole', *Nouvelle Critique* 82 (March), pp. 47–53.
'L'Ordre mental', preface to *Les Femmes et la folie*, Phyllis Chesler (Payot).
'Le Rire de la Méduse', *L'Arc* 61, pp. 39–54. Reprinted in Maïté Albistur and Daniel Armogathe (eds), *Le Grif des femmes 2: Anthologie de textes féministes du Second Empire à nos jours* (Hier and Demain, 1978).
1976
'Etre femme-juive', *Les Nouveaux Cahiers* 46 (autumn).
'Fort-sein', *Poétique* 26, p. 131.
'Je me souviens de mon corps d'enfant', *Quotidien de Paris* (April).
'Lorsque je n'écris pas, c'est comme si j'étais morte', *Le Monde* (9 April).
'La Missexualité ou jouis-je?', *Poétique* 26, pp. 383–402. Reprinted in *Entre l'Ecriture* (Des femmes, 1986), pp. 75–96.
'Un Morceau de Dieu', *Sorcières* 1 (January), pp. 14–17.
'Une Passion, l'un peu moins que rien', *Samuel Beckett, Cahiers de l'Herne* 31, pp. 396–413.
'Le Sexe ou la tête', *Cahiers du Grif* 13 (October), pp. 5–15.
'Textes de l'imprévisible: Grâce à la différence', *Les Nouvelles Littéraires* (26 May), pp. 18–19.
1977
'Aller à la mer', *Le Monde* (28 April).
1978
'L'Approche de Clarice Lispector', *Poétique* 40 (November), pp. 408–19. Reprinted in *Entre l'écriture* (Des femmes, 1986), pp. 115–38.

'L'Ecriture comme placement', *L'Art de la fiction chez Henry James*, ed. Michel Zéraffe (Collection d'Esthétique).
1979
'Commence par a', *Des femmes en mouvement hebdo* 4 (21 November), pp. 15–17.
'O Grand-mère que vous avez de beaux concepts!', *Des femmes en mouvement hebdo* 1 (9 November), pp. 11–12.
'Poésie e(s)t politique', *Des femmes en mouvement hebdo* 4 (30 November), pp. 28–33.
'Quant à la pomme de texte', *Etudes Littéraires* (December), Québec, pp. 412–23.
1980
'Extrait de *Illa*', *Revue Nouvelle* (November), p. 504.
1981
'La Grâce d'une autre politique', *Le Quotidien de Paris* (April).
'La Poésie comme contrepoison, *Nouvel Observateur* (May).
1982
'La Dernière Phrase', *Corps écrit* 1, pp. 93–104.
1983
'Allant vers Jérusalem, Jérusalem à l'envers', *Nouvelle Barre du Jour* 132, Québec, pp. 113–26.
'Cahier de métamorphose', *Corps écrit* 6, pp. 65–76.
'Freincipe de plaisir ou paradoxe perdu', preface to James Joyce's *Finnegan's Wake* (Gallimard). Reprinted in *Entre l'écriture* (Des femmes, 1986), pp. 99–112.
'Suitée de Jérusalem', *Land* 5/6 (5 June), pp. 36–42.
'Tancrède continue', *Etudes Freudiennes* 21/22 (March), pp. 115–31. Reprinted in *Entre l'écriture* (Des femmes, 1986), pp. 141–68.
1985
'C'est l'histoire d'une étoile', *Roméo et Juliette*, translated and adapted from William Shakespeare by Gervais Robin (Papiers).
'Les Gardiens de notre grandeur', *Le Monde* (26 May).
'Sonia Rykiel en traduction', *Sonia Rykiel* (Herscher).
1986
'Cela n'a pas de nom, ce qui se passait', *Le Débat* 41 (September–November), pp. 153–8.
'Un Fils', *Hamlet* (Papiers).
'Le Pays des autres', *Réouverture de la Monnaie*, ed. Gérard Mortier, Brussels.
'La Séparation du gâteau', *Pour Nelson Mandela* (Gallimard).
1987
'Clarice Lispector: Titane délicate', *Quinzaine Littéraire* 484 (April), p. 10.
'Extrême Fidélité', *Travessia* 14, Florianopolis, Brazil, pp. 11–45.
1988
'Comment arriver au théâtre', *Lettre internationale* 17 (April), pp. 55–6.
'Jean-Jacques Mayoux', *Quinzaine Littéraire* (16–31 January), p. 7.

'Marina Tsvetaeva: Le Feu éteint celle . . .', *Les Cahiers du Grif* 39, pp. 87–96.
'Noir émoi', *Corps écrit* 26 (June), pp. 37–43.
1989
'Je me souviens', *Globe* (November).
'Je suis plutôt un être de bord', *Quinzaine Littéraire* 352 (May), p. 10.
'Le Sens de la forêt', *Qui vive: Autour de Julien Gracq* (José Corti).
'Théâtre enfoui', *Europe* 726 (October), pp. 72–7.
1990
'L'Arrêt du train, ou résurrections d'Anna', preface to *Karine Saporta* (Colin).
'Clarice Lispector – Marina Tsvetaeva – Portraits', *Avant Garde* 4, Rodopi, Amsterdam, pp. 147–55.
'De la scène de l'Insconscient à la scène de l'Histoire: Chemin d'une écriture', in Françoise Van Rossum-Guyon and Myriam Diaz-Diocaretz (eds), *Hélène Cixous: Chemins d'une écriture* (Presses Universitaires de Vincennes, Saint-Denis, and Rodopi, Amsterdam), pp. 15–34.
'Des pieds et des mains', *Corps écrit* 34 (June), pp. 105–10.
'Ecoute avec les mains', *Etats généraux des femmes* (Des femmes).
1991
'Le Décollage du Bourreau', *Repentirs* (Réunion des musées nationaux), pp. 55–64.
1994
'L'Amour du loup', *La Métaphore* 2 (spring), pp. 15–37.

Interviews

1969
'L'Exil de Joyce', with Gilles Lapouge, *Quinzaine Littéraire* (1–15 March), pp. 6–8.
'Hélène Cixous, une grande fille pas simple: Le Prix Médicis', with Ginette Guitard-Auviste, *Nouvelles Littéraires* (27 November), p. 7.
1973
'C'est la culture qui est enfouie dans *Tombe*', with Claudine Jardin, *Le Monde* (2 June).
1976
'Avec Hélène Cixous', with Jacqueline Sudaka, *Nouveaux Cahiers* 46, pp. 92–5.
'Entretien avec Alain Clerval sur *Souffles*', *Infoartitudes* (April).
'Le Grand JE au féminine: Un Entretien avec Hélène Cixous', with Nicole Casanova, *Nouvelles Littéraires* 54 (8 April), p. 6.
'Hélène Cixous et le *Portrait de Dora*', with Claire Devarrieux, *Le Monde* (26 February), p. 15.
'Je me souviens très bien de mon corps d'enfant', with Jean-Louis de Rambures, *Le Monde* (9 April).
'Lorsque je n'écris pas c'est comme si j'étais morte', with Jean-Louis de

Rambures, *Comment travaillent les écrivains*, Jean-Louis de Rambures (Flammarion).

'Quelques questions posées à Hélène Cixous', with Françoise Collin, *Les Cahiers de Grif* 13 (October), pp. 16–20.

1977

'Entretien avec Françoise van Rossum-Guyon', *Revue des Sciences Humaines* XLIV/168 (October–December), pp. 479–93.

'L'Etrange Traversée d'Hélène Cixous', with Lucette Finas, *Le Monde* (13 May).

'Le *Portrait de Dora*', with Madeleine Gagnon, Philippe Haeck and Patrick Straramn, *Chroniques* 1, Montreal.

'Le Quitte ou double de la pensée féminine', with Nicole Casanova, *Nouvelles Littéraires* (22 September), p. 8.

1978

'Entretien avec Hélène Cixous: Un destin révolu', with Colette Godard, *Le Monde* (28 July).

1980

'Hélène Cixous commente *Illa*', with Salim Jay, *Mots pour mots* (June), pp. 39–43.

1981

'Biographie de l'écriture', with Alain Poirson, *Révolution magazine* (31 July), pp. 18–19.

1982

'Dossier Jean Genet', *Masques* 12 (winter), pp. 59–63.

'Hélène Cixous ou le rêve de l'écriture', with François Coupry, *Libération* (22 December).

1983

'Hélène Cixous reçoit le rêve de l'écriture', with Anne Laurent, *Libération* (30 December).

1984

'Le Roman d'aujourd'hui', with Henri Quéré, *Fabula* 3, Lille (March), pp. 147–58.

1985

'*L'Histoire terrible mais inachevée de Norodom Sihanouk roi du Cambodge*', with Gisèle Barret, *Jeu*, Montreal (October), pp. 131–53.

1986

'Une Témérité tremblante', with Véronique Hotte, *Théâtre Public* (March–April), pp. 22–5.

1988

'Les Motions contre l'émotion de l'Histoire', with Dominique Le Coq, *Politis* (7 July), pp. 77–80.

'Le Tragique de la partition', with Bernard Golfier, *Théâtre Public* (June), pp. 81–4.

1989

'Hélène Cixous', with Pascale Hassoun, Chantal Maillet et Claude Rabant, *Patio* 10, pp. 59–76.

1990

'A Propos de *Manne*', with Françoise Van Rossum-Guyon, in Françoise Van Rossum-Guyon and Myriam Diaz-Diocaretz (eds), *Hélène Cixous: Chemins d'une écriture* (Presses Universitaires de Vincennes, Saint-Denis, and Rodopi, Amsterdam), pp. 213–34.

'L'Auteur entre texte et Théâtre', with Marie-Claire Ropars et Michèle Lagny, *Hors Cadre* 8, pp. 31–65.

1992

'Le Lien de l'autre', with Frédéric Regand, *Logique de Traverses*, pp. 11–26.

1994

'Questions à Hélène Cixous', with Christa Stevens, in Susan Van Dijk and Christa Stevens (eds), *En(jeux) de la communication romanesque* (Rodopi, Amsterdam), pp. 321–32.

Interviews in English

1976

'Hélène Cixous: Interview with Christiane Makward', transl. Beatrice Cameron and Ann Liddle, *Substance* 13, pp. 19–37.

1979

'Rethinking Differences', transl. by Isabelle de Courtivron, in Elaine Marks and Georges Stambolian (eds), *Homosexualities and French Literature* (Cornell University Press, New York).

1982

'Comment on Women's Studies in France', *Signs* (spring), pp. 721–2.

1984

'An Exchange with Hélène Cixous', with Verena Andermatt Conley, in Verena Andermatt Conley, *Hélène Cixous: Writing the Feminine* (University of Nebraska Press, Lincoln).

'Voice 1', with Verena Andermatt Conley, *Boundary 2 Symposium on Feminine Writing* 12/2 (winter), pp. 51–67.

1985

'Hélène Cixous', with Susan Sellers, *The Women's Review* (May 7), pp. 22–3.

1988

'Conversations', with Susan Sellers, in Susan Sellers (ed.), *Writing Differences: Readings from the Seminar of Hélène Cixous* (Open University Press, Milton Keynes, and St Martin's Press, New York).

1989

'A Realm of Characters', 'The Double World of Writing', 'Listening to the Heart', 'Writing as a Second Heart', in Susan Sellers (ed.), *Delighting the Heart: A Notebook by Women Writers* (The Women's Press, London, reissued 1994).

'Exploding the Issue "French" "Women" "Writers" and the "Canon"', with Alice Jardine and Anne Menke, *Yale French Studies* 75, pp. 235–8.

1989
'Interview with Hélène Cixous', with Catherine Franke and Roger Chazal, *Qui Parle: A Journal of Literary and Critical Studies* 3/1 (spring), pp. 152–79.
1993
'Hélène Cixous', in Alice Jardine and Anne Menke (eds), *Shifting Scenes: Interviews on Women, Writing, and Politics in Post-68 France* (Columbia University Press, New York, 1993).

Translations of Cixous' work into English

1972
The Exile of James Joyce, transl. Sally Purcell (David Lewis, New York, and John Calder, London, 1976; Riverrun, New York, 1980).
1974
'The Character of Character', transl. Keith Cohen, *New Literary History* 5/2 (winter), pp. 383–402.
'Political Ignominy: Ivy Day', in William M. Chace (ed.), *Joyce: A Collection of Critical Essays* (Prentice Hall, Englewood Cliffs, New Jersey).
1975
'At Circe's or the Self Opener', transl. Carol Bové, *Boundary* 2, p. 397.
1976
'Fiction and its Phantoms: A Reading of Freud's "Das Unheimliche" ("The Uncanny")', transl. R. Denommé, *New Literary History* 7/3 (spring), pp. 525–48.
'The Fruits of Femininity', Manchester, *Guardian* (16 May).
'The Laugh of the Medusa', transl. Keith and Paula Cohen, *Signs* 1–4 (summer), pp. 875–93. This translation is reprinted in Isabelle de Courtivron and Elaine Marks (eds), *New French Feminisms* (University of Massachusetts Press, Minneapolis, and Harvester, Brighton, 1981).
1977
'Boxes', transl. Rosette C. Lamont, *Centerpoint*, New York (fall), pp. 30–1.
'*La Jeune Née*: An Excerpt', transl. Meg Bortin, *Diacritics* 7/2 (summer), pp. 64–9.
'*Partie*: An Extract', transl. Keith Cohen, *Triquarterly* 38 (winter), pp. 95–100.
1979
Portrait of Dora, transl. Anita Barrows (John Calder, London).
1980
'Come the Following Chapter', *Enclitic* 4/2 (fall), pp. 45–58.
'Poetry is/and (the) political', transl. Ann Liddle, *Bread and Roses* 2/1, pp. 16–18.
'Sorties: Where Is She . . .', transl. Ann Liddle, in Isabelle de Courtivron and Elaine Marks (eds), *New French Feminisms* (University of Massachusetts Press, Minneapolis, and Harvester, Brighton, 1981).
1981
'Castration or Decapitation?', transl. Annette Kuhn, *Signs* 7/1 (autumn),

pp. 41–55. Reprinted in Robert Davis and Ronald Schleifer (eds), *Contemporary Literary Criticism: Literature and Cultural Studies* (Longman, New York, 1989).

1982

'Introduction to Lewis Carroll's *Through the Looking Glass* and *The Hunting of the Snark*', transl. Marie Maclean, *New Literary History* 13/2 (winter), pp. 231–51.

'The Step', transl. Jill MacDonald and Carole Darring Paul, *The French American Review* 6/1, pp. 33–41.

1984

'August 12, 1980', transl. Betsy Wing, *Boundary* 2, pp. 8–39.

'Going to the Seashore', *Modern Drama* 27/4 (December 1984), pp. 546–8.

'Joyce, the (R)use of Writing', transl. Judith Still, *Poststructuralist Joyce* (Cambridge University Press, Cambridge).

'Reading Clarice Lispector's "Sunday Before Going to Sleep"', transl. Betsy Wing, *Boundary* 2, pp. 41–8.

1985

Angst, transl. Jo Levy (John Calder, London).

1986

'The Conquest of the School at Madhubai', transl. Deborah Carpenter, *Women and Performance* 3, pp. 59–95.

Inside, transl. Carol Barko (Shocken Books, New York).

'The Language of Reality', in Harold Bloom (ed.), *Twentieth Century British Literature 3: James Joyce: Ulysses* (Chelsea House, New York).

'The Last Word', transl. Ann Liddle and Susan Sellers, *The Women's Review* 6 (April), pp. 22–4.

The Newly Born Woman, transl. Betsy Wing (Minnesota University Press, Minneapolis).

1987

'The Book of Promethea', transl. Deborah Carpenter, *Frank* 6/7, pp. 42–4.

'Foreword', transl. Verena Andermatt Conley, to Clarice Lispector, *The Stream of Life* (Minnesota University Press, Minneapolis).

'Her Presence Through Writing', transl. Deborah Carpenter, *Literary Review* 30 (spring), pp. 445–53.

'Life Without Him Was Life Without Him', *New York Times Book Review* (1 November), pp. 2–35.

'The Parting of the Cake', transl. Franklin Philips, in Jacques Derrida and Mustapha Tlili (eds), *For Nelson Mandela* (Seaver Books, New York).

1988

'Extreme Fidelity', transl. Ann Liddle and Susan Sellers, in Susan Sellers (ed.), *Writing Differences: Readings from the Seminar of Hélène Cixous* (Open University Press, Milton Keynes, and St Martin's Press, New York).

'Tancrede Continues', transl. Ann Liddle and Susan Sellers, in Susan Sellers (ed.), *Writing Differences: Readings from the Seminar of Hélène Cixous* (Open University Press, Milton Keynes, and St Martin's Press, New York).

1989
'From the Scene of the Unconscious to the Scene of History', transl. Deborah Carpenter, in Ralph Cohen (ed.), *The Future of Literary Theory* (Routledge, New York and London, 1989).
'Writings on the Theatre: Dedication to the Ostrich', transl. Catherine Franke, *Qui Parle: A Journal of Literary and Critical Studies* 3/1 (spring), pp. 120–52.
1990
'Difficult Joys', in Helen Wilcox, Keith McWatters, Ann Thompson and Linda R. Williams (eds), *The Body and the Text: Hélène Cixous, Reading and Teaching* (Harvester Wheatsheaf, Hemel Hempstead).
Reading With Clarice Lispector, ed. and transl. Verena Andermatt Conley (Minnesota University Press, Minneapolis, and Harvester Wheatsheaf, Hemel Hempstead).
'The Two Countries of Writing: Theater and Poetical Fiction', in Juliet Flower MacCannell (ed.), *The Other Perspective in Gender and Culture: Rewriting Women and the Symbolic* (Columbia University Press, New York).
1991
The Book of Promethea, transl. Betsy Wing (University of Nebraska Press, Lincoln).
'Coming to Writing' and Other Essays, transl. Sarah Cornell, Deborah Jensen, Ann Liddle and Susan Sellers (Harvard University Press, Cambridge, Mass.).
1992
'Manna for the Mandelas for the Mandelstams', transl. Catherine MacGillivray, *Lit: Literature Interpretation Theory* 4/1, pp. 1–16.
Readings: The Poetics of Blanchot, Joyce, Kafka, Kleist, Lispector and Tsvetayeva, transl. Verena Andermatt Conley (Harvester Wheatsheaf, Hemel Hempstead).
1993
'Bathsheba or the Interior Bible', transl. Catherine MacGillivray, *Lit: Literature Interpretation Theory* 24 (autumn), pp. 820–36.
Three Steps on the Ladder of Writing, transl. Sarah Cornell and Susan Sellers (Columbia University Press, New York).
'Without End – No – State of Drawingness – No –, Rather: The Executioner's Taking Off', transl. Catherine A. MacGillivray, *New Literary History: A Journal of Theory and Interpretation* 24/1 (winter), pp. 87–103.
1994
The Hélène Cixous Reader, ed. Susan Sellers (Routledge, London).

BOOKS AND ARTICLES ON HÉLÈNE CIXOUS

Albérès, René-Marill, 'Jeux de miroirs', *Les Nouvelles Littéraires* (25 November–1 December 1974), p. 5.

Alexandrescu, Liliana, '*Norodom Sihanouk*: L'inachevé comme lecture shakespearienne de l'Histoire contemporaine', in Françoise Van Rossum-Guyon and Myriam Diaz-Diocaretz (eds), *Hélène Cixous: Chemins d'une écriture* (Presses Universitaires de Vincennes, Saint-Denis, and Rodopi, Amsterdam, 1990).

Allen, Jeffner, 'Poetic Politics: How the Amazons Took the Acropolis', *Hypatia* 3 (summer 1988), pp. 107–22.

Alonso, H, 'Review of Hélène Cixous' and Catherine Clément's *The Newly Born Woman*', *Choice* 24/4 (December 1986), p. 619.

Alonzo, Anne-Marie, 'Ecrire pivoine et penser fleur', *La Nouvelle Barre du Jour* 125 (April 1973), pp. 77–80.

——, 'Review of Hélène Cixous' *(With) Ou l'art de l'innocence*', *La Nouvelle Barre du Jour* 109 (January 1982), pp. 89–91.

Andersen, Marguerite, 'Review of Hélène Cixous' *Entre l'Ecriture*', *Resources for Feminist Research/Documentation sur la Recherche Féministe* (Toronto), (March 1988), pp. 12–13.

Anderson, Linda, 'At the Threshold of the Self: Women and Autobiography', in Moira Monteith (ed.), *Women Writing: A Challenge to Theory* (Harvester, Brighton, Sussex, and New York, 1986).

Aneja, Ann, 'The Mystic Aspect of L'Ecriture Féminine: Hélène Cixous' *Vivre l'orange*', *Qui Parle: A Journal of Literary and Critical Studies* 3/1 (spring 1989), pp. 189–201.

——, 'The Medusa's Slip: Hélène Cixous and the Underpinnings of Ecriture Féminine', *Lit: Literature Interpretation Theory* 4/1 (1992), pp. 17–28.

Armbruster, Carol, 'Hélène Clarice: Nouvelle Voix', *Contemporary Literature* 24/2 (summer 1983), pp. 145–57.

Atherton, J.S., 'Between Fact and Fiction', *Times Literary Supplement* (13 August 1976).

Banting, Pamela, 'The Body as Pictogram: Rethinking Hélène Cixous' *écriture féminine*', *Textual Practice* 6/2 (summer 1992), pp. 225–46.

Barnet, Andrea, 'Review of Hélène Cixous' and Catherine Clément's *The Newly Born Woman*', *New York Times Book Review* (24 August 1986).

Barr, Marleen, 'Feminist Fabulation: The Feminist Anglo-American Critical Empire Strikes Back', *Restant* 15/3 (1987), pp. 105–99.

Benmussa, Simone, 'Introduction: "Portrait of Dora": Stage Work and Dream Work', in *Benmussa Directs: Portrait of Dora by Hélène Cixous* (Calder, London, and Riverrun Press, Dallas, 1979).

Bergonzi, Bernard, 'Joyce without Laughs', *Observer*, London (14 March 1976), p. 31.

Binhammer, Katherine, 'Metaphor of Metonymy? The Question of Essentialism in Cixous', *Tessera* 10 (summer 1991), pp. 65–79.

Blue, Denise, 'Joyce and Poetic Identity', *Comparative Literature* 27/2 (spring 1975), pp. 184–8.

Bonnefoy, Claude, 'Les Aventures du texte', *Les Nouvelles Littéraires* 50 (12–18 June 1972), p. 5.

——, 'Les Pouvoirs de l'écriture', *Les Nouvelles Littéraires* 51 (23–29 April 1973), p. 7.

Bott, François, 'Un Roman d'amour fou: *Dedans* d'Hélène Cixous', *Le Monde* (13 September 1969), pp. i–ii.

Bouraoui, H.A., 'Le Vide enfin dépassé', *Etudes Françaises* (Montreal) 7/1 (February 1971), pp. 79–84.

Boutin, Richard, 'Le Courrier du coeur', *La Nouvelle Barre du Jour* (Quebec) 135 (February 1984), pp. 66–74.

Bowlby, Rachel, 'The Feminine Female', *Social Text* 7 (spring–summer 1983), pp. 55–68.

——, 'Flight Reservations: Cross-Cultural Positions in Contemporary Feminist Theory', *Oxford Literary Review* 10/1–2 (1988), pp. 71–2.

Boyle, Robert, 'James Joyce', *Contemporary Literature* 15/2 (spring 1974), pp. 264–5.

Boyman, Anne, 'Dora or the Case of L'Ecriture Féminine', *Qui Parle: A Journal of Literary and Critical Studies* 3/1 (spring 1989), pp. 180–8.

Brivic, Sheldon, 'Review of Hélène Cixous' *The Exile of James Joyce*', *Journal of Modern Literature* 3/3 (February 1974), pp. 678–9.

Brooke-Rose, Christine, 'Paris Letter: Dramatics', *Spectator* (28 February 1976), p. 25.

——, 'Woman as a Semiotic Object', *Poetics Today* 6/1–2 (1985), pp. 12, 20.

Burke, Carolyn Greenstein, 'Report from Paris: Women's Writing and the Women's Movement', *Signs* 3/4 (summer 1978), pp. 848–54.

Calle-Gruber, Mireille, *Du Féminin* (Le Griffon d'Argile, Sainte-Foy, 1992).

——, 'Afterword: Hélène Cixous' Book of Hours, Book of Fortune', transl. Agnes Conacher and Catherine McGann, in Susan Sellers (ed.) *The Hélène Cixous Reader* (Routledge, London and New York, 1994).

Camelin, Colette, 'La Scène de la fille dans *Illa* d'Hélène Cixous', *Littérature* 67 (October 1987), pp. 84–101.

Cameron, Beatrice, 'Letter to Hélène Cixous', *SubStance* 17 (1977), pp. 159–65.

Camp, André, 'Ouvrages de dames', *L'Avant-Scène Théâtre* 818 (15 November 1987), pp. 43–4.

Canning, Charlotte, 'The Critic as Playwright: Performing Hélène Cixous' *Le Nom d'Oedipe*', *Lit: Literature Interpretation Theory* 4/1 (1992), pp. 43–55.

Carpenter, Deborah, 'Hélène Cixous and North African Origin: Writing "L'Orange"', *Celfan Review* 6/1 (November 1986), pp. 1–4.

——, 'Translator's Introduction to "Her Presence Through Writing" by Hélène Cixous', *Literary Review: An International Journal of Contemporary Writing* 30/3 (spring 1987), pp. 441–53.

Chapsal, Madeleine, 'Dora: Un rêve de Freud', *L'Express* (1–7 March 1976), p. 20.

——, 'Hélène Cixous contre Freud', *L'Express* (28 June–4 July 1976), p. 64.

——, 'Hélène Cixous: Noces de nymphes', *L'Express* (19–25 June 1978), pp. 85–6.

Christ, Ronald, 'Review of Hélène Cixous' *The Exile of James Joyce*', *Books Abroad* 47/3 (summer 1973), pp. 564–5.

Clédat, Françoise, 'L'Ecriture du corps', *Magazine Littéraire* 180 (January 1982), pp. 20–2.

Clement, Catherine Backès, 'Introduction to Hélène Cixous' "La Déroute du sujet, ou le voyage imaginaire de Dora"', *Littérature* 1/3 (October 1971), pp. 79–80.

——, 'La Taupe et le Phénix', *Les Lettres françaises* (14 June 1972).

——, 'Le Temps pour vivre et la durée pour respirer', *L'Art du Théâtre* 9 (fall 1988), pp. 74–7.

Cohen, Danielle, 'Review of Hélène Cixous' and Catherine Clément's *La Jeune née*', *Sorcières* 1 (January 1976), pp. 57–8.

Coldwell, Joan, 'The Beauty of the Medusa: Twentieth Century', *English Studies in Canada* 11/4 (December 1985), pp. 432–7.

Colville, Georgiana, 'Review of Hélène Cixous' and Catherine Clément's *La Jeune née*', *French Review* 50/4 (March 1977), pp. 666–7.

——, 'Hélène Cixous' *La*', *French Review* 11/2 (December 1977), pp. 325–6.

Conley, Verena Andermatt, 'Missexual Mystery', *Diacritics* 7/2 (summer 1977), pp. 70–82.

——, 'Writing the Letter: The Lower-Case of Hélène Cixous', *Visible Language* 12/3 (summer 1978), pp. 305–18.

——, 'Hélène Cixous and the Uncovery of a Feminine Language', *Women and Literature* 7/1 (winter 1979), pp. 38–48.

——, *Writing the Feminine: Hélène Cixous* (University of Nebraska Press, Lincoln, 1984).

——, 'Approaches', *Boundary* 12/2 (winter 1984), pp. 1–7.

——, 'Saying "Yes" to the Other', *Dalhousie French Studies* 13 (fall–winter 1987), pp. 92–9.

——, 'Hélène Cixous', in Catherine Savage Brosman (ed.), *French Novelists Since 1960* (Detroit, MI, Gale Research, 1989).

——, 'Délivrance', in Françoise Van Rossum-Guyon and Myriam Diaz-Diocaretz (eds), *Hélène Cixous: Chemins d'une écriture* (Presses Universitaires de Vincennes, Saint-Denis, and Rodopi, Amsterdam, 1990).

——, 'Hélène Cixous', in Eva Martin Sartori and Dorothy Wynne Zimmerman (eds), *French Women Writers: A Bio-Bibliographical Source Book* (Greenwood, New York, 1991).

——, *Hélène Cixous* (University of Toronto Press, Toronto, and Harvester Wheatsheaf, Hemel Hempstead, 1992).

——, 'Le Goût du nu', *Lendemains: Etudes Comparées sur la France/ Vergleichende Frankreichforschung* 13/51, pp. 92–8.

Cornell, Sarah, 'Hélène Cixous' *Le Livre de Promethea*: Paradise Refound', in Susan Sellers (ed.), *Writing Differences: Readings from the Seminar of Hélène Cixous* (Open University Press, Milton Keynes, and St Martin's Press, New York, 1988).

——, 'Hélène Cixous and "les Etudes Féminines"', in Helen Wilcox, Keith

McWatters, Ann Thompson and Linda R. Williams (eds), *The Body and the Text: Hélène Cixous, Reading and Teaching* (Harvester Wheatsheaf, Hemel Hempstead, 1990).

Corredor, Eva, 'The Fantastic and the Problem of Re-Presentation in Hélène Cixous' Feminist Fiction', *Papers in Romance* 4/3 (autumn 1982), pp. 173–9.

Coste, Didier, 'Rehearsal: An Alternative to Production/Reproduction in French Feminist Discourse', in Ihab Hassan and Sally Hassan (eds), *Innovation/Renovation: New Perspectives on the Humanities* (University of Wisconsin Press, Madison, 1983).

Courtivron, Isabelle de, 'Rethinking Differences', in George Stambolian and Elaine Marks (eds), *Homosexualities and French Literature: Cultural Contexts/Critical Texts* (Cornell, Ithaca, 1979).

Crecelius, Kathryn J., 'La Voix de Tancrède: de Cixous à Sand', in Françoise Van Rossum-Guyon and Myriam Diaz-Diocaretz (eds), *Hélène Cixous: Chemins d'une écriture* (Presses Universitaires de Vincennes, Saint-Denis, and Rodopi, Amsterdam, 1990).

Crowder, Diane, 'Amazons and Mothers? Monique Wittig, Hélène Cixous and Theories of Women's Writing', *Contemporary Literature* 24/2 (summer 1983), pp. 117–44.

Daly, Pierette, *Heroic Tropes: Gender and Intertext* (Wayne State University Press, Detroit, 1993).

Daubenton, Annie, 'Le Sang et l'essence', *Les Nouvelles Littéraires* 52 (8–14 April 1974), p. 7.

Davis, Robert Con, 'Woman as Oppositional Reader: Cixous on Discourse', *Papers on Language and Literature: A Journal for Scholars and Critics of Language and Literature* 24/3 (summer 1988), pp. 265–82.

——, 'Cixous, Spivak, and Oppositional Theory', *Lit: Literature Interpretation Theory* 4/1 (1992), pp. 29–42.

Day, R., 'James Joyce à la mode', *Sewanee Review* 82 (winter 1974), pp. 130–8.

Defromont, Françoise, 'Faire la femme: Différence sexuelle et énonciation', *Fabula* 5 (1985), pp. 95–112.

——, 'L'Epopée du corps', in Françoise Van Rossum-Guyon and Myriam Diaz-Diocaretz (eds), *Hélène Cixous: Chemins d'une écriture* (Presses Universitaires de Vincennes, Saint-Denis, and Rodopi, Amsterdam, 1990).

——, 'Metaphorical Thinking and Poetic Writing in Virginia Woolf and Hélène Cixous', in Helen Wilcox, Keith McWatters, Ann Thompson and Linda R. Williams (eds), *The Body and the Text: Hélène Cixous, Reading and Teaching* (Harvester Wheatsheaf, Hemel Hempstead, 1990).

Deleuze, Gilles, 'L'Ecriture stroboscopique', *Le Monde* (11 August 1972).

Derrida, Jacques, 'Preface' to Susan Sellers (ed.), *The Hélène Cixous Reader* (Routledge, London and New York, 1994).

Diaz-Diocaretz, Myriam, with Françoise Van Rossum-Guyon (eds), *Hélène*

Cixous: Chemins d'une écriture (Presses Universitaires de Vincennes, Saint-Denis, and Rodopi, Amsterdam, 1990).

Didier, Béatrice, 'La Chambre et la mère', *Corps Ecrit* 8 (December 1983), pp. 164–5.

Duchen, Claire, *Feminism in France: From May '68 to Mitterrand* (Routledge & Kegan Paul, London and Boston, 1986).

——, 'Review of Hélène Cixous' *Angst*', *Modern Languages Review* 82/1 (January 1987), pp. 214–15.

Duportail, Guy-Félix, 'Une Ouïe multiforme', *La Quinzaine Littéraire* 359 (16–30 November 1981), p. 14.

Duren, Brian, 'Cixous' Exorbitant Texts', *SubStance* 32 (1982), pp. 39–51.

Ego, Ariane, 'L'Exil au fond de soi', *L'Express* (24–30 November 1969), p. 56.

Elbaz, André, '*Dedans* ou l'exil intérieur de Hélène Cixous', *Liberté* (Montreal), 12/2 (March–April 1970), pp. 136–41.

Ertel, Evelyne, 'Entre l'imitation et la transposition', *Théâtre/Public* 68 (March–April 1986), pp. 25–9.

Eslin, Jean-Claude, 'La Chute de la Maison Cambodge', *Esprit* 2 (February 1986), pp. 97–8.

Esonwanne, Uzoma, 'Feminist Theory and the Discourse of Colonialism', in Shirley Neuman (ed.), *ReImagining Women: Representations of Women in Culture* (University of Toronto Press, Toronto, 1993).

Evans, Martha Noel, '*Portrait of Dora*: Freud's Case History as Reviewed by Hélène Cixous', *SubStance* 36 (1982), pp. 64–71.

Fabre-Luce, Anne, 'L'Aventure du texte', *Quinzaine littéraire* (1 mai 1972).

Faris, Wendy, 'Desyoizacion: Joyce, Cixous, Fuentes and the Multi-Vocal Text', *Latin American Literary Review* 9/19 (1981), pp. 31–9.

Feldman, Marie, 'Le Troc des femmes ou la révolte de Dora', *Paroles Gelées: UCLA French Studies* 8 (1991), pp. 21–9.

Feral, Josette, 'The Powers of Difference', in Hester Eisenstein and Alice Jardine (eds), *The Future of Difference* (G.K. Hall, Boston, 1980).

——, 'Ecriture et déplacement: La femme au théâtre', *The French Review: Journal of the American Association of Teachers of French* 56/2 (December 1982), pp. 281–92.

——, 'Writing and Displacement: Women in Theater', *Modern Drama* 27/4 (December 1984), pp. 549–63.

Ferrer, Olga Prjevalinskaya, 'Review of Hélène Cixous' *Partie*', *World Literature Today* 51 (summer 1977), pp. 404–5.

——, 'Review of Hélène Cixous' *Illa*', *World Literature Today* 55 (spring 1981), pp. 268–9.

Finas, Lucette, 'Le Critique exilé', *Critique* 270 (November 1970).

——, 'Le pourpre du neutre', *Critique* 305 (October 1972).

——, 'L'Etrange traversée d'Hélène Cixous', *Le Monde* (13 May 1977), p. 21.

Fisher, Claudine Guégam, 'Hélène Cixous' Window of Daring through Clarice Lispector's Voice', in Eunice Myers and Ginette Adamson (eds), *Continental, Latin-American and Francophone Women Writers* (University Presses of America, Lanham, 1987).

——, 'Refractions shakespeariennes et humour noir chez Hélène Cixous', *Thalia: Studies in Literary Humour* 10/1 (spring–summer 1988), pp. 30–4.

——, 'Cixous' North/South Feminist Dichotomy', *Lit: Literature Interpretation Theory* 2/3 (1991), pp. 231–7.

——, 'Cixous' Concept of "Brushing" as a Gift', *Lit: Literature Interpretation Theory* 4/1 (1992), pp. 79–86.

Fitz, E., 'Hélène Cixous' Debt to Clarice Lispector: The Case of "Vivre l'Orange" and L'Ecriture Féminine', *Revue de Littérature comparée* 64/1 (January–March 1990), pp. 235–49.

Fletcher, John, 'Review of Hélène Cixous' *Un Vrai jardin*', *French Review* 46/4 (March 1973), pp. 851–2.

Fleuret, Maurice, 'Oedipe en Avignon: Un opéra plein sens du terme où une large place est laisée au théâtre', *Le Nouvel Observateur* (12–18 August 1978), p. 54.

Forrester, Viviane, 'Les Relectures d' Hélène Cixous', *La Quinzaine Littéraire* (16–31 January 1975), p. 6.

Fournier, Danielle, 'Jouir auprès des femmes', *Spirale* (Quebec) 35 (June 1983), p. 22.

——, 'L'Oeuil louche, l'amour. Oh, l'amour', *Spirale* 43 (May 1984), p. 12.

Franke, Catherine Anne, 'Dossier: Hélène Cixous', *Qui Parle: A Journal of Literary and Critical Studies* 3/1 (spring 1989), pp. 113–201.

Freeman, Barbara, 'Plus-Corps-Donc-Plus-Ecriture: Hélène Cixous and the Mind–Body Problem', *Paragraph: A Journal of Modern Critical Theory* 11/1 (March 1988), pp. 58–70.

Friedman, Ellen, 'Utterly Other Discourse: The Anticanon of Experimental Women Writers from Dorothy Richardson to Christine Brooke-Rose', *Modern Fiction Studies* 34/3 (autumn 1988), pp. 357–69.

Friedman, Melvin, 'Review of Hélène Cixous' *Les Commencements*', *French Review* 45/1 (October 1971), pp. 197–8.

Frosh, Stephen, *The Politics of Psychoanalysis: An Introduction to Freudian and Post-Freudian Theory* (Macmillan, Basingstoke, 1987).

Gagné, Sylvie, 'Mots d'elle', *La Barre du Jour* (Quebec) 56–7 (May–August 1977), pp. 35–49.

Galey, Matthieu, 'Avignon: Oedipe à l'envers', *L'Express* (7–13 August 1978), p. 17.

Gallop, Jane, 'Keys to Dora', in *The Daughter's Seduction: Feminism and Psychoanalysis* (Cornell University Press, New York, 1982).

Galvin, Thomas, 'Review of Hélène Cixous' *The Exile of James Joyce*', *Library Journal* 98/2 (15 January 1973), p. 167.

Gamarra, Pierre, 'Les Livres nouveaux: La *La*', *Europe* 54 (June 1976), pp. 249–51.

Garcia, Irma, *Promenade femmilière: Recherches sur l'écriture féminine* (Editions Des femmes, Paris, 1981).

Gibbs, Anna, 'Hélène Cixous and Gertrude Stein: New Directions in Feminist Criticism', *Meanjin Quarterly* 38/3 (September 1979), pp. 281–93.

Gilbert, Sandra, 'Introduction: A Tarantella of Theory', *The Newly Born Woman* (University of Minnesota Press, Minneapolis, 1986).

——, 'Sexual Linguistics: Gender, Language, Sexuality', in Catherine Belsey and Jane Moore (eds), *The Feminist Reader: Essays in Gender and Politics of Literary Criticism* (Macmillan, Basingstoke, and Blackwell, New York, 1989).

——, and Susan Gubar, *No Man's Land: The Place of the Woman Writer in the Twentieth Century*, vol. 1: *The War of the Words;* vol. 2: *Sexchanges* (Yale University Press, New Haven, CT, 1988).

Godard, Barbara, 'Translating (With) the Speculum', *Traduction, Términologie, Rédaction: Etudes sur le texte et ses transformation* 4/2 (1991), pp. 85–121.

Godard, Colette, 'Portrait de Dora', *Le Monde* (29 February–1 March 1976), p. 19.

——, '*Portrait of Dora*: Woman's Play', *Manchester Guardian Weekly* (16 May 1976), p. 14.

——, 'Images cruelles d'un rêve de paix: *L'Indiade* par le Théâtre du Soleil', *Le Monde* (10 October 1987), p. 19.

Goldman, Arnold, 'Brother Cannibal', *New Statesman* (16 April 1976), pp. 513–14.

Goldsmith, Francisca, 'Review of Hélène Cixous' *Inside*', *Library Journal* 111/16 (1 October 1986), p. 108.

Goy-Blanquet, Dominique, 'An Indian Dream', *Times Literary Supplement* (16–22 October 1987), p. 140.

Granjon, Marie-Christine, 'Les Femmes, le langage et l'écriture', *Raison Présente* 39 (July–September 1976), pp. 25–32.

Graver, David, 'The Théâtre du Soleil, Part Three: The Production of *Sihanouk*', *New Theatre Quarterly* 2/7 (August 1986), pp. 212–15.

Greenberg, J.L., 'Review of Hélène Cixous' *Limonade tout était si infini*', *World Literature Today* 58/1 (winter 1984), p. 70.

Hanrahan, Mairéad, 'Hélène Cixous' *Dedans*: The Father Makes an Exit', in Margaret Atack and Phil Powrie (eds), *Contemporary French Fiction by Women: Feminist Perspectives* (Manchester University Press, Manchester, 1990).

——, 'Une Porte du *Portrait du soleil* ou la succulence du sujet', in Françoise Van Rossum-Guyon and Myriam Diaz-Diocaretz (eds), *Hélène Cixous: Chemins d'une écriture* (Presses Universitaires de Vincennes, Saint-Denis, and Rodopi, Amsterdam, 1990).

Hart, Stephen, 'On the Threshold: Cixous, Lispector, Tusquets', in Lisa Conde and Stephen Hart (eds), *Feminist Readings on Spanish and Latin-American Literature* (Mellen, Lewiston, New York, 1991).

Hector, Josette, 'Le Jeu du "je"', *La Quinzaine Littéraire* 184 (1–15 April 1974), p. 9.

Hill, Gerald, 'Bardes d'apotropes: Anglo-American Response to "Le Rire de la Méduse"', *Canadian Review of Comparative Literature* 19/1–2 (March–June 1992), pp. 225–36.

Hite, Molly, 'Writing – and Reading – the Body: Female Sexuality and

Recent Feminist Fiction', *Feminist Studies* 14/1 (spring 1988), pp. 122–3, 138–42.

Huston, Nancy, 'Review of Hélène Cixous' *Souffles*', *Sorcières* 1 (January 1976), p. 52.

——, 'Review of Hélène Cixous' *Angst*', *Sorcières* 11 (January 1978), p. 54.

Irving, Nicole, 'The Explosive Turn', *Times Literary Supplement* (21 March 1986), p. 306.

Jardine, Alice, 'Death Sentences: Writing Couples and Ideology', *Poetics Today* 6/1–2, pp. 124–5. Reprinted in Susan Rubin Suleiman (ed.), *The Female Body in Western Culture: Contemporary Perspectives* (Harvard University Press, Cambridge, MA, 1985).

——, *Gynesis: Configurations of Woman and Modernity* (Cornell University Press, Ithaca and London, 1985).

Jean, Raymond, 'Les Mythologies d'Hélène Cixous', *Le Monde* (10 May 1973), p. 19.

——, 'La Voix d'Hélène Cixous', *Matin de Paris* (15 April 1977).

——, 'Le Texte-amant de Cixous', in *Pratique de la littérature: Roman/poésie* (Editions du Seuil, Paris, 1978).

——, 'L'Incantation d'Hélène Cixous', *Le Monde* (4 August 1978), p. 12.

Jones, Ann, 'Writing the Body: Toward an Understanding of "l'Ecriture Féminine"', *Feminist Studies* 7/2 (summer 1981), pp. 247–63. This article is reprinted in Gayle Greene and Coppelia Kahn (eds), *Making a Difference: Feminist Literary Criticism* (Methuen, London, 1985); Elaine Showalter (ed.), *The New Feminist Criticism: Essays on Women, Literature and Theory* (Pantheon, New York, 1985); and Mary Eagleton (ed.), *Feminist Literary Theory: A Reader* (Basil Blackwell, Oxford, 1986).

Jouve, Nicole Ward, 'Oranges et sources: Colette et Hélène Cixous', in Françoise Van Rossum-Guyon and Myriam Diaz-Diocaretz (eds), *Hélène Cixous: Chemins d'une écriture* (Presses Universitaires de Vincennes, Saint-Denis, and Rodopi, Amsterdam, 1990).

——, 'Hélène Cixous: From Inner Theatre to World Theatre', in Helen Wilcox, Keith Mcwatters, Ann Thompson and Linda R. Williams (eds), *The Body and the Text: Hélène Cixous, Reading and Teaching* (Harvester Wheatsheaf, Hemel Hempstead, 1990). Reprinted in Nicole Ward Jouve *White Woman Speaks with Forked Tongue; Criticism as Autobiography* (Routledge, London, 1991).

——, 'The Faces of Power: Hélène Cixous', *Our Voices Ourselves: Women Writing for the French Theatre* (Peter Lang, New York, 1991).

Juncker, C., 'Writing (with) Cixous', *College English* 50/4 (1988), pp. 424–36.

Kattan, Naïm, 'Remplir le vide: Hélène Cixous romancière', *Synthèses: Revue Internationale* (Brussels) 26 (October–November 1971), pp. 80–2.

Kelertas, Violeta, 'Review of Hélène Cixous' *Un K. incompréhensible: Pierre Goldman*', *World Literature Today* 51 (winter 1977), pp. 60–1.

Kerchove, Arnold de, 'Cixous', *Revue Générale* (Brussels) 105/9 (November 1969), pp. 115–17.

Kiernander, Adrian, 'The King of Cambodia', *Plays and Players* 386 (November 1985), pp. 17–18.

——, 'The Orient, the Feminine: The Use of Interculturalism by the Théâtre du Soleil', in Laurence Senelick (ed.), *Gender in Performance: The Presentation of Difference in the Performing Arts* (University Press of New England, Hanover, New Hampshire, 1992).

Kitch, Sally, 'French Feminist Theories and the Gender of the Text', in Eunice Myers and Ginette Adamson (eds), *Continental, Latin-American and Francophone Women Writers* (University Presses of America, Lanham, 1987).

Klein-Lataud, 'La Nourricriture ou l'écriture d'Hélène Cixous, de Chantal Chawaf et d'Annie Leclerc', in Suzanne Lamy and Irène Pagès (eds), *Féminité, subversion, écriture* (Les Editions du Remue-Ménage, Montreal, 1983).

Knapp, Bettina, 'Review of Hélène Cixous' *Manne aux Mandelstams aux Mandelas*', *World Literature Today*, (spring 1989), 63(2):281.

Kogan, Vivian, 'I Want Vulva! Hélène Cixous and the Poetics of the Body', *L'Esprit créateur* 25/2 (summer 1985), pp. 73–85.

Kohn, Ingeborg, 'Review of Hélène Cixous' *Limonade tout était si infini*', *French Review* 57/6 (May 1984), pp. 906–7.

Kolk, Mikeke, 'La Vengeance d'Oedipe: Théorie féministe et pratique du théâtre', in Françoise Van Rossum-Guyon and Myriam Diaz-Diocaretz (eds), *Hélène Cixous: Chemins d'une écriture* (Presses Universitaires de Vincennes, Saint-Denis, and Rodopi, Amsterdam, 1990).

Kuhn, Annette: 'Introduction to Hélène Cixous' "Castration or Decapitation?"', *Signs: Journal of Women in Culture and Society* 7/1 (autumn 1981), pp. 36–40.

La Bardonnie, Mathilde, 'Le Nom d'Oedipe à Avignon', *Le Monde* (28 July 1978), p. 16.

Lafontaine, Dominique, 'Review of Hélène Cixous' *Préparatifs de noces au delà de l'abîme*', *Les Cahiers du GRIF* 23–24 (December 1978), pp. 181–2.

—— and Geneviève Lorent, 'Si l'écriture des femmes', *Les Cahiers du GRIF* 23–24 (December 1978), pp. 153–6.

Lamar, Celita, 'Traduit du Cixous', *Le Figaro* (June 26–7, 1976), 1571:15.

——, 'Norodom Sihanouk, A Hero of our Times: Character Development in Hélène Cixous' Cambodian Epic', in Karelisa Hartigan (ed.), *From the Bard to Broadway* (University Presses of America, Lanham, 1987).

Lambert, Annie, 'Quelques remarques à propos de certains "textes de femmes"', *Lendemains* (Berlin) 7 (1982), pp. 149–56.

Lamont, Rosette, 'Review of Hélène Cixous' *Angst*', *World Literature Today* 52/5 (spring 1978), p. 250.

——, 'Review of Hélène Cixous' *With ou l'art de l'innocence*', *World Literature Today* 56/3 (summer 1982), p. 479.

——, 'The Off-Center Spatiality of Women's Discourse', in Gabriela Mora and Karen S. Van Hooft (eds), *Theory and Practice of Feminist Literary Criticism* (Bilingual Press/Editorial Bilingüe, Michigan, 1982).

——, '*The Terrible But Unended Story of Norodom Sihanouk: King of Cambodia* by Hélène Cixous', *Performing Arts Journal* 10/1 (1986), pp. 46–50.

——, 'The Reverse Side of a Portrait: The Dora of Freud and Cixous', in Enoch Brater (ed.), *Feminine Focus: The New Women Playwrights* (Oxford University Press, Oxford, 1989).

Larose, Jean, 'Le Temps d'une voix', *Etudes Françaises* 17/3–4 (October 1981), pp. 87–96.

Laureillard, Rémi, 'Les Paysages intérieurs', *La Quinzaine Littéraire* 34 (1 August 1967), p. 11,

Le Clec'h, Guy, 'Hélène Cixous ou l'illusion cosmique', *Le Figaro Littéraire* (1–7 December 1969), p. 19.

Le Clézio, Marguerite, 'Psychanalyse-poésie: Le rite de Cixous la Méduse', *Les Bonnes Feuilles* (Pennsylvania State University) 9/1–2 (fall 1980), pp. 92–103.

Le Roux, Monique, 'Un Sampeâh shakespearien', *La Quinzaine Littéraire* 457 (16–28 February 1986), pp. 24–5.

Lecerf, Yves, 'Des poèmes cachés dans des poèmes', *Poétique* 18 (1974), pp. 148–9.

Leonardini, Jean-Pierre, 'Un battement d'ailes lyrique: Hélène Cixous écrit "Le cantique des cantiques" des femmes . . .', *L'Humanité* (23 June 1978), p. 10.

Lewis, Janet, 'Review of Hélène Cixous' *The Exile of James Joyce*', *Humanities Association Bulletin* (summer 1973), pp. 231–3.

Libertin, Mary, 'Challenging the Language', *Belles Lettres* 2/11 (July–August 1987).

Lie, Sissel, 'Pour une lécture féminine', in Helen Wilcox, Keith Mcwatters, Ann Thompson and Linda R. Williams (eds), *The Body and the Text: Hélène Cixous, Reading and Teaching* (Harvester Wheatsheaf, Hemel Hempstead, 1990).

Lindsay, Cecile, 'Body/Language: French Feminist Utopias', *The French Review: Journal of the American Association of Teachers of French* 60/1 (October 1986), pp. 46–55.

Lonchampti, Jacques, 'Cette Plainte de toutes les femmes: L'Oedipe de Cixous et Boucourechilev', *Le Monde* (30 May 1978), p. 24.

Luccioni, Eugénie, 'Review of Hélène Cixous' *Souffles*, *La* and *Angst*', *Esprit* 6 (June 1977), pp. 127–8.

——, 'Métaphores', *Quinzaine Littéraire* 312 (15 November 1979), pp. 10–11.

MacCabe, Colin, 'Separation and Loss', *Times Higher Education Supplement* (19 March 1976), p. 19.

Mairs, Nancy, 'Carnal Acts', *TriQuarterly* 75 (spring–summer 1989), pp. 61–70.

Makward, Christiane, 'To Be or Not to Be . . . A Feminist Speaker', transl. Marlène Barsoum, Alice Jardine and Hester Eisenstein, in Hester Eisenstein and Alice Jardine (eds), *The Future of Difference* (G.K. Hall, Boston, 1970).

——, 'Structures du silence/du délire: Marguerite Duras/Hélène Cixous', *Poétique* 35 (September 1978), pp. 314–24.

——, 'Les Editions des femmes: Histoire, politique et impact', *Contemporary French Civilization* 5 (spring 1981), pp. 347–55.

——, 'The Theater of Genocide', *Women's Review of Books* 3/6 (March 1986), pp. 17–18.

Mambrino, Jean, 'Carnet de théâtre: *L'Histoire terrible mais inachevée de Norodom Sihanouk* de Cixous par le Théâtre du Soleil', *Etudes* 363/6 (December 1985), pp. 641–2.

Marcus, Jane, 'Daughters of Anger/Material Girls: Con/Textualizing Feminist Criticism', *Women's Studies* 15/1–3 (1988), pp. 287–91.

Marks, Elaine, 'Woman and Literature in France', *Signs* 3/4 (summer 1978), pp. 832–42.

——, 'Review of Hélène Cixous' *Préparatifs de noces au delà de l'abîme*', *French Review* 52/2 (December 1979), pp. 309–10.

Marrero, Mara Négron, 'Comment faire pour écrire l'Histoire poétiquement ou comment faire pour ne pas oublier', in Françoise Van Rossum-Guyon and Myriam Diaz-Diocaretz (eds), *Hélène Cixous: Chemins d'une écriture* (Presses Universitaires de Vincennes, Saint-Denis, and Rodopi, Amsterdam, 1990).

Mauriac, Claude, 'Une génération débâillonnée', *Le Figaro* (29 November 1975), p. 16.

McCallum, Pamela, 'New Feminist Readings: Women as Ecriture or Woman as Other?', *Canadian Journal of Political and Social Theory/Revue Canadienne de Théorie Politique et Sociale* 9/1–2 (winter–spring 1985), pp. 127–32.

Mechtilt, Greiner, 'Le Portrait de Dora', *Kunst en Cultur* (1 April 1976), pp. 26–7.

Meese, Elizabeth, *Crossing the Double-Cross: The Practice of Feminist Criticism* (University of North Carolina Press, Chapel Hill and London, 1986).

Mezei, Kathy, 'Writing the Risk in, Risking the Writing', *Tessera* 10 (summer 1991), pp. 13–21.

Micha, René, 'La Tête de Dora sous Cixous', *Critique* 33 (1977), pp. 114–21.

Michel, Frann, 'Displacing Castration: *Nightwood*, *Ladies Almanack* and Feminine Writing', *Contemporary Literature* 30/1 (spring 1989), pp. 34–9.

Miller, Judith, 'Jean Cocteau and Hélène Cixous: Oedipus', in James Redmond (ed.), *Drama, Sex and Politics* (Cambridge, Cambridge University Press, 1985).

Miller, Nancy, *Subject to Change: Reading Feminist Writing* (Columbia University Press, New York, 1988).

Miner, Madonne, 'Lizzie Borden Took an Ax: Enacting Blood Relations', *Literature in Performance: A Journal of Literary and Performing Art* 6/2 (April 1986), pp. 10–21.

Minh-Ha, Trinh T., 'Linnécriture: Féminisme et littérature', *French Forum* 8/1 (January 1983), pp. 45–63.

Misurella, Fred, 'Review of Hélène Cixous' *The Exile of James Joyce*', *Philological Quarterly* 52/2 (spring 1974), pp. 282–3.

Mnouchkine, Ariane, 'Au fil d'Ariane: Indiade ou L'Inde de leurs rêves d'Hélène Cixous, à la Cartoucherie', *Le Nouvel Observateur* (25 September–1 October 1987), pp. 58–9.

Moi, Toril, 'Hélène Cixous: An Imaginary Utopia', in *Sexual/Textual Politics: Feminist Literary Theory* (Methuen, London, 1985).

——, 'Feminist, Female, Feminine', in Catherine Belsey and Jane Moore (eds), *The Feminist Reader: Essays in Gender and the Politics of Literary Criticism* (Macmillan, Basingstoke and Blackwell, New York, 1989). Reprinted from her 'Feminist Literary Criticism', in Ann Jefferson and David Robey (eds), *Modern Literary Theory: A Comparative Introduction* (Barnes & Noble, Totowa, NJ, and London, Batsford, 1982).

Moore, Jane, 'Review of Hélène Cixous' and Catherine Clément's *The Newly Born Woman*', *Quinquereme* 11/1 (January 1988), pp. 108–9.

Moreau, Jean, 'Question de personne', *Critique* 31 (March 1975), pp. 297–306.

Morgan, Amy, 'Journeys in the Neighbourhood of Heidegger and Cixous', *Ellipsis* 1/1 (1989).

Moss, Jane, 'Women's Theater in France', *Signs* 12/3 (spring 1987), pp. 554–9.

Motard-Noar, Martine, *Les Fictions d'Hélène Cixous: Une autre langue de femme* (French Forum, Lexington, 1991).

——, 'Manne ou Man: Où en est l'écriture d'Hélène Cixous?', *The French Review: Journal of the American Association of Teachers of French* 66/2 (December 1992), pp. 286–94.

——, 'Reading and Writing the Other: Criticism as Felicity', *Lit: Literature Interpretation Theory* 4/1 (1992), pp. 57–68.

Moynahan, Julian, 'Review of Hélène Cixous' *The Exile of James Joyce*', *New York Times Book Review* (11 February 1973), p. 21.

Mutter, John, 'Review of Hélène Cixous' *Angst*', *Publishers' Weekly* (29 November 1985), p. 43.

Neill, Anna, 'Review of Hélène Cixous' *Angst*', *Landfall: A New Zealand Quarterly* 42/168 (December 1988), pp. 458–9.

Norris, Christopher, 'Portrait in Depth', *Books and Bookman* 21/10 (July 1976), pp. 54–6; 'Portrait in Depth 2', *Books and Bookman* 21/11 (August 1976), pp. 48–9.

Nye, Andrea, 'French Feminism and the Philosophy of Language', *Nous*, 20/1 (March 1986), pp. 45–51. Also in 'The Voice of the Serpent: French Feminism and the Philosophy of Language', in Ann Garry and Marilyn Pearsall (eds), *Women, Knowledge and Reality: Explorations in Feminist Philosophy* (Unwin Hyman, Boston and London, 1989).

——, 'The Inequalities of Semantic Structure: Linguistics and Feminist Philosophy', *Metaphilosophy* 18 (July–October 1987), pp. 222–38.

Oxenhandler, Neal, 'Review of Hélène Cixous' *Le Troisième corps*', *French Review* 45/5 (April 1972), pp. 1041–2.

Pachet, Pierre, 'Un Débordement impressionnant', *Quinzaine Littéraire* 257 (1–15 June 1977), pp. 8–9.

Pavlides, Merope, 'Restructuring the Traditional: An Examination of

Hélène Cixous' *Le Nom d'Oedipe*', in Karelisa Hartigan (ed.), *Within the Dramatic Spectrum* (University Presses of America, Lanham, 1986).

Piatier, Jacqueline, 'Review of Hélène Cixous' *Le Prénom de Dieu*', *Le Monde* (14 June 1967), pp. i–ii.

——, '*La* ou l'avènement de la femme', *Le Monde* (25 November 1969), p. 28.

——, 'Une Moderne Sibylle', *Le Monde* (16 October 1970), pp. 15–16.

Picard, Anne-Marie, 'L'Indiade: Ariane and Hélène Conjugate Dreams', *Modern Drama* 32/1 (March 1989), pp. 24–38.

——, 'L'Indiade ou l'Inde de leurs rêves', *Dalhousie French Studies* 17 (fall–winter 1989), pp. 17–26.

Picaud, Christian, 'Peinture poésie: Vers le portrait de Dieu', in Françoise Van Rossum-Guyon and Myriam Diaz-Diocaretz (eds), *Hélène Cixous: Chemins d'une écriture* (Presses Universitaires de Vincennes, Saint-Denis, and Rodopi, Amsterdam, 1990).

Pidoux, Jean-Yves, 'Le Soleil de la tragédie', *Théâtre/Public* 75 (May–June 1987), pp. 5–12.

Poirot-Delpech, Bertrand, 'I'inconscient à l'œuvre', *Le Monde* (8 March 1974), p. 19.

——, 'Freud, lecteur: Essais de Sarah Kofman et Hélène Cixous', *Le Monde* (26 December 1974), p. 9.

——, 'Review of Hélène Cixous' *Un K. incompréhensible*', *Le Monde* (12 December 1975), p. 19.

——, 'Illisibles', *Le Monde* (6 August 1976), p. 7.

——, 'Corps-écrit', *Le Monde* (1 June 1979), p. 19.

Pujade-Renaud, Claude, 'Du corps féminin à l'écriture', *Esprit* 62 (February 1982), pp. 107–21.

Rabine, Leslie, 'Ecriture Féminine as Metaphor', *Cultural Critique* 8 (winter 1987–8), pp. 19–44.

Rajan, Gita, 'A Feminist Rereading of Poe's "The Tell-Tale Heart"', *Papers on Language and Literature: A Journal for Scholars and Critics of Language and Literature* 24/3 (summer 1988), pp. 283–300.

Rambures, Jean-Louis de, *Comment travaillent les écrivains*, Flammarion, (Paris, 1978).

Ravelli, Catherine, 'De l'Intérêt de la féminitude pour le féminisme', *La Revue d'en Face* 4 (November 1978), pp. 18–23.

Remy, Monique, 'Cixous en langues ou les jeux de la féminité' in Françoise Van Rossum-Guyon and Myriam Diaz-Diocaretz (eds), *Hélène Cixous: Chemins d'une écriture* (Presses Universitaires de Vincennes, Saint-Denis, and Rodopi, Amsterdam, 1990).

Richman, Michèle, 'Sex and Signs: The Language of French Feminist Criticism', *Language and Style* 13/4 (fall 1980), pp. 62–80.

Robinson, Sally, 'The "Anti-Logos Weapon": Multiplicity in Women's Texts', *Contemporary Literature* 29/1 (spring 1988), pp. 105–24.

Rone, Ruth, 'Review of Hélène Cixous' and Catherine Clément's *The Newly Born Woman*', *Poetics Today* 9/3 (1988), pp. 670–1.

Rossman, Charles, 'Review of Hélène Cixous' *The Exile of James Joyce*', *James Joyce Quarterly* 10/3 (spring 1973), pp. 360–4.

Rossum-Guyon, Françoise Van, with Myriam Diaz-Diocaretz (eds), *Hélène Cixous: Chemins d'une écriture* (Presses Universitaires de Vincennes, Saint-Denis, and Rodopi, Amsterdam, 1990).

Roy, Claude, 'James Joyce, le fabuleux "voleur" de Dublin: Enorme comme Falstaff et maigre comme Don Quichotte', *Le Monde* (22 February 1969), pp. i–ii.

Running-Johnson, Cynthia, 'The Medusa's Tale: Feminine Writing and "La Genet"', *Romanic Review* 80/3 (May 1989), pp. 438–95.

——, 'Themes in Drama II: Feminine Writing and Its Theatrical "Other"', in James Redmond (ed.), *Women in Theatre* (Cambridge University Press, Cambridge, 1989).

——, 'Genet's "Excessive" Double: Reading *Les Bonnes* through Irigaray and Cixous', *The French Review: Journal of the American Association of Teachers of French* 63/6 (May 1990), pp. 959–66.

Sabouraud, Frédéric, 'Coup de soleil pour Sihanouk', *Le Nouvel Observateur*' (6–12 September 1985), pp. 52–4.

Sage, Lorna, 'Past Eternal', *Observer* (London) (12 January 1986), p. 46.

Salesne, Pierre, 'Hélène Cixous' *Ou l'art de l'innocence*: The Path to You', in Susan Sellers (ed.), *Writing Differences: Readings from the Seminar of Hélène Cixous* (Open University Press, Milton Keynes and St Martin's Press, New York, 1988).

——, 'L'émoi d'Hélène Cixous en langues d'autres', in Françoise Van Rossum-Guyon and Myriam Diaz-Diocaretz (eds), *Hélène Cixous: Chemins d'une écriture* (Presses Universitaires de Vincennes, Saint-Denis, and Rodopi, Amsterdam, 1990).

Sallenave, Danièle, 'Review of Hélène Cixous' *Portrait de Dora*', *Les Nouvelles Littéraires* 54 (11 March 1976), p. 29.

——, 'Review of Hélène Cixous' *La*', *Les Nouvelles Littéraires* 54 (15 April 1976), p. 23.

Salvaggio, Ruth, 'Theory and Space, Space and Woman', *Tulsa Studies in Women's Literature* 7/2 (fall 1988), pp. 257–77.

Sankovitch, Tilde, 'Hélène Cixous: The Pervasive Myth', *French Women Writers and the Book: Myths of Access and Desire* (Syracuse University Press, Syracuse, 1988).

Santellani, Violette, 'Femmes sans figure et figures de femmes', in Françoise Van Rossum-Guyon and Myriam Diaz-Diocaretz (eds), *Hélène Cixous: Chemins d'une écriture* (Presses Universitaires de Vincennes, Saint-Denis, and Rodopi, Amsterdam, 1990).

Savona, Jeannette Laillou, 'French Feminism and Theatre: An Introduction', *Modern Drama* 27/4 (December 1984), pp. 540–5.

——, 'In Search of Feminist Theater: Portrait of Dora', in Enoch Brater (ed.), *Feminine Focus: The New Women Playwrights* (Oxford University Press, Oxford, 1989).

——, '*Portrait de Dora* d'Hélène Cixous: A la recherche d'un théâtre féministe', in Françoise Van Rossum-Guyon and Myriam Diaz-Diocaretz (eds), *Hélène Cixous: Chemins d'une écriture* (Presses Universitaires de Vincennes, Saint-Denis, and Rodopi, Amsterdam, 1990).

Schmidt, Ricarda, 'E.T.A. Hoffmann's "Der Sandmann": An Early Example of Ecriture Féminine? Critique of Trends in Feminist Literary Criticism', *Women in German Yearbook: Feminist Studies and German Culture* 4 (1988), pp. 21–45.

Schneider, Judith Morganroth, 'Review of Hélène Cixous' *La*', *World Literature Today* 51 (spring 1977), p. 238.

Sellers, Susan, 'Writing Woman: Hélène Cixous' Political "Sexts"', *Women's Studies International Forum* 9/4 (1986), pp. 443–7.

——, (ed.), *Writing Differences: Readings from the Seminar of Hélène Cixous* (Open University Press, Milton Keynes, and St Martin's Press, New York, 1988).

——, 'Biting the Teacher's Apple: Opening Doors for Women in Higher Education', in Ann Thompson and Helen Wilcox (eds), *Teaching Women: Feminism and English Studies* (Manchester University Press, Manchester, 1989).

——, 'Learning to Read the Feminine', in Helen Wilcox, Keith Mcwatters, Ann Thompson and Linda R. Williams (eds), *The Body and the Text: Hélène Cixous, Reading and Teaching* (Harvester Wheatsheaf, Hemel Hempstead, 1990).

——, 'Blowing up the Law', 'Masculine and Feminine', 'The Mother's Voice', 'Woman's Abasement', 'Writing the Other', 'Writing Other Worlds', in *Language and Sexual Difference: Feminist Writing in France* (Macmillan, Basingstoke, and St Martin's Press, New York, 1991).

——, (ed.), *The Hélène Cixous Reader* (Routledge, London and New York, 1994).

Setti, Nadia, 'Les Noms de l'amour', in Françoise Van Rossum-Guyon and Myriam Diaz-Diocaretz (eds), *Hélène Cixous: Chemins d'une écriture* (Presses Universitaires de Vincennes, Saint-Denis, and Rodopi, Amsterdam, 1990).

Sherzer, Dina, *Representation in Contemporary French Fiction* (University of Nebraska Press, Lincoln, 1986).

Shiach, Morag, 'Their "Symbolic" Exists, it Holds Power – We, the Sowers of Disorder, Know it Only Too Well', in Teresa Brennan (ed.), *Feminism and Psychoanalysis* (Routledge, London, 1989).

——, *Hélène Cixous: A Politics of Writing* (Routledge, London, 1991).

Showalter, Elaine, 'Feminist Criticism in the Wilderness', *Critical Inquiry* 8/2 (winter 1981), pp. 184–6. Reprinted in Elizabeth Abel (ed.), *Writing and Sexual Difference* (University of Chicago Press, Chicago, 1982).

Siebers, Tobin, 'The Ethics of Sexual Difference', in *The Ethics of Criticism* (Cornell University Press, Ithaca, 1988).

Silverstein, Marc, 'Body-Presence: Cixous' Phenomenology of Theater', *Theatre Journal* 43/4 (December 1991), pp. 507–16.

Silvert, Eileen Boyd, 'Lelia and Feminism', *Yale French Studies* 62 (1981), pp. 45–66.

Simpson-Zinn, Joy, 'The Différence of L'Ecriture Féminine', *Chimères: A Journal of French and Italian Literature* 18/1 (autumn 1985), pp. 77–93.

Singer, Linda, 'True Confessions: Cixous and Foucault on Sexuality and Power', in Jeffner Allen and Marion Young (eds), *The Thinking Muse: Feminism and Modern French Philosophy* (Indiana University Press, Bloomington, 1989).

Sipriot, Pierre, 'Vivre sa vie', *Le Figaro* (21–2 May 1977), p. 20.

Slama, Béatrice, 'Entre amour et écriture: *Le Livre de Promethea*', in Françoise Van Rossum-Guyon and Myriam Diaz-Diocaretz (eds), *Hélène Cixous: Chemins d'une écriture* (Presses Universitaires de Vincennes, Saint-Denis, and Rodopi, Amsterdam, 1990).

Spivak, Gayatri, 'French Feminism in an International Frame', in *In Other Worlds: Essays in Cultural Politics* (Methuen, New York, 1987).

Staley, Thomas, 'Recent Joyce Criticism', *Studies in the Novel* 6/4 (winter 1974), pp. 486–7.

Stanton, Domna C., 'Language and Revolution: The Franco-American Dis-Connection', in Hester Eisenstein and Alice Jardine (eds), *The Future of Difference* (Hall, Boston, 1980).

——, 'Difference on Trial: A Critique of the Maternal Metaphor in Cixous, Irigaray and Kristeva', in Nancy K. Miller (ed.), *The Poetics of Gender* (Columbia University Press, New York, 1986).

Stary, Sonja, 'Review of Hélène Cixous' *Un K. incompréhensible: Pierre Goldman*', *French Review* 50/5 (April 1977), pp. 808–9.

Steinberg, Sybil, 'Review of Hélène Cixous' *Inside*', *Publishers Weekly* 230/12 (19 September 1986), p. 124.

Stéphane, Nell, 'Review of Hélène Cixous' *Prénoms de personne*', *Europe* 53 (March 1975), p. 241.

Still, Judith, 'A Feminine Economy: Some Preliminary Thoughts', in Helen Wilcox, Keith Mcwatters, Ann Thompson and Linda R. Williams (eds), *The Body and the Text: Hélène Cixous, Reading and Teaching* (Harvester Wheatsheaf, Hemel Hempstead, 1990).

Sudaka, Jacqueline, 'Review of Hélène Cixous' *Un Vrai jardin*', *Nouveaux Cahiers* 27 (winter 1971–2), pp. 71–2.

Suleiman, Susan Rubin, '(Re)Writing the Body: The Politics and Poetics of Female Eroticism', in *The Female Body in Western Culture: Contemporary Perspectives* (Harvard University Press, Cambridge, MA, 1986).

——, 'Writing Past the Wall or the Passion According to H.C.', in Hélène Cixous, *'Coming to Writing' and Other Essays*, transl. Sarah Cornell, Deborah Jensen, Ann Liddle and Susan Sellers (Harvard University Press, Cambridge, MA, 1991).

Temkine, Raymonde, 'Le Théâtre: Femmes', *Europe* 54 (September 1976), pp. 196–9.

——, 'Théâtre: La Cartoucherie, cette ruche', *Europe* 64 (January–February 1986), pp. 183–4.

Thorburn, David, 'Portraits of the Artist', *Partisan Review* 40/2 (1973), pp. 306–9.

Todd, Janet, *Feminist Literary History* (Routledge, New York, 1988).

Tostevin, Lola Lemire, 'Breaking the Hold on the Story: The Feminine Economy of Language', in Shirley Neuman and Smaro Kambourelli (eds), *A Mazing Space: Writing Canadian Women Writing* (Longspoon, Edmonton, 1986).

Turner, Pamela, 'Hélène Cixous: A Space Between – Women and (Their) Language', *LIT: Literature Interpretation Theory* 4/1 (1992), pp. 69–77.

Tytell, Paméla, 'Hélène Cixous: *Préparatifs de noces au-delà de l'abîme*', *Magazine Littéraire* 140 (September 1978), pp. 45–6.

Upton, Lee, 'Coming to God: Notes on Dickinson, Bogan, Cixous', *Denver Quarterly* 27/4 (spring 1993), pp. 83–94.

Vaccaro, Barbaro Pietro, 'Review of Hélène Cixous' *Révolutions pour plus d'un Faust*', *Culture Française* 23 (1976), pp. 341–2.

Van Buren, Jane Silverman, *The Modernist Madonna: Semiotics of the Maternal Metaphor* (Indiana University Press, Bloomington and Indianapolis; Karnac Books, London, 1989).

Van Laere, François, 'Review of Hélène Cixous' *L'Exil de James Joyce*', transl. H. Stewart, *James Joyce Quarterly* 7/3 (spring 1970), pp. 259–66.

Vandenschrick, Jacques, 'Hélène Cixous: Un cri d'absence', *Revue Nouvelle* 51/2 (February 1970), pp. 210–12.

Villelaur, Anne, 'Le Médicis à Hélène Cixous', *Les Lettres Françaises* 1310 (26 November–2 December 1969), p. 3.

——, 'Encerclement et solitude', *Les Lettres Françaises* 1312 (10–16 December 1969), p. 10.

Vuarnet, Jean-Noël, 'Review of Hélène Cixous' *Le Troisième corps* and *Les Commencements*', *Europe* 49 (February–March 1971), pp. 277–8.

——, 'Review of Hélène Cixous' *Portrait du soleil*', *Les Lettres Nouvelles* 4 (September–October 1974).

Walt, J., 'Review of Hélène Cixous' *Tombe*', *Books Abroad* 48/3 (summer 1974), p. 536.

Watson, Christine, 'Review of Hélène Cixous' *Inside*', *West Coast Review of Books* 12/4 (1986), p. 29.

Weedon, Chris, *Feminist Practice and Post-Structuralist Theory* (Blackwell, Oxford, 1987).

Weidemann, Barbara, 'The Search for an Authentic Voice: Hélène Cixous and Marguerite Duras', *Journal of Durassian Studies* 1 (fall 1989), pp. 99–114.

Wierlys, Hélène de, 'Arabesques', *La Quinzaine Littéraire* 103 (1–15 October 1970), p. 8.

Willis, Sharon, 'Portrait de Dora: The Unseen and the Un-scene', *Theatre Journal* 37/3 (October 1985), pp. 287–301.

——, 'Mis-Translation: *Vivre l'orange*', *Studies in the Novel* 18/4 (winter 1986), pp. 76–83. Reprinted in *SubStance: A Review of Theory and Literary Criticism* 16/1 (1987), pp. 76–83.

——, 'Mistranslation, Missed Translation: Hélène Cixous' *Vivre l'orange*', in

Lawrence Venuti (ed.), *Rethinking Translation: Discourse, Subjectivity, Ideology* (Routledge, London, 1992).

Wilson, Ann, 'History and Hysteria: Writing the Body in "Portrait of Dora" and "Signs of Life"', *Modern Drama* 32/1 (March 1989), pp. 73–88.

Wiseman, Susan, '"Femininity" and the Intellectual in Sontag and Cixous', in Helen Wilcox, Keith Mcwatters, Ann Thompson and Linda R. Williams (eds), *The Body and the Text: Hélène Cixous, Reading and Teaching* (Harvester Wheatsheaf, Hemel Hempstead, 1990).

Wolfromm, Jean-Didier, 'Jean Didier Wolfromm a lu: *Dedans* par Hélène Cixous', *Le Magazine Littéraire* 35 (December 1969), p. 43.

Worsham, Lynn, 'Writing against Writing: The Predicament of Ecriture Féminine in Composition Studies', in Patricia Harkin and John Schilb (eds), *Contending With Words: Composition and Rhetoric in a Postmodern Age* (Modern Languages Association of America, New York, 1991).

Wright, Elizabeth and Dianne Chisholm, 'Review of Hélène Cixous' and Catherine Clément's *The Newly Born Woman*', *Modern Languages Review* 84/2 (April 1989), pp. 418–19.

Yaeger, Patricia, 'Honey-Mad Women', in her *Honey-Mad Women: Emancipatory Strategies in Women's Writing* (Columbia University Press, New York, 1988).

Zéraffa, Michel, 'Review of Hélène Cixous' *Dedans*', *Le Nouvel Observateur* (13–19 October 1969), p. 49.

Index